WITHDRAWN
UTSA LIBRARIES

RENEWALS 458-4574
DATE DUE

A PARTICIPATORY APPROACH TO URBAN PLANNING

A PARTICIPATORY APPROACH TO URBAN PLANNING

Edmund M. Burke, Ph.D.

*Boston College,
Chestnut Hill, Mass.*

HUMAN SCIENCES PRESS
72 Fifth Avenue 9 Henrietta Street
NEW YORK, NY 10011 ● LONDON, WC2E 8LU

Library of Congress Catalog Number 78-31107

ISBN: 0-87705-393-6

Copyright © 1979 by Human Sciences Press
72 Fifth Avenue, New York, New York 10011

All rights reserved. No part of this work may be reproduced or utilized in any form or by any means, electronic or mechanical, including photocopying, microfilm and recording, or by any information storage and retrieval system without permission in writing from the publisher.

Printed in the United States of America
9 987654321

Library of Congress Cataloging in Publication Data

Burke, Edmund M
   A participatory approach to urban planning.

  Bibliography: p.
  Includes index.
  1. City planning—Citizen participation. I. Title.
HT166.B86   309.2'62   78-31107
ISBN 0-87705-393-6

To Lee and our four sons—
Brian, Chris, Tom, and Ted

ACKNOWLEDGMENTS

This book is a collaborative effort. A great many individuals—some knowingly, others unknowingly—were involved in its preparation.

Students were a particular source of help and, also, inspiration. Their reactions and comments helped to sharpen definitions and examples. Practicing planners who were exposed to some of the material in institutes and workshops contributed ideas and examples that greatly improved the final results.

I am indebted, too, to colleagues who read all or parts of the manuscript. Richard Bolan, Victor Capoccia, and Audrey Faulkner provided thoughtful comments and suggestions.

Preparations of the manuscript involved a number of typists over varying drafts. I am particularly thankful to Grace Anastasia, Lisa Hubbard, Barbara Simons, and Virginia Richardson.

Chestnut Hill, Mass.
October 1978

CONTENTS

Acknowledgments   7
Introduction   11

PART I

1. Characteristics of Community Decision-Making   25

2. The Principle of Legitimacy   45

3. The Citizen Participation Characteristics in Planning   65

4. The Strategies of Citizen Participation   89

5. Planning and Social Change   108

PART II

6. Introduction to Part II   147

7.	Developing Legitimacy for Planning	158
8.	Developing the Motivation to Plan	177
9.	Goal Setting and Plan Elements	195
10.	The Decision Phase of Planning: Part I	215
11.	The Decision Phase of Planning: Part II	238
12.	Introducing and Carrying Out the Plan: Final Decision and Plan Cut-over Phases	255
13.	The Role of the Planner	268
14.	Typologies of Planning	285
Index		301

INTRODUCTION

Prior to the 1950s community planning was the exclusive domain of a single organization—the city planning agency or department. Its function was precise and uncomplicated: namely, to provide for the orderly and systematic growth of the community. The product was a master plan, which was used as a basis to guide the development of the community.

The planning method was also precise and uncomplicated. The approach was a rational form of analysis, the ultimate aim of which was to be as comprehensive as possible. The format followed a pattern in which the planner:

- Was guided by a goal.
- Began to set out the range of alternative solutions or means for achieving the goal.
- Detailed the consequences of each alternative.
- Weighed and ranked each alternative for the purpose of selecting one alternative as opposed to another.
- Selected the preferred set of consequences approaching or meeting the goal.

The planner, moreover, occupied a singular position. It was taken for granted that he (rarely she) was a professional whose expert advice and opinion reflected the needs and best interests of the community. He was often the lone arbiter of developmental needs.

Human services or social planning was virtually nonexistent—at least at the magnitude we know today. In a few communities, a health and welfare council existed. It functioned primarily for the then called Community Chest or Red Feather agencies. Human services planning was considered to be the province of the voluntary agencies.

Since the 1950s, however, numerous events have occurred that alter this conception of planning. Three changes in particular—multiple planning centers, citizen participation, and changed decision environment—have markedly affected the scope, practice, and objectives of planning in local communities.

Multiple Planning Centers

In addition to the city planning agency, there is now a number of functional agencies planning for specific groups or categories of special needs. Area agencies on aging, comprehensive health planning agencies, community development agencies, environmental planning agencies, community action agencies, and youth service planning agencies are just a few examples. Then, too, direct service agencies, such as public welfare and mental health departments, have been mandated to engage in community and state planning activities.

The objectives of the city planning agency have also changed. It no longer focuses exclusively on land use planning but engages in a wide range of community planning activities from housing, transportation, the environment, and in some instances, social welfare.

Similar changes are occurring in the field of human services planning. In fact, the more dramatic and rapid changes have taken place in the human services field. Almost 2,000 local communities are now served by a voluntary health and welfare planning council or similar United Way planning organization. In metropolitan communities, there are also voluntary planning agencies serving specialized needs—for example, housing, education, and mental retardation.

The major change in the field of human services planning, however, is the increased role of the government. Since the poverty program, governments at all levels have taken a more direct interest in coordinating and planning programs to alleviate social problems. In fact, of all the planning organizations that have emerged in the past few years, the vast majority are for human services, and the vast majority have been initiated by federal, state, or local governments.

The consequence of the multiple planning centers development has been to shift the practice emphasis of planning. Specialization is the objective, and the planning agency assumes the role of advocate around its particular specialization. The focus of the planning method becomes *problem* oriented rather than *goal* oriented.

Citizen Participation

A second change has been the opening up of the planning process to citizen involvement. Begun as a means to induce cooperation in urban renewal and then added, almost as an afterthought, to protect the rights of the poor in the poverty program, the function of citizen participation in planning has become fairly common in community planning activities. This is not to say that it is widely or amicably accepted. In some instances this is true. In other instances it is grudgingly accepted. But in almost all instances it is required by federal law or regulations. In fact, the President's National Commission on Neighborhoods reports that 62 pieces of federal legislation mandate citizen participation.

The type and scope of citizen participation in planning

differs from one class of planning organization to the next and, indeed, differs even within the same class of organization. In some states, for example, the extent of citizen participation in the development of an annual social services plan (Title XX of the Social Security Act) may mean merely the opportunity to respond to a proposed plan at a regionwide public hearing. In other states, citizen groups may be actively engaged in a variety of planning and decision-making tasks in preparing the plan. Regardless, however, of the type and structure of citizen participation, it has significantly altered the course of planning in America. Indeed, of all the changes this has had the most effect on planning practice and methods.

Planning no longer is the exclusive domain of technical experts. The task facing planners today is that of determining who should be involved, how they should be involved, what function citizens should serve, and how to adapt a planning method to a process involving a wide range of interests and groups. The planner has become both technical expert *and* organizer.

Decision Environment

The third change is the uncertain decision environment for planning. At one time the decision center for community planning was fixed, known, and centralized. Studies now reveal, however, that the decision-making procedure varies from one community to the next or, indeed, even from one issue to the next. What worked as a strategy for making a decision in one context may be incorrect or inappropriate in another.

The one valid conclusion that can be made is that decision-making in American communities is dispersed among a number of decision centers, formal and informal. Decision-making, moreover, tends to be a resultant, a consequence of a series of actions. It is not entirely the product of a scientific search; that is, the rational choice of a decision arrived at after examining alternative courses of action, as depicted at the outset of this chapter.

Moreover, the planner and planning organization appear no longer to be the single arbiter of decision-making recommendations. A number of organizations and groups vie both with one another and with the planning organization to influence decision choices. Success in influencing decisions seems not to be related to the wisdom or worthiness of a decision but rather to the politics of choice.

The consequence of this change has been to cast doubt on the traditional model of planning. That model assumed a centralized decision center; precluded, except at the planner's discretion, the involvement of anyone other than the planner; and did not allow for the existence of competing planning organizations. When at one time, the method of community planning was defined and understood, it is now confused and frustrating.

In response to the inappropriateness of the traditional model, several alternative approaches to planning have been proposed. Each is addressed to one or more faults of the traditional model. The disjointed incrementalism strategy of Braybrooke and Lindblom,[1] for example, eschews comprehensiveness and focuses on the remedial and incremental character of planning. Paul Davidoff promotes an advocacy/quasi–private-interest role for planning.[2] Amitai Etzioni emphasizes the relationship between controls and the need for consensus to guide planning.[3] Morris and Binstock stress the need to relate planning aims to the feasibility of implementing those aims.[4] And one of the newer approaches is to view planning as a form of social learning that occurs in the transactions between planners and clients.[5] The object of such planning is the innovative adaptation of social organizations to a constantly shifting environment, but its ultimate purpose is to support and enhance the individual's own development as a person in the course of transforming action itself.[6]

What is significant in these newer approaches to planning is that each represents a shift away from a rational mode of planning dominated by a planner to a *process* of planning that recognizes the influence of other individuals in defining planning objectives. The emphasis, moreover, is on the achievement of particular plans as opposed to the development of master plans to guide day-by-day decisions. And finally, there is the recognition that the planner and the planning organization is just one of a number of influences on community decision-making.

COGNITIVE AND SOCIAL PROCESSES OF PLANNING

This is the general thrust of community planning described in this book. Planning is viewed as part of a social change process that depends on the participation of citizens and groups, both for the *effectiveness* of its results and the *achievement* of its objectives. Planning is defined here as the application of conscious and deliberate methods to capture the future for the purpose of either altering the present to redirect the future, or changing the future in order to preserve the present. Planning, furthermore, is an activity in which the purpose is not only to solve a problem but also to seek acceptance and implementation of the solution.

Consequently, the activity of planning requires three distinct yet interrelated ways of thinking:

1. Ways of understanding the past and the present.
2. Ways of imagining the future.
3. Ways of achieving the future.[7]

The first two ways of thinking are termed the substantive process of planning. This is the ordinary and familiar conception of planning. Fact-finding, study, examination of alternative courses of action, and the proposing of solutions are the common tasks.

The third way of thinking—that is, achieving the future—is the social process aspect of planning. This is the conception of planning as part of a political process in which the planner intervenes into a set of existing or newly constructed social networks for the purpose of achieving planned social change. This intervention generates a process of planning that is collaborative in nature. It is also a conception of planning that recognizes that successful intervention requires a mandate or permission to intervene as well as an appropriate strategy to influence decision outcomes.

It is the social process aspect of planning that is emphasized in this book. That is not to imply that the substantive process of planning is any less important. Not at all. There are, however, any number of texts available to the reader stressing the technical or design characteristics of planning. It is the social process characteristics of planning, on the other hand, that have proved to be of current concern and interest. Designing the future is important, but achieving the future is equally, if not more, important.[8]

A Note on the Meaning of the Term "Community Planning"

Throughout this book, the terms "planning" and "community planning" are used interchangeably. For our purposes they mean the same. Also, the term "community" is not meant to suggest that the planning process described here is relevant only at the community level. Planning goes on at a variety of different levels today—neighborhood, municipal, county, region, state, and national. What is described in this text is applicable to all levels of planning, except possibly the national level.[9] National planning has a tradition more in common with economic development than in planned social change, which is the emphasis here. Whether or not a model stressing a social process orientation is applicable to national planning is difficult to say. There has not been enough analysis of national planning efforts to make this judgment at this time.

Another term used in a universal context is "agency" or "planning agency." Although it is customary to think of community planning within an *agency* perspective, the term may be misleading. Planning today is performed in a variety of different organizational contexts. Planning may be:

- An exclusive function of a single organization, such as a city planning commission, a council of governments, an urban redevelopment authority, a community welfare council, or a municipal human services planning department of the mayor's office.
- A specialized function within an organization offering direct services, such as a state department of mental health, a public social services agency (Title XX agency), or a voluntary federated fund-raising organization.
- A major function within an organization that provides other ancillary functions, such as a state aging planning agency or a council of daycare providers.
- A part-time responsibility of a staff person whose primary job is to administer or supervise direct services, such as in a Title XX agency in a sparsely populated state.
- A joint activity of two or more agencies, such as a coordinated planning activity carried on by a county social services agency and the area planning agency on aging.

When the term "agency" is used, we mean it to apply to all types of planning organizations and activities. No distinction is made between the type of planning carried on in one agency as opposed to another.

Obviously there are distinctions. Planning styles can and do differ from one organization to the next. There is growing evidence that structure and planning style are interrelated variables. This is discussed in Chapter 14.

The point we are making here, however, and which needs reemphasizing, is that the focus of this book is the *social* and *political* processes of planning. This is common in varying degrees to all styles of planning. An equally important and interrelated aspect is the participatory character of planning. A major purpose of this book is to outline a method and rationale for involving individuals and groups in community planning activities.

STRUCTURE OF BOOK

This book is divided into two parts. Part I is an explanation of planning as a social and political process. The characteristics of the process are outlined and include the following:

- The influence of the decision environment on the planning process (Chapter 1).
- The necessity for sanction and legitimacy to influence decision outcomes (Chapter 2).
- The participatory base of planning (Chapter 3).
- The various strategies for involving participants in planning (Chapter 4).
- The relationship between planning and social change (Chapter 5).
- The types of social change (Chapter 5).

Part II is the application of the social and political processes of planning to a strategy of community planning. A planning diagram (Chapter 6) outlines six phases in the planning process. The objective in Part II is to identify techniques related to each of the six phases of planning. Based on principles explained in Part II of the text, the techniques describe methods of organizing planning constituencies, developing motivation for planning, setting goals, diagnosing the acceptance of planning objectives, developing strategies for decision-making, and implementing a plan.

NOTES

1. David Braybrooke and Charles E. Lindblom, *A Strategy of Decision* (New York: Free Press, 1963).

2. Paul Davidoff, "Advocacy and Pluralism in Planning," *Journal of the American Institute of Planners,* Vol. XXXI (November 1965) pp. 331–337.

3. Amitai Etzioni, *The Active Society: A Theory of Society and Political Processes,* (New York: Free Press, 1968) and "Towards Theory of Guidance," Sarajane Heidt and Amatai Etzioni (eds.) *Societal Guidance: A New Approach to Social Problems* (New York: Crowell, 1969).

4. Robert Morris and Robert W. Binstock, *Feasible Planning for Social Change* (New York: Columbia University Press, 1966).

5. The following are cited as examples: Donald N. Michael, *On Learning to Plan—and Planning to Learn* (San Francisco: Jossey-Bass, 1973); John Friedmann, *Retracking America: A Theory of Transactive Planning* (Garden City, N.Y., Anchor Doubleday, 1973); John Friedmann and Barclay Hudson, "Knowledge and Action: A Guide to Planning Theory," *Journal of the American Institute of Planners,* Vol. 40, No. 1 (January 1974) pp. 2–16, and Donald A. Schon, *Beyond the Stable State* (New York: Random House, 1971.)

6. Friedmann and Hudson, op. cit., p. 7, and Friedmann, op. cit., pp. 223–242. Interestingly, the emphasis that the objective of planning is to promote man's development can also be found in early social work planning literature. The primary objective of community organization oriented planning was not a plan—a new daycare center or a housing project —but increasing the capacity of people to learn how to work together in order to form a cooperative and collaborative society. See Murray G. Ross, *Community Organization* (New York: Harper and Row, 1955) pp. 48–50.

7. Richard S. Bolan, "Mapping the Planning Theory Terrain," David R. Godschalk (ed.) *Planning in America: Learning from Turbulence* (Washington, D.C.: American Institute of Planning, 1974), pp. 13–34.

8. Some have suggested that the social process of planning is planning's dominant feature, and it is only incidentally a technical task. See Frederick L. Ahearn, Jr., Richard S. Bolan, and Edmund M. Burke, "A Social Action Approach for Planning Education in Social Work," *Journal of Education for Social Work,* Vol. 11, No. 3 (Fall 1975), pp. 5–11.

9. Friedmann and Hudson, op. cit., pp. 3–4 and 11–12.

Part I

Chapter 1

CHARACTERISTICS OF COMMUNITY DECISION-MAKING

Organization theorists contend that two functions are critically necessary for the effective operation of an organization. One is the securing of sufficient information and wisdom for the purpose of making organizationally rational decisions. The second is the coordinating function: coordinating the behaviors of the organization's members in respect to decisions once they are made.[1]

The former is defined as *expertise;* that is, securing decisions of a high quality of rationality and effectiveness—or, in other words, the adoption of a *good* decision. The coordinating function on the other hand is aimed at the adoption by all members of an organization or group of the *same* decision.[2]

Expertise is an advisory function. It is a framework or background for decisional premises. Coordination, however, is an operational or administrative function. Indeed, coordination is the very essence of management.[3]

Planning that is a means of arriving at decisions of high quality is a function of expertise. It is a device for influencing decisions,[4] and as a consequence, defined as a staff rather than as a line function. The planner or planning agency *advises* decision centers. The decision center or managing function decides whether or not the premises of the planner are "correct" for decision-making. If they are correct, the planner's "plan" is implemented.

This is a very common and logical conception of the relationship between planning and decision-making. It is, however, deceptively misleading; indeed, probably the most misleading conception in planning. No such dichotomous nor disinterested relationship is possible.

For one thing, community decision centers function in a *political* environment. They are subject to all the conditions of community politics that may and frequently do include bargaining and negotiation in arriving at a decision. The concept of planning as a source of expertise in advising decision centers may be useful in industry where efficiency is a guide, but it is inappropriate in communities where the competing guides of the common good, getting reelected, maintaining a job, and serving a constituency are the rule.

Secondly, it fails to recognize that community planning assumes action. A basic premise of planning is change. As Bolan has observed, "To prepare a plan is to promote a cause."[5] A characteristic of community planning is that it intervenes into the process of decision-making in order to influence the decision outcome.

The relationship between planning and the community decision environment will be examined in this chapter. The reason why community planning intervenes into the decision-making process will be discussed in the next chapter.

THE CHARACTERISTICS OF DECENTRALIZATION

It is true that up until about the mid-1950s, planners and local government officials generally assumed that community decision-making was centralized. Communities, it was believed, were governed in a fairly formal and consistent manner. The leadership of a community comprised mainly public officials and prominent private individuals representing major interests in the community.

Doubtless, this pattern of a decision system did exist, particularly in cities with "boss" control. Doubtless, too, it does exist in some cities today. But it is rare.[3] A number of studies have indicated that community decision-making emerges out of a process involving a number of individuals, groups, and organizations. Individuals, groups, and organizations vie with one another to influence decisions either to protect or to promote their own self-interest.[7]

Moreover, the increasing role of citizen participation that began in the mid-1950s has further diminished the capacity of community decision-making to be centralized. The role of citizens in community planning activities tends to vary, as we shall see in Chapters 3 and 4. Experience reveals, however, that once citizens are permitted to participate in a community activity, they tend to demand increased influence. It is safe to predict therefore, that citizens will exert more rather than less influence in future community planning activities.

One characteristic of the community decision environment, therefore, is that it is *not* centralized. Few if any community issues are decided on by a single individual acting arbitrarily and autonomously.

A number of individuals can be expected to play a role in deciding and influencing community issues. A study of community decision-making in Syracuse, New York, identified seven roles involved in the exercise of community power.

One is the *initiator,* the person who proposes an issue for resolution. Another is the *expert,* the individual with substantive knowledge about a particular issue. A third is the *publicist,* who brings an issue out on the community agenda for problem solving. The *influentials,* because of their resources and their stake in the community, play a significant and substantial role in deciding community issues. A fifth role is one of acting as a *broker,* or negotiator, for the influentials. A similar role for the governmental decision centers is the *transmitter* of influence, that is, the person who can reach governmental officials, such as the head of a political party. (The last two roles, incidentally, can better be conceptualized as *gatekeepers.* Gatekeepers are those who monitor entry to a decision center.)

The final role is that of the assigned or *nominal decision center.* This role is enacted by those officials who are responsible for the adoption of a planning proposal—mayor, agency director, legislative committee, and the like.[8]

The successful adoption of a planning proposal, therefore, depends, first, on identifying the appropriate actors integral to the adoption of a plan; and, second, it depends on the development of an organizational schema that relates such actors to the planning and decision-making activity. Techniques for achieving both of these objectives are outlined in Chapter 8.

STATUS QUO CHARACTERISTIC

Another characteristic of the decision environment is the preference to maintain the status quo. Change in general is more often than not resisted. Community change, however, is frequently resisted. A community decision is usually the consequence of competing and conflicting claims and values. To approve one decision will please one group and displease another. Decision centers prefer to displease no one.

Secondly, decision-making represents more than just approving or disapproving a proposal. It involves hard choices in which there may be winners and losers. Decision-makers can be expected to shrink from such choices. Indeed, it has been said that decision centers spend more time trying to avoid making a decision than in making and carrying out the consequences of a decision.

It is necessary for the planner to understand that he or she operates in a decision environment that is frequently negative.

Planning represents change. The achievement of planning objectives, consequently, will require strategies that will overcome the common resistance to change.

Characteristic of Community Power

A long-held tenet of community politics is the concept of the power behind the throne. The belief that a small group of influentials control a community's destiny goes back even further than the writings of Machiavelli. It is an important topic in decision-making and also one that is replete with misunderstandings, contentions, and myth. It is, moreover, a significant topic because the long-held belief does have considerable credibility.

The important questions of community power are: Who has power? How is it exercised? At what costs? Toward what end?

Perhaps the seminal work on community power theory must be credited to Floyd Hunter,[9] a social work professor. Hunter's interest in community power structure grew out of the frustrations of his former students who were employed in voluntary welfare planning councils. Reporting they had little influence over social welfare decisions, they assumed someone else outside the formal decision-making structure did.

Hunter went to Atlanta (he called it "Regional City") to study the structure of community influence. He began by studying newspaper accounts, then interviewed civic and community leaders; finally by using a panel of judges, he saw a pattern of influence emerge. The pattern resembled a pyramid with an industrial and business elite at the top, followed by bank vice-presidents, small business people (owners), top public officials, attorneys, followed by civic organization personnel, newspaper writers, selected organization executives, and concluding at the base with professionals, such as ministers, teachers, and social workers.[10]

Each level in the pyramid structure had its own functions. The elites at the top ruled; frequently and preferably behind the scenes. Actors within other levels could initiate action but did so only with the assent of the power elite. Yet it was not uncommon, according to Hunter, for the ruling elite to involve others in decision-making, not for the purpose of abdicating its ruling function, but to create a sense of community-wide participation.[11]

Initially acclaimed, Hunter's study later generated critics. The methodology was questioned. If one started out by asking, "Who has power?" said the critics, "You will generate a self-fulfilling prophecy and discover a pyramid of power."

A later study by Dahl in New Haven, employing a different methodology, arrived at conclusions that differed from Hunter's.[12] Dahl examined specific community issues (urban renewal, public education and political nominations) to determine who were involved in such issues in contradistinction to Hunter's reputational method of study.

Similar to Hunter, Dahl discovered a hierarchy of power resembling a pyramid. Unlike Hunter, however, what Dahl discovered was not a single pyramid of community power but a series of pyramids each structured around a specific issue. Moreover, elites active in one issue area were not active in other issue areas, leading Dahl to conclude:

1. Many different resources for influencing officials are available to different citizens.
2. With few exceptions, these resources are unequally distributed.
3. Individuals best off in their access to one kind of resource are often badly off with respect to many other resources.
4. No one influence resource dominates all the others in all or even in most key decisions.
5. With some exceptions, an influence resource is effective in some issue areas or in some specific decisions, but not in all.

6. Virtually no one, and certainly no group of more than a few individuals, is entirely lacking in some influence resource.[13]

Dahl's conclusions were also criticized, again for methodological reasons. The issue areas, it was said, were so divergent that it precluded the possibility of overlap in elite participation.[14] There may have been a power pyramid in New Haven, but the structure of the study ruled out the possibility of discovering it. To conclude, too, that no group is lacking in influence is questionable. Underprivileged groups responded by rioting in American cities in the early 1960s precisely because they could not use traditional means for influencing community decision-making.

These early disputes of community power studies have not been settled. Some continue to insist that communities are ruled by an elite, usually a corporate elite. Others contend that a much more diffuse pattern of power exists. Yet, there is increasing evidence to suggest that a variety of structures exists among American communities. No one pattern fits all cities and towns, but rather diversity is the rule. One analyst has suggested four types of power or decision-making structures.[15] (See Figure 1–1.)

Type 1, the mass participation model, assumes active members who participate in all decisions. This may be characteristic of small New England towns and a small number of experimental communities that emerged in the 1960s and 1970s.

The monolithic model, Type 2, represents the structure Hunter describes. The polylithic model, Type 3, approximated Dahl's findings and assumes that there is a number of different issue areas, although each issue area is characterized by a monolithic decision-making structure. Most large American communities tend to be characterized by this type of decision-making structure. The trend, moreover, because of the increasing scale of society or urbanization, is toward this type of decision-making structure.[16]

Type 4, or what Clark calls the pluralistic model, which

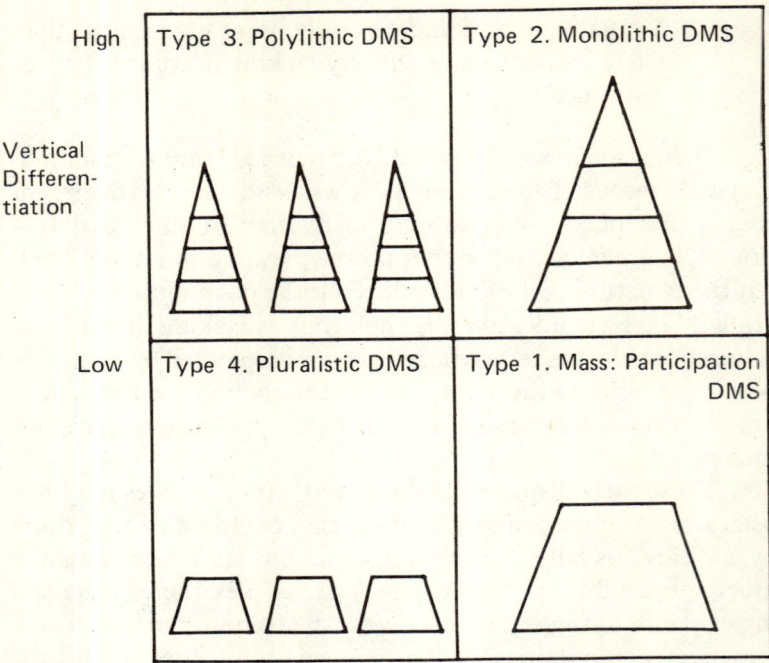

Figure 1–1 Four types of decision-making structures. (From Terry N. Clark, "Social Stratification, Differentiation and Integration," Terry N. Clark, Ed., *Community Structure and Decision Making: Comparative Analyses;* San Francisco: Chandler, 1968, p. 37.)

Type 4, or what Clark calls the pluralistic model, which is a term he uses in a more limited way than others, is characterized by many different influence hierarchies in distinct issue areas. There is little differentiation in influence among the actors. This type of structure may be found in small wealthy American suburbs.

To summarize the issue of community power at this point: There is no hard-and-fast rule about how power is structured in American communities. It tends to be related to the type of community. Planners should examine the type of community before making generalizations on how power is structured in their own communities.

Further Refinements of Community Power Theory

How power is structured, we have learned, is only one facet of the concept of community power. Community power and decision-making is somewhat more complex, involving such factors as transactions among actors, the changing base of power and influence, and the effect of organized efforts on influencing decisions.

One refinement suggests that the exercise of power is not a unilateral process but one that involves a transaction between the actor employing influence and the actor being influenced. Moreover, the transaction is bounded and constrained by the consequence of using the influence (that is, the gains and losses in the actor's stock of influence), the issue itself and the decision behavior of the community social system. To explain this, let us start with a definition.

Banfield's definition is the most useful for our purposes. He explains that power is the ability to control an actor who has authority over assenting to or withholding action requisite to the adoption of a proposal.[17] A *requisite* action is one that is necessary for the adoption of a proposal. An actor who can perform a requisite action is one who has *authority* over that action. An actor who has power over individuals having authority over requisite actions is defined as an actor having control.[18]

Banfield uses a diagram (Figure 1–2) to depict the relationship between actors having authority over a requisite action and actors having control. This is a simple representation that assumes that control is centralized. When control is not centralized, which we can assume is more common, there may be multiple pyramids involving different actors with authority and different actors with control (Figure 1–3).

An important distinction between an actor having control and an actor exercising control needs to be made. Control is not exercised without the assent of the actor to whom the control is directed. An actor chooses to place himself or herself under

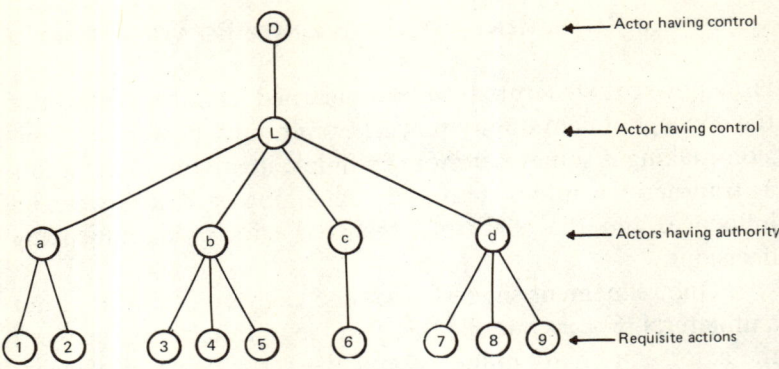

Figure 1–2 Relationship of requisite actions to actors having authority and control where control is centralized. (From Edward C. Banfield, *Political Influence;* New York: Free Press, 1961, p. 309.)

the control of another. "No actor," explains Banfield, ". . . ever gives a requisite action unless control over him has first been established by an exercise of power. That is to say, the actor must be persuaded, deceived, bribed, or otherwise induced to accept control, or else he will not give the requisite action."[19]

Power, then, is exercised in terms of costs. What will it cost to induce another individual to accept control?

Power, however, cannot be exercised at any cost. Individuals have limited stocks of power. It can either be consumed (spent) or invested (used to maintain or generate more power). The latter is the general rule. As Banfield points out:

> Every actor seeks to maintain or increase his stock of power. That is, capital is always "invested," never "consumed." An actor exercises power only when he thinks doing so will improve his net position (he may, of course, invest to minimize losses) when there are alternative investment possibilities, he always chooses the one he thinks will be most profitable.[20]

Before an individual exercises power, assuming, of course, that the individual has sufficient stock of power to exercise, he

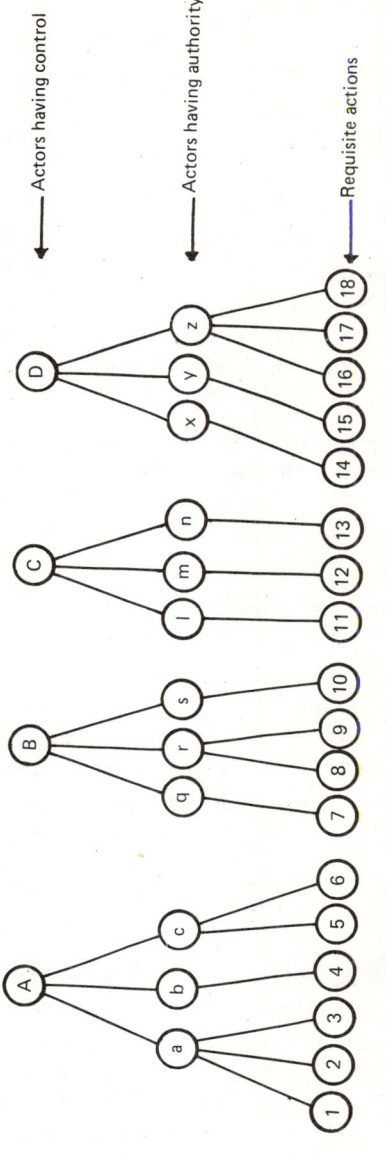

Figure 1-3 Relationship of requisite actions to actors having authority and control where a proposal is related to multiple actors having control. (From Edward C. Banfield, *Political Influence;* New York: Free Press, 1961, p. 311.)

or she assesses the benefits and losses that will result before inducing someone to come under his or her control. What will it cost? Is the issue itself worth the investment? What returns can be expected? ... Further power? ... Control over future actions? ... Payment of past debts? ... Benefit from the issue itself?

On the other hand, the actor to whom the power is directed asks similar questions. What will be the benefits and losses for agreeing to come under the control of another; and obversely, what will be the benefits and losses for refusing? The important point is that either implicitly or explicitly, a transaction takes place and power is not exercised without an awareness of the transaction.

The reader, however, should be cautioned. The typology of power and its use, as borrowed from Banfield, is an "ideal type" representation. It makes an assumption, similar to the assumptions of economists, that actors have almost omniscient rationality. It assumes that each actor is aware of all benefits and losses, knows the consequences of all alternative actions, and weighs the benefits and losses of each alternative action.

This is obviously absurd. Not only are there limitations to knowing alternatives and consequences for any course of action, but also individuals act in response to social and psychological influences. An individual may act impulsively in one situation and not in another; angrily in one instance and not in another; foolishly (at least in terms of squandering his or her stock of power) on one issue and knowledgeably on another.

Despite this caution, the Banfield analysis is extremely useful in understanding the nature of power and influence. It correctly identifies the transactional aspect of utilizing influence. It points out, as well, that in the adoption of a proposal a number of requisite actions are necessary. In turn, this provides a model for identifying requisite and influential actors in the adoption of a proposal.

Changing Character of Influence

A second refinement of community power theory, derived from the work of Nuttall, Scheuch, and Gordon, suggests that a dichotomous distinction defining an actor with or without power is misleading.[21] In fact, the term "power" may be too limited. The important distinction is what resources are required for influencing a decision and how is influence related to decision outcomes?

An influence resource is defined as anything that allows one actor to control, provide, or apply a sanction (positive or negative) to another actor.[22] Such resources would include legitimated authority, control over votes, access to information, the ability to destroy or enhance reputations, or money. Personal characteristics, intelligence, expertise, a likeable personality, persistence, and friendship networks are also resource sources.[23] In this sense there are few, if any, individuals without an access to influence resources. Often the effectiveness of influence is related to the way in which resources can be organized.

Nuttall and his colleagues suggest there are four types of influence. They are:

1. *Manifest influence:* an actor having a resource and also credited with having it.
2. *Potential influence:* an actor having access to a resource but not being credited with it.
3. *Reputed influence:* an actor not having access to a resource but being credited with the ability to use influence.
4. *Without influence:* the most simple type; an actor without influence and recognized as not having influence.[24]

This typology is an important reference point for two reasons. One, it identifies the actual categories of influence. Two, it allows for change in resource attributes. It is misleading to suggest that resource attributes change simply from no influence to influence, or from influence to no influence. The simplest example is an actor with potential influence who moves to the category of manifest influence by virtue of changing the potential attributes to one of actual attributes.

This can be seen more readily in relation to the decision process of community issues. Issues move through several decision modes.[25] Furthermore, a community often is faced with many issues at the same time. Consequently, decisions are being made often and are being made at various stages in the development of several issues. Who is involved in each decision varies greatly with the issue and with its stage in a decision process.

In turn, this can affect the resource attributes of the actors who become involved in the various stages of the decision process. For example, planning agency officials may have manifest influence in the beginning stages of planning a highway route; that is, achieving initial approval, securing planning funds, and even beginning preliminary acquisition along the planned route. At later stages, as the plan becomes more visible and threatening, other individuals may organize, form into groups and coalitions of groups, and move from a category of potential influence to actors with manifest influence. Similarly, the planning officials can move from a category of manifest influence to one of reputed influence or even no influence.

It is more likely that the planning officials will move to the category of potential influence rather than to no influence. Because of their initial manifest influence, they would be perceived to have some measure of influence.

Organized Efforts to Obtain Influence

A third refinement of community power theory indicates that an organized campaign effort on behalf of community change may be even more significant than merely the involvement of community elites. In a study of the role of reputational leaders affecting the outcome of issues in 18 New England communities, William Gamson discovered that in those issues (52 in number) in which community leaders were involved, there was more likelihood of success (in almost 50 per cent of the campaigns) than if community leaders were not involved. If, however, the leaders are active and united, that is, engaged in an organized campaign effort on behalf of the issue, they were successful 75 per cent of the time. In addition, the side supporting change wins only 30 per cent of the time without the united support of reputational leaders but 66 per cent of the time with it.[26]

The implication of Gamson's findings suggest that influence is but one part of the community decision behavior question. Techniques of persuasion, public relations and education, and an organized constituency effort play a significant role in the adoption of plans and proposals. These will be discussed in a later chapter.

The Characteristic of Organizational Behavior

To single out an organization as an actor distinct from other actors as a source of influence in community decision-making may be not entirely correct. Organizations are merely a subset of a class of actors attempting to influence community decisions. Nonetheless, because of their uniqueness, and more important, their maintenance behavior, they need to be highlighted as a special characteristic in the decision environment.

Organizations, community organizations in particular, are continually engaged in a process of influence survival. They are forced to provide satisfactions for their various members in order to maintain their membership as a whole. To provide satisfactions, organizations need to engage in activities that will increase or at least maintain their supply of influence. It is a form of self-protection. Organizations, therefore, as Banfield has noted, engage in opportunistic decision-making, they "extemporize, meeting each crisis as it arises."[27]

The reasons lying behind this conclusion will be explained in a later chapter. At this point, however, a simple example can be used to illustrate the principle. United Way organizations have to be keenly sensitive to any change in public welfare regulations. Many of their supported agencies are partially financed through contracts with state and local public welfare departments. Any change in the welfare regulations can seriously affect the funding balance of the individual agencies. When a change is proposed or even contemplated, United Way organizations intervene into the decision-making process to determine the decision's effect on their member agencies. If it is found to be affecting the agencies negatively, there will be an attempt to influence and change the decision outcome.

This behavior is not unique. The network of interdependence among organizations, public and private, built up since the early 1960s has created a situation in which the decision of one set of organizations can critically affect the survival of others. Organizations, consequently, are forced to attempt to control the external environment. They do so by attempting to influence community decisions.

The role organizations play in influencing decision is probably more crucial than the role of a group of elites. The motivation to influence decisions on the part of organizations is survival. Whereas the motivation on the part of elites may range from altruism through increasing power to self-interest or even self-gain. However powerful some of these motivations may be, they are not as compelling as survival.

SUMMARY

The objective of this chapter has been to outline the characteristics of the decision environment as they affect planning. The following principles have been deduced:

1. Because of the wide range of community groups and organizations involved in influencing community decisions, as well as the increasing trend toward participation in governmental programs, decision-making tends to be decentralized in American communities.
2. Although there may be variability of decision-making structures among communities, it is safe to assume that urban communities are characterized by power structures that are polylithic rather than monolithic or elitist.
3. The use of power to influence decisions is a transactional process between the actor exercising power and the actor to whom the power is directed. At the very least, actors generally attempt to maintain their supply of influence.
4. There are several resources that can be used to develop or enhance influence. Influence attributes, moreover, are capable of changing.
5. The adoption of any proposal requires a number of requisite actions to be made.
6. There are several different decision points along the process of adopting a proposal and each decision point is subject to different sets of influence.
7. The influence attributes of actors can change from one decision phase to another within the same proposal.
8. Organized campaign efforts on behalf of a proposal is a form of influence.
9. Because of their need for survival, community organizations play a compelling role in influencing decisions.

NOTES

1. Herbert A. Simon, *Administrative Behavior* (New York: Macmillan, 1961), pp. 136–140.
2. Ibid.
3. Chester I. Barnard, *The Functions of the Executive,* (Cambridge, Mass.: Harvard University Press, 1946), pp. 215–234.
4. Simon, op. cit., p. 228.
5. Richard S. Bolan, "The Social Relations of the Planner," *Journal of the American Institute of Planners,* Vol. 37, No. 6 (November 1971), p. 395.
6. Francine Rabinovitz's study of planning in New Jersey reveals two cities that closely resemble this type of political leadership. See Francine F. Rabinovitz, *City Politics and Planning* (New York: Atherton Press, 1969), pp. 59–78, 63–64.
7. Martin Myerson and Edward C. Banfield, *Politics, Planning and the Public Interest* (New York: Free Press, 1950); Altshuler, op. cit.; Rabinovitz, op. cit.; Roscoe Martin and Frank Munger, et al., *Decisions in Syracuse* (Garden City, N.Y.: Doubleday, 1965) and Edward C. Banfield, *Political Influence* (New York: Free Press, 1961).

8. Martin and Munger, et al., op. cit., pp. 323–331.
9. Floyd Hunter, *Community Power Structure* (Chapel Hill: University of North Carolina Press, 1953).
10. Ibid., p. 109.
11. Hunter provides an example of this in his description of the establishment of an international trade council in Regional City, ibid., pp. 172–174.
12. Robert Dahl, *Who Governs?* (New Haven, Conn.: Yale University Press, 1961).
13. Ibid., p. 228.
14. H. W. Bruck, "Book Review," *Journal of the American Institute of Planners,* Vol. 28, No. 4 (November 1962), pp. 293–295.
15. Terry N. Clark, "Social Stratification, Differentiation and Integration," Terry N. Clark (Ed.), *Community Structure and Decision Making: Comparative Analyses* (San Francisco: Chandler, 1968), pp. 25–44. For further illustration of the diversity of leadership concept, see Harold L. Nix, *The Community and Its Involvement in the Study Planning Action Process* (Atlanta: U.S. Department of Health, Education, and Welfare, 1977), pp. 19–24.
16. This conclusion is drawn from a study of 166 communities conducted by Claire Gilbert, as well as Terry Clark's findings. See: Claire W. Gilbert, "Community Power and Decision Making: A Quantitative Examination of Previous Research"; Clark, op. cit., pp. 139–156.
17. Banfield, op. cit., p. 348.
18. Ibid., pp. 309–312.
19. Ibid., p. 312.
20. Ibid., p. 313.
21. Ronald L. Nuttall, Erwin K. Scheuch, and Chad Gordon, "On the Structure of Influence," Clark, op. cit. pp. 349–380.
22. Ibid., pp. 352–353.
23. Ibid., p. 353.
24. Ibid., pp. 360–364.
25. Ibid., pp. 356–357.

26. William A. Gamson, "Reputation and Resources in Community Politics," *The American Journal of Sociology,* Vol. 72, No. 2, (September 1966), pp. 121–131.
27. Edward C. Banfield, "Ends and Means in Planning," *UNESCO International Social Science Journal,* Vol. XI, No. 3 (1959), p. 363.

Chapter 2

THE PRINCIPLE OF LEGITIMACY

Decision-making is not an event that occurs independently of other events. It is part of a chain of activities ranging from a point at which a choice is made to make a decision and the decision itself. There are, therefore, activities antecedent to a decision indicating that decision-making is not a discrete activity but a *process*.

Some antecedent activities may be haphazard or unexplained—capriciousness, reflex actions; some may be routine—habit, standard procedures; while others may be purposive and deliberate—reflection, analyses, planning. What is significant about planning as an antecedent activity, however, is its interactional characteristic. Planning, as we noted, is rarely ever purely an advisory function. It *intervenes* into the process of decision-making. More important, the intention is to influence the outcome. The influence may be subtle or it may be open and pronounced, but it exists; and it exists because of the stake both the planner and planning agency have in the outcome of a plan.

The planner's stake is purely personal, and is a consequence of his or her involvement in the planning activity. The involvement in the planning process creates a commitment to the plan, and therefore, a personal investment to influence the plan's outcome. This is a basic principle of human behavior. Individuals who are engaged in an activity with meaning for them are motivationally disposed to accomplish that activity.[1]

Frequently, planners view this as a part of their *professionalism*. Employed as professionals, they see themselves called upon to exercise autonomous judgments, a recognized attribute of a profession. This, however, merely provides added sanction to intervene. Despite the prescription of professionalism, the compelling force for intervening and attempting to influence the decision outcome is the involvement in the planning activity itself.

There is an exception to this. If an individual's involvement in an activity is an academic exercise or if his or her contributions are repeatedly rebuffed, then there is no stake, or, indeed, interest in the outcome. Planning becomes an academic exercise. The United States' requirement for a comprehensive plan as part of an entitlement for developmental funds under the Alliance for Progress led to plans that were ritualistic exercises. Recent studies of state social services planning under Title XX of the Social Security Act reveal similar behaviors. Plans in some states have become compliance documents merely to fulfill federal regulations.[2]

Nonetheless this does not obviate the principle.[3] Our interest, moreover, is not in compliance planning, but in planning in which developmental outcomes are desired.

The organization's commitment, on the other hand, is related to the principle of organizational survival referred to in the preceding chapter. Organizational theorists[4] report that an organization is governed in part by the way in which it can offer inducements or incentives to attract and sustain the contribution of its members. Incentives are "payments" made by or through an organization to its participants in return for the contribution the participant makes to the organization. An individual will continue the participation in an organization only so long as the incentives or inducements offered to him or her are as great or greater (measured in terms of values and in terms of the alternatives open to him or her) than the contribution he or she is asked to make. If an organization does not have sufficient inducements to offer, it cannot attract and sustain the contribution of its members or participants.[5] Consequently, as Chester Barnard has noted, "Hence, in all sorts of organizations the affording of adequate incentives becomes the most definitely emphasized task in their existence."[6]

Community organizations have a limited supply of incentives. Status and power is one set, and often the most crucial. Ideal benefactions is another. The term "ideal benefactions" refers to the capacity of the organization to satisfy the personal ideals of the participants, such as identification with the organization and its purpose, altruistic service, and the satisfaction of individual motives. Of lesser importance but still useful as incentives are the social compatibility of the members with one another and the opportunity to be engaged in what could be an important event or course of events.[7]

It is important to note here that reference to organizational members is not limited to paid employees. Organizational membership includes all those who are active in any capacity in support of the organization or any one of its activities, such as volunteers.

An organization develops its incentives through its own accomplishments.[8] The more successful an organization is in achieving its objectives the more likely it is that it can offer a wider range of incentives, which in turn can be used to recruit more influential participants and thereby further increase the status of the organization or make it easier to accomplish other objectives. Organizations, therefore, will use techniques and strategies and define objectives in ways that will lead to the successful accomplishment of the objectives—or, in other words, influence the achievement of the objective.

But community organizations, such as planning agencies,

are particularly vulnerable to losing their stock of incentives, because they are frequently in competition with other organizations over a limited supply of incentives. They may, too, be in competition with one another over the same issue. They are forced, then, to act to protect their supply of incentives. We have situations, therefore, in which organizations may intervene into a decision-making process not in response to community or social needs but in order to obtain advantages vis-á-vis other organizations. In this case organizations are acting opportunistically.

Now the reader is cautioned that there is an assumption of omniscient rationality here. Not all organizations act wisely or successfully in all instances. Hindsight often reveals that some organizations intervened in issues when they should not have, and some did not intervene when they should have.

To intervene, however, there must be a sanction to do so. Permission, in other words, must be given to the planner and planning agency to intervene and influence decision outcomes. That permission is termed *legitimacy*. Legitimacy is defined as an allowance bestowed on an organization[9] that sanctions its right to intervene into and influence the decisions of another organization or decision center.

In this definition, the character of legitimacy is determined not by the organization itself, but by an external agent; that is, the organization or the decision center the organization is attempting to influence. Another organization, in other words, permits its behavior to be guided by the planning agency.

That permission, it should be pointed out, need not arise willingly. It can result from collaboration, negotiation, or pressure. Nonetheless, legitimacy is permissive behavior whether or not it is granted openly, grudgingly, or rebelliously.

Legitimacy should not be confused with authority, although there are similarities between the two. Authority is also transactional. An authoritive relationship exists only when the superior and subordinate accept the relationship. Moreover, the determination of authority, as Chester Barnard has pointed out, lies with the subordinate individuals,[10] just as a planning agency's legitimacy lies with the organization toward which the planning agency is directing its activities.

The concept of authority is governed by the fact that an individual accepts an order not blindly, but according to certain conditions. These conditions are that the order is understandable, that it is not contrary to the purpose of the organization, that it is compatible with the individual's own personal interest, and that the individual is able, physically and mentally, to comply with this order.[11]

Beyond these conditions, or zone of acceptance, in Herbert Simon's terms, orders will not be accepted.[12] The magnitude of the zone of acceptance is determined by the sanctions an organization is able to command. Sanctions are obtained through the initial acceptance of the organization's objectives and purpose. They are also obtained through persuasion and influence.

These are the sanctions or means by which legitimacy is obtained. But here is where the similarity between authority and legitimacy ends. The fundamental distinction is that authority implies a relationship between a superior and a subordinate. There is a line of authority in an administrative organization that has "the right to the last word," whenever disagreement cannot be resolved by discussion, persuasion, or other means of communication.[13]

No planning agency in the American system has ever been guaranteed the "right to the last word," even though there may be a legislative prescription that this type of authority exists—as, for example, the authoritative prescriptions granted to health planning agencies.

As part of this regulatory function, Health System Agencies (regional comprehensive health planning agencies) certify the need for medical services expansion in excess of $150,000. In Boston, the famous Leahy Clinic's planned relocation from the city to a suburb was rejected by the Health Systems Agency. The Leahy Clinic, in turn, went over the head of the HSA and successfully appealed to the state legislature.

Formal authority may be explicit—and, indeed, planning agencies as we shall see have sought authority—but the quest has been illusive. It is legitimacy, not authority, that sanctions the influence of the planning agency.

All planning activities, therefore, require legitimacy. The extent of actions necessary to obtain the legitimacy will vary. It will depend on the reason for initiating a plan, the nature of the plan, the specific planning solution, and most important, the relationship of the planning agency to a decision center.

A planning activity, for example, that cuts across and is designed to affect a number of different organizations will have to depend on extensive efforts to legitimize its activities for the purpose of influencing a number of decision centers. A planning effort, on the other hand, that emerges at the request of a decision center with the authority and willingness to act on a planning recommendation—such as an agency executive who requests a plan that will affect only the internal activities of his or her own organization—will require minimal legitimizing activities.

Let us be cautious, however. Even when a decision center confers legitimacy on a planning effort, it is not possible to presume that the planning decision will be accepted once the plan is completed.

Machiavelli's advice to the prince, Lorenzo De' Medici, should serve as a caveat for all planners.

> It should be borne in mind that there is nothing more difficult to arrange, more doubtful of success, and more dangerous to carry through than initiating changes.... The innovator makes enemies of all those who prospered under the old order, and only lukewarm support is forthcoming from those who would prosper under the new. Their support is lukewarm partly from fear of their adversaries, who have the existing laws on their side, and partly because men are generally incredulous, never really trusting new things unless they have tested them by experience.[14]

The technology for obtaining legitimacy is described in Chapter 8. At this point, however, we would like to describe the types of legitimacy that are necessary for planning. There are three: *positional, organizational,* and *role.* In describing the three types of legitimacy we will also explain how they emerged historically as a reference for planning.

Positional Legitimacy

Positional legitimacy is conferred. It is derived from the position or place within an organizational hierarchy. It exists, furthermore, regardless of who holds the position. Consequently, it can be passed on from one set of actors to another.

Significantly, prior to the early 1900s, city planning agencies did not have positional legitimacy. Initially, city planning operated under voluntary rather than local government auspices. Voluntarism was discarded, however, because all too often attempts to implement city plans met with consistent opposition. Daniel Burnham, for example, prepared a plan for the city of San Francisco, which incidentally the American Institute of Architects considered so exceptional that it recommended the plan as a model for other cities; yet it was completely ignored despite the fact that it was prepared, almost as if providentially, just before the earthquake. Similar difficulties were faced in other cities. St. Louis officials refused to implement its city plan and Burnham's famous plan for Chicago in 1909 initially met the same fate.

The failure to adopt exceedingly good and highly praised plans was attributed to the voluntary character of city planning. Indeed, considerable activity during the early 1900s on the part of such city planning leaders as Frederick Law Olmstead, Flavel Shurtleff, and Harland Bartholomew, was directed toward seeking sanction for planning within the framework of municipal government.[15] Looking back on this development, Harland Bartholomew commented:

> It was discovered that citizen committees, no matter how prominent, could not bring about the planning and preplanning of

American cities by voluntary action. Something more was needed. The mayor and city officials did not share the enthusiasm of the citizen committees. Without official sanction, no city plan could be carried out.[16]

The solution was to create a mandate for planning, to give it legislative sanction within the local government. In 1912, the first city planning commission was established in Hartford, Connecticut. Authority, or what was perceived to be authority, became fixed. Although the debate about the need for governmental status is raised occasionally,[17] the principle is clear.

The commitment of the planner to his creation led to the desire to intervene. It was a positional adaptation to authority. Sanction was viewed as a function of location. The assumptions were twofold: one, that position within an organizational entity determines sanction,[18] and second, that authority is prescribed in specific office holders, in this case, mayors and city officials.

Since the first city planning commissions, a variety of planning agencies have been given positional legitimacy. Renewal agencies, interstate planning commissions, and comprehensive health planning agencies are examples. Each has been given a mandate over a specific sphere of activities.

Yet positional legitimacy, despite legislative mandate, is limited also by the expectation of others. Authority, as we have seen, involves behaviors on the part of both those in positions of authority and those subject to authority. "When, and only when, these behaviors occur does a relation of authority exist between the two persons involved. When the behaviors do not occur there is no authority, whatever may be the 'paper' theory of organization."[19]

Comprehensive health planning agencies even with specific state and federal legislative sanction have found their mandate frustrated. The mandate is frustrated because influential organizations, teaching hospitals, powerful medical schools, are *unwilling* and at the same time *able* to reject the communicated decisions of the planning agency. Positional legitimacy, therefore, is not sufficient, in and of itself, to legitimate planning activities.

In summary, positional legitimacy is legislated and conferred upon an organization. It provides a formal mandate for an organization to engage in an activity (in our case planning) within a defined jurisdictional sphere. The jurisdiction is not exclusive. Other organizations may act within the same jurisdiction. Voluntary organizations are clear examples.

The mandate derived from positional legitimacy, however, does not extend to decision-making itself. Decision-making is reserved to a legislative or administrative entity; mayor, city council, county commissioner, legislature, agency administrator, for example. Nor does positional legitimacy guarantee the planning agency any more influence than any other organization, governmental or voluntary.

What it does guarantee is:

1. *Jurisdictional rights.* While other organizations may have to depend on other influence resources to sanction its intervention into a particular planning activity, an agency with positional legitimacy presupposes that jurisdictional sanction by virtue of a legislative mandate. An urban renewal agency, for example, has a mandate to be involved in slum clearance. A citizens group or private housing agency may also want to become involved whether to oppose or modify the slum clearance objectives. It, however, has to depend upon its own force of influence or the renewal agency's acquiescence to become involved.

2. *Formalized relationship to a decision center.* A planning agency with positional legitimacy has a *sanctioned* relationship to a decision center; an urban renewal agency has a sanctioned relationship with a city council for example. This means that its case can always at least be heard by the decision center. Organizations without positional legitimacy or organiza-

tions acting outside their jurisdiction, have no guarantee that they can present a plan to a decision center, let alone attempt to influence that decision center.

ORGANIZATIONAL LEGITIMACY

Where positional legitimacy is conferred and exists for the life of an organization, *organizational legitimacy* is earned and can be ephemeral. It derives from the planning organization's capacity to create sanctions for its activities from a variety of individuals, interest groups, and other organizations that may have influence upon decisions.

The necessity for organizational legitimacy for planning agencies is derived from the experience of community planning agencies in the 1960s. The Myerson-Banfield analysis of public housing planning in Chicago is the earliest and probably best illustration of the concept of organizational legitimacy.[20] Moreover, it is an excellent example of an attempt on the part of planners and a planning agency both to intervene into and to influence the decision-making process.

In summary, the Myerson-Banfield analysis represents a study of community decision-making in the planning of public housing in Chicago. (The reader, of course, is advised to examine the primary source.) Although the principal issue was the selection of sites for low-rent public housing, the planning agency (Chicago Housing Authority) and more specifically, the staff envisioned its role as an attempt to relate a specific housing program to an overall comprehensive or master plan for the city.[21] Admittedly, the agency was unable to frame its site selection decisions on a master plan because none existed, nor did the agency have time to develop a master plan. Nevertheless, the agency did base its decisions on its own conceptions, a priori, of the development needs of a city and what it saw as the needs of citizens in an urban city.[22] Equally, and if not more important, the agency staff viewed its role as a disinterested agent in protecting the public interest: "one function of planning, and especially of comprehensive planning, was to assert the supremacy of the public interest over private, partial or special interests."[23]

The planning proposals of the Chicago Housing Authority were repeatedly rebuffed. The initial plan represented a series of compromises involving in one form or another the mayor, aldermen, newspaper editors, consultants, party leaders, neighborhood groups, public officials, civic organizations, business leaders, trade union officials, and, it was suspected, even the President of the United States. The decision was nominally in the hands of the Chicago city council. It in turn was subject to the leadership of the mayor or chairman of the council finance committee. Neither the council nor its leadership could, or more correctly, would, agree to a decision, however rational, that did not meet the approval of a wide range of individuals and groups.

Despite the intentions of the Chicago Housing Authority, the accepted plan was determined not by any objective criteria or need but by bargaining, negotiation, and compromise among competing interest groups. The Chicago Housing Authority was just another interest group. Indeed, the planning agency once engaged in winning support for the plan abandoned its disinterested public interest role and became an active private interest group. On at least a half dozen occasions, the planning agency staff intervened directly in an attempt to influence decision-making. It encouraged, supported, and advised an advocate group of influential citizens;[24] it directly attempted to influence local elected officials including the mayor;[25] and twice sought to use federal officials to intervene on the planning agencies' behalf.[26]

It was a case, however, of too little too late. Other groups more adept at the politics of decision-making made better use of organizational tactics and strategies. Nonetheless, the Chicago planners did recognize that in addition to a cause and a position of presumed authority they also needed to persuade others about the merits of their cause.

Where the planners of the early 1900s sought a positional adaptation to the *mechanics* of community decision-making, the Chicago planners sought to create an *organizational* adaptation to the *process* of decision-making. Further case studies[27] have explicated the Myerson and Banfield findings.

The significant conclusion is that organizational legitimacy is necessary because of the character of community-decision in America.

As we pointed out in Chapter 1, decision-making is no longer centralized. The consequence is that the arena in which the decision-making takes place is widened, and it is this widened locus of decision-making that creates the need for organizational legitimacy. Indeed, because of the decentralized and competitive character of community decision-making, organizational legitimacy is both a necessary and sufficient condition of planning.

Positional legitimacy, on the other hand, is merely a sufficient condition. Voluntary organizations, for example, do not have positional legitimacy, yet they can and do play a part in shaping, initiating, and implementing plans and issues.

This in no sense is meant to imply that positional legitimacy is unimportant. Voluntary social planning agencies, to continue with the example, have consistently had their effectiveness curtailed because they have not had a legislate mandate for their activities. While there have been suggestions for the establishment of social planning commissions, and as well, the emergence of poverty planning and model cities agencies, this has not diminished the continued growth of voluntary planning agencies.

In the absence of positional legitimacy, however, voluntary agencies have to rely exclusively on organizational legitimacy, that is *organizing and involving individuals and groups who will sanction the agencies' right to intervene into and influence decision-making.* It is for this reason that voluntary organizations place emphasis on organizing techniques and the development of structures that allow for widespread citizen support. Voluntary planning agencies, for example, may have a structure that includes a delegate body, a board of directors, and a number of committees. Voluntary organizations, moreover, are forced to place continued stress on publicizing their activities to maintain their legitimacy.

ROLE LEGITIMACY

Occasionally in city planning literature, there are suggestions that the planner should create personal sanctions for his or her activities. Robert Walker, writing in the early 1940s, for example, recommended that the planning agency should cultivate harmonious personal relations with local politicians and operating agency personnel.[28] Robert Dahl, cognizant of the influence of organizations and actors outside government, suggested the term "technipol" to describe the function of the planner in legitimating his or her activities. The planner as technipol becomes skillful in using himself or herself to gain proposal support from among a number of organizations, groups and individuals.[29]

Both Walker and Dahl are essentially recommending a stylized adaptation to planning; that is an adaptation that is wholly dependent on the personal style and traits of the planner in creating relationships that will provide the planner legitimacy for his or her activity. This is a limited view and does not address the issue of the planner's role nor the necessary skills for planning.

One extensive analysis of planning role by Bolan and Nuttall[30] started out by postulating nine major process roles (See Figure 2-1). The analysis, incidentally, was not confined to a study of the planner's role alone but all process roles.

After a study of four planning cases (Inner Belt, Boston; Lower Manhattan Expressway, New York City; Great High Schools, Pittsburgh; and Affiliated Hospital Center, Boston) the nine roles were reduced to seven (Figure 2-1). What is signifi-

Original Model	Adjusted Model
1. Community knowledgeable informant	1. Veto power holder
2. Initiator, planner [a]	2. Public leader
3. Technical expert, analyst	3. Community knowledgeable informant
4. Expert on process, strategist	4. Mediator, arbitrator, negotiator
5. Public leader	5. Coalition maker, organizer
6. Mediator, arbitrator, negotiator	6. Expert on process, strategist
7. Judge, evaluator	7. Initiator, planner
8. Possessor of veto power	
9. Coalition maker, organizer	

[a] The term is used in a general sense and is not necessarily confined to the formal role of professional planner.

Figure 2-1 Major process roles in planning. (From Richard S. Bolan and Ronald L. Nuttall, *Urban Planning and Politics;* Lexington, Mass.: Heath, 1975, pp. 26 and 121-122.)

cant is that the role of technical expert was dropped; that is the role that has traditionally defined the function of the planner. Bolan and Nuttall report:

> In none of the cases, individually or combined was the role of Technical Expert relevant to importance to outcome. This does not mean that Technical Experts were not essential to the deci-

sion-making process. Obviously, the complex plans could not have been developed nor could this intricate financial and legal operation have been conducted without technical experts. Nonetheless, the men and women who were called upon to do them, by virtue of their roles as Technical Experts, were not of much influence in the actual decision process (unless they simultaneously played some other role).[31]

What can be assumed, and it is a tentative assumption, is that the traditionally defined role of the planner or a technical expert is taken for granted. Other roles, however, may appear to be necessary to legitimize the function of the planner.

When skills are examined a similar pattern emerges. Bolan and Nuttall hypothesized eight actor skills (again they were examining all process skills in planning, not just the planners' skills). The skills were:

1. General intelligence
2. Factual knowledge of issue
3. Background knowledge
4. Experience
5. Social-professional contacts
6. Verbal communication skill
7. Written communication skill
8. Popularity[32]

After the case study analysis, they were reduced to two: viz., *cognition skills* and *social relation skills*.[33] In effect, therefore, two general skills appear to be necessary. One is related to the technical skills of planning, and the other is related to the planner's ability to interact with other actors both within and outside the planning agency. The former skill is termed *procedural* and the latter *interactional.*

The procedural skills are basically cognate skills. The emphasis is upon methods and procedures. Knowing how to plan, collect, analyze, and interpret data; knowledge of economic, spatial, and urban theories is one set of examples. Knowledge of group behavior; and ability to interpret communication patterns, both verbal and nonverbal; knowledge of committee processes, public relations techniques, and administration is another set of procedural skills.

The interactional role demands an entirely different set of skills. It is related to the planner's personal ability as an agent of change. The reference point is the planner's skill in establishing sanctioned working relationships with individuals and groups. Often it is interpreted as the planner's ability to "get along" with people, but this is merely a manifestation of the skill. Fundamentally, it is the understanding the planner has of himself or herself as he or she is interacting. This requires sensitivity, of course, but just as critical an empathetic understanding. Empathy is the capacity to understand another and thereby understand his attitude and response patterns.

Both procedural skills and interactional skills are necessary to legitimate the role of the planner. Demonstrated knowledge and creativity are obviously important for the planner to create trust in his or her own ability. The ability to work with others in a dynamic participatory process is equally important. As with organizational legitimacy, role legitimacy is a necessary and sufficient condition of planning.

Summary

In this chapter we have indicated that planning is fundamentally interventionist in character. The involvement that the planner has in the process of planning creates a commitment to the planning outcome. The planning organization is equally committed to influencing the outcome of planning, but its interest is based on its own survival. Human behavior theory explains the motivation of the planner; organizational theory explains the actions of the planning agency.

In order to intervene, the planning agency and the planner need a permission or sanction to do so. Sanction is derived from legitimacy. One form of legitimacy is positional and is secured through legislative authority. As the arena in which decision-making becomes broadened, so too do other types of legitimation become necessary. Organizational legitimacy is the ability to develop sanction from among groups and organizations that exercise influence over community decision centers. The planner is also required to legitimate his or her role. Both the planner's knowledge and his or her capacity to create cooperative relationships are skills that are necessary to sanction his or her planning activities.

NOTES

1. See Talcott Parsons and Edward S. Shils (Eds.), *Toward a General Theory of Action,* (Cambridge: Harvard University Press, 1962), pp. 114–120.

2. Edmund M. Burke and Victor A. Capoccia, *Social Service Planning Under Title XX: A Report to HEW,* (Mimeographed, 1978).

3. This observation has been supported by other studies of city planning activities. See Francine F. Rabinovitz, *City Politics and Planning* (New York: Atherton Press, 1969), pp. 11–12. See also International City Managers' Association. *Principles and Practice of Urban Planning* (Washington, D.C.: Author, 1968), p. 3 for the recognition that the planner's intervention into decision-making is accepted part of practice.

4. Two of the most noted theorists are Chester I. Barnard and Herbert Simon. See Chester I. Barnard, *The Functions of the Executive,* (Cambridge Mass.: Harvard University Press, 1946), and Herbert A. Simon, *Administrative Behavior,* (New York: Macmillan, 1961).

5. James G. March and Herbert A. Simon, "The Theory of Organizational Equilibrium," in Amitai Etzioni, *Complex Organizations* (New York: Holt, Rinehart and Winston, 1966), pp. 61–62.

6. Barnard, op. cit., p. 139.

7. Ibid., pp. 139–149.
8. The accomplishments of an organization are achieved because of the contributions of the members. It is more correct to say, therefore, that the contributions provided by the members are the source from which the organization manufactures incentives. See March and Simon, op. cit., p. 62. We will return to this aspect of incentives in a later chapter.
9. Legitimacy also applies to individuals. For clarity, we are using the term organization. The reader should know that it could read "individual *and* organization."
10. Barnard, op. cit., pp. 161–177.
11. Ibid., p. 165.
12. Simon, op. cit., p. 12.
13. Ibid., p. 129.
14. Nicolò Machiavelli, *The Prince* (Baltimore: Penguin, 1961), p. 37.
15. Mel Scott, *American City Planning Since 1890,* (Berkeley: University of California Press, 1969), pp. 141–146. The quote is attributed to Frederick Law Olmstead, Ibid., p. 142.
16. Harland Bartholomew, *Development and Planning of American Cities,* (Pittsburgh: Carnegie Institute of Technology, 1950), pp. 9–10.
17. One example is Robert A. Walker, *The Planning Function in Urban Government,* (Chicago: University of Chicago Press, 1941), pp. 166–175.
18. Herbert Simon rejects the positional argument for planning by commenting that, "the proper location for planning or designing unit is apt to be highly inconclusive, and may hinge on the personalities in the organization and their relative enthusiasm, or lack of it, toward the planning function." This, of course, is a recognition of the social organization element of planning discussed in the next example. Simon, op. cit., p. 244.
19. Simon, op. cit., p. 125.
20. Martin Myerson and Edward C. Banfield, *Politics, Planning and the Public Interest,* (New York: Free Press, 1955).
21. Ibid., pp. 52–53.
22. Ibid., pp. 156–159.
23. Ibid., p. 54.

24. Ibid., pp. 138, 248.
25. Ibid., pp. 203.
26. Ibid., pp. 206, 243.
27. Alan A. Altshuler, *The City Planning Process*, (Ithaca N.Y.: Cornell University Press, 1965); Francine F. Rabinovitz, *City Politics and Planning*, (New York: Atherton Press, 1969); Richard S. Bolan and Ronald L. Nuttall, *Urban Planning and Politics*, (Lexington, Mass.: Heath, 1975).
28. Walker, op. cit., pp. 366–367.
29. Robert Dahl, *Who Governs?* (New Haven, Conn.: Yale University Press, 1961), pp. 126–130.
30. Richard S. Bolan and Ronald L. Nuttall, *Urban Planning and Politics* (Lexington Mass.: Heath, 1975).
31. Ibid., pp. 122–123.
32. Ibid., p. 122.
33. Ibid., pp. 122, 124.

Chapter 3

THE CITIZEN PARTICIPATION CHARACTERISTICS IN PLANNING

When the planner (obviously, the planning organization, as well) intervenes into the decision-making process, collaboration is inevitable. By intervening into a set of existing or newly created entities, the planner and planning organization become enmeshed in a network of interpersonal and interorganizational networks. Individuals and organizations external to the planner and planning organization become involved in some or all stages of the planning process, and consequently, may and frequently do, have an effect on the outcome of a plan. It is axiomatic to conclude that planning is *participatory*.

The issue, therefore, is not whether planning is participatory or not, but what is the nature of participation in planning? Who are the participants? What roles do they serve? What is the process of decision-making in planning with participants? And what functions do the participants in planning serve?

Who are the Participants?—Turning Points in the Participation of Citizen in Public Planning

Citizen Participation Prior to Legislative Prescriptions

Since the mid-1950s, the participation of citizens in planning has emerged as a matter of *right* whether acknowledged or not. Even prior to the mid-1950s, however, planners made an accommodation to the participatory character of planning. The nature of the response varied, however, and varied principally according to the planner's conception of the environment within which planning and decision-making took place. A common and early response, for example, was to take into account tacitly the opinions of selected formal and informal community leaders either by associating with them or by presuming their needs and desires. For planning to be effective, as one planner boldly stated, "The planner must gain the confidence of important community leaders."[1] Effectiveness is defined, obviously, in terms of a plan's acceptance.

Basically the planner acknowledged the influence of community leaders. It was an informal mechanism of participation. The planner responded to elites for pragmatic reasons, that is, to achieve acceptance of planning goals.

Citizen Participation in Urban Renewal

The advent of urban renewal in 1954 brought about an outright rather than a tacit acknowledgement of participatory planning. Moreover, it widened the scope of participants and required a *formal* structuring of individuals and groups. Again, however, the response was primarily pragmatic in terms of achieving planning goals; not, incidentally, in response to specific federal legislation. It was basically a recognition of one more class of actors who were believed to have an influence on plan acceptance.

In the development of urban *redevelopment* legislation in 1949, no consideration was given to any role of citizens in the process. Authority boards were created composed of "leading citizens," but these were instituted to allow for a borrowing capacity outside of the state legislative requirements. Primary attention was devoted to developing a mechanism that would provide a planned unfragmented approach to slum clearance.

In the mid-1950s, the objective was changed from purely slum clearance and redevelopment to include rehabilitation of homes and businesses. To reflect this change, the name urban *redevelopment* was changed to urban *renewal.* The change also brought about a new relationship with individual citizens and groups. The Urban Renewal Administration insisted that local renewal agencies provide a means for citizen involvement. It is interesting to examine the substantive reasons.

A number of studies in the early 1950s began to question seriously the effectiveness of redevelopment. On the one hand it wasn't achieving the aims that it had set for itself. Slums continued to proliferate often faster than urban redevelopment programs could demolish them. Both Baltimore and Chicago, for example, had ambitious redevelopment programs between 1950 and 1955, yet the slum clearance activities could not keep pace with the rapidly deteriorating housing.

One of the administrative requirements which emerged out of the 1954 act was called "Citizen Participation." For most renewal agencies, however, citizen participation meant the creation or continuation of anywhere from a seven- to a 15-member advisory board composed principally of (again) "citizen leaders." For clearance objectives this made practical sense. So-called citizen leaders had access to those who could make development work; i.e., contractors, bankers, developers, legislators.

Grass roots, or any kind of broad scale citizen participation was negligible for a number of years. "In clearance areas," according to one urban renewal director, "you don't organize citizens, you prepare people for moving."[2] At the same time as urban renewal activities began to encompass rehabilitation objectives, the involvement of citizens in renewal planning began to emerge. One study of 95 renewal agencies conducted in 1965 reveals that grass roots citizen participation was confined almost exclusively to renewal agencies engaged in rehabilitation.[3] A little more than a dozen had any organized program involving citizens in planning agencies. These few agencies accounted for two-thirds of all the nation's rehabilitation projects at that time.[4]

In this respect, citizen participation became less a value ideal than a practical necessity. To achieve rehabilitation goals, dwellings and businesses had to be fixed up and repaired. The citizens, in effect, controlled implementation of renewal goals. The renewal agency in order to achieve citizen cooperation held out the inducement of participation in planning. The involvement of citizens became a quid pro quo; the agency would take the deficiencies out of the neighborhood if the citizens would rehabilitate their houses.

Unlike participatory techniques prior to renewal, which aimed at developing sanction and legitimacy from among community leaders, the involvement of neighborhood groups in renewal planning sought two objectives: legitimacy and a change in citizen attitude. Prior to renewal, there was little necessity, pragmatically, to involve community leaders formally. A perception of community and political leaders' needs led the planner to devise courses of action beneficial to these groups. Community and political leaders benefited from the planner's efforts. This is not to suggest that the planner was a tool of the community and political leaders. Not necessarily. It occurred because the planner and the leaders shared the same value premises. The function of the planner was to improve the city and more often than not this meant improvement for business leaders, and it should be added, at the total community's expense.

Rehabilitation costs, on the other hand, cannot be spread across the community. Some can, of course. Public improvement is an example. But the main costs of rehabilitation are born by the homeowners and the tenants. Techniques other than outright grants are necessary to induce them to make these improvements. Their attitude has to be modified, changed to an orientation favorable to rehabilitation objectives.

Participation is used as the technique. By sharing in agency decision-making it was hoped that neighborhood citizens would come to share the aims of the planning activities. It was to be hoped that their attitudes would become positive toward the agency's goals. Indeed, the Urban Renewal Administration cited this as an objective of citizen participation: "The willingness of individuals to accept these [rehabilitation] standards and do their part in creating a better neighborhood can be stimulated if they have a part in the development of the standards."[5]

Despite the pragmatic nature of the response to participation, the urban renewal program was the first governmental program to broaden the scope of participation beyond the community elites. The urban renewal program, moreover, introduced into the lexicon of planning the term "citizen participation."

Citizen Participation in Poverty Program

Beginning with the poverty program in the 1960s, the concept of citizen participation took on a new meaning. Newer actors were identified: the victims of poverty itself. It was a personal commitment, assured R. Sargent Shriver, the poverty program's first director, "that the poor themselves actively participate in the planning, implementation, and administration of these programs."[6]

The intention was less pragmatic than urban renewal. Where urban renewal described citizen participation as a means of gaining citizen cooperation, the poverty program announced that citizens should have a voice in programs and plans affecting their destiny. Citizens should also contribute substantively to the planning process by pointing out solutions and devising the means to solve problems. Other reasons were also offered. Some defined citizen participation as therapeutic for the poor; a way for the poor to learn how to overcome hopelessness and despair. Others saw it as a means for giving the poor power. In any event, the poverty program was the first federal program that stated clearly that a particular group of citizens should have a voice in planning.

From the outset the poverty program was marked by confusion and contention. It was doubtlessly the most controversial government program ever initiated. Disputes between mayors and local poverty officials marked the first sign of contention. The Bureau of the Budget, then Congress, and finally federal administrators lost their initial enthusiasm for the poverty program.[7]

While support was given to a number of programs, such as Headstart and Neighborhood Legal Services, begun by the Office of Economic Opportunity, support in the late 1960s began to diminish for the Community Action Program (CAP) agencies. The CAP agencies were the fundamental organ for involving the poor in planning.

Under Nixon, an outspoken foe of the "War on Poverty," the poverty program came under repeated attacks. A number of programs were transferred to existing federal agencies and departments. An attempt was made to phase out the CAP programs. The attempt failed. Two reasons can be offered.

After the initial conflicts that erupted in some of the nation's cities (Newark, Syracuse, Oakland, Pittsburgh, to name a few) the contention began to wane. The local CAP agencies began to find their way into the local structure of city government. The CAP agencies became an instrument for relating the poor to the programs of city government. Local mayors, once hostile, began to realize it might be difficult to live without CAP agencies, especially in administering a number of neighborhood programs that OEO had invented.[8]

Significantly, an amendment had been added in the 1967 Economic Opportunity Act providing that local governments would have the option of bringing their CAP agency under official control of city government. The purpose of the amendment was to assuage local officials and to serve as a threat to local CAP agencies that they could be taken over by local officials if they were uncooperative with City Hall. But the amendment was not needed. The conflict techniques that precipitated the backlash against the poverty program dropped out of use by local CAP agencies. In the six months following the passage of the amendment, only five per cent of the CAP agencies were taken over by City Hall.[9]

A second reason for failure to wipe out community action agencies was the successful lobbying efforts by local constituents. The CAP agencies organized the poor not only for purposes of planning but also as a loyal constituency base. This was not an immediate objective, but served as an objective when the poverty program came under fire, particularly during the Nixon reign. The CAP agencies emerged as an interest group, supported by a wide range of followers, who successfully defended the program in their local communities, before Congress and in the courts—a practical example of the behavioral hypothesis that if people are involved in a decision-making activity, they are likely to support and defend that decision.

The poverty program spawned three legacies for citizen participation in planning. One is that the base of participation has been legislatively widened to include specifically identified individuals and groups. In the case of the poverty program, this was originally defined as "residents of the areas and members of groups involved in local programs"; or, more simply, "the poor." Since the poverty program this definition has been broadened. Citizens are now defined as those who share an interest in a particular planning organization as well as those who would be affected by a plan or program of service. The latter are often referred to as "consumers."

A second legacy is that the purpose of citizen participation has shifted. Citizen participation is now seen as serving two purposes: one is organizational support. Citizens who are involved in planning activities will tend to endorse and support such activities. They become constituents of their own actions. The second is that the citizen participants are seen as a source of information and collective wisdom. Decisions tend to reflect widespread rather than narrow preferences. It will not ensure better decisions, nor, as Zbigniew Brzezinski advises, will it ensure political or social responsibility, "but it might make for a society that more readily approaches both."[10]

The third legacy is that citizen participation has become institutionalized. As each governmental planning program has emerged from Model Cities through health planning to human services planning, other legislation and federal regulations have required some form of citizen participation. It has become a normal part of the planning process, and as we noted in the Introduction, required in over 60 pieces of federal legislation.

Citizen Participation in Issue Politics

The civil rights struggle in the 1960s was instructive for Americans for a number of reasons. For one thing, it did awaken America to the contradictions between the promise of freedom and the practice of freedom. It not only brought about a wide number of legislative changes, but also changed the attitudes—albeit, still not sufficiently—of a significant number of people.

Another legacy was the dramatic illustration of the power of citizen participation. The participation was for the purpose of securing the rights of individuals in collective action. Marches, picketing, and sit-ins were the techniques of the collective action. The essence of the action was the organization of individuals around a common cause—an *issue.*

The 1970s witnessed the broadening of such participatory activities. There are organizations devoted to a wide spectrum of issues, such as women's rights, the protection of children, the legal rights of the mentally ill, the environment, disarmament, suburban rezoning, housing, and the like. Each defines its function as acting to protect the interests and aims of its constituency. The role of the organization is *advocacy*—promoting or proposing the adoption of an issue through judicial, legislative, or regulatory means. Frequently the organizations engage in adversary relationships with other organizations or governmental agencies.

Some issue-oriented organizations engage in planning—in the traditional sense of the term. The organization may initiate and develop a plan on behalf of its constituency. One example is a plan for public housing in a wealthy suburb proposed by a low income planning organization. An organization, on the other hand, may develop a plan as an alternative or competitive proposal to another organization's plan. A group, for example, may suggest an alternative income supplement proposal to that of the state welfare agency's proposal. A still further illustration is an organization that uses the courts to force another organization to develop a plan. A common example is when a mental health association gets a court order requiring the state department of mental health to develop more realistic plans for deinstitutionalizing state mental hospitals.

The significant factor in this development is that the operations of governmental agencies are more easily challenged. The citizen as a member of an issue-centered organization is provided an opportunity to influence decisions, to safeguard rights, or to force public organizations to initiate corrective action. The consequence is that the base of decision-making is even further widened. Citizens not only have the opportunity to influence decisions through the involvement in a planning agency's activities, but also citizens can influence decisions as members of organizations external to a planning agency.

This, of course, offers the potential, if not the actuality, of altering the "planning with citizens" orientation of planning agencies. Citizens active in planning agencies find their role to be not merely defending the planning agency and its plans before decision centers, such as legislators and city council members, but also before other citizen groups and organizations. More than one organization, all with citizen representation, may vie to influence decision centers over competing plans. The base and function of citizen participation has become expanded.

CITIZEN ROLES IN PLANNING

The roles citizens can and do play in planning organizations vary widely from one organization to the next. The lack of any consistent definition of citizen participation accounts for the variation. What determines the role is a variety of factors including organizational objectives and need, legislation and regulations, citizen pressures and demands, and, at times, issues of the moment.

Despite these variations, it is possible to identify a range of five roles. Each is based on the extent of influence the citizens have in deciding on planning issues and outcomes—from little influence to major or primary influence. They are a variation of the roles first proposed by Sherry Arnstein in her widely quoted article "Ladder of Citizen Participation."[11]

Although identified as discrete roles, they should be seen as part of a continuum. The roles, moreover, are additively inclusive; citizens, in other words, performing one role are assumed to be able to perform all predecessor roles. More than one role can be used in a planning organization.

Review and Comment

The role of citizens in the review and comment type of citizen participation is precisely as the title suggests. Citizens are given an opportunity to review proposed plans. Comments can be made, but the planning organization is under no commitment to alter or modify the plan.

It is a passive role designed primarily to provide information to citizens and groups.

This type of citizen participation is easily recognized because it relies on media techniques—newspaper advertising and radio announcements—and public hearings. The public hearings are formal, at which citizens are allowed to present testimony to a panel.

Consultation

The function of a consultant is to provide expert advice for the purpose of improving the effectiveness of a decision. Acting in this role citizens are recruited and asked for specific advice and information. The method for obtaining the advice is through meetings and questionnaires. The role of the citizen as a consultant is to be a part of framing planning decisions.

A secondary objective is to locate potential obstacles to planning issues and proposals. The use of meetings with a wide range of individuals and groups is a helpful technique in searching out attitudes toward a plan.

Similar to the previous role, the decision to accept or reject the advice is the exclusive judgement of the planning organization. Unlike the review and comment role, however, the intent goes beyond just providing information to citizens. It is a two-way process of communications in which the main objective is to improve planning decisions.

Advisory

This is a formal organizational role. Citizens are recruited to the organization and placed on policy and planning committees within the planning organization. The committees, however, are *advisory*. Nonetheless, by virtue of membership in the organization, the degree of influence for citizens is greater than the degree of influence in the predecessor roles.

The objective of this role is to seek out both information and organized support for planning activities.

Shared Decision-Making

This role describes the participation of citizens and planners acting as partners in planning and decision-making. The roles of each are recognized as essential in the planning process. The intention is to arrive at decisions that reflect the preference of the citizen-planner planning team.

This role is recognized by the formal participation of citizens in a wide variety of committees and tasks.

Controlled Decision-Making

In this role citizens exercise ultimate authority over all policy and planning decisions. The role of the professional staff is to facilitate decision-making—to act as advisers and provide information for citizen decision-making.

This role of citizen participation is common to voluntary organizations. There are some examples of the controlled decision-making role in public agencies, but they are rare.[12] It has been assumed that in public agencies ultimate decision-making is a responsibility of an elected legislative entity—city council, chief executive, state legislature, and the like.

DECISION-MAKING CHARACTERISTICS OF CITIZEN PARTICIPATION IN PLANNING

There are two processes for decision-making in planning with citizens. One is legislative and the other is interest group.

Legislative Decision-Making

The legislative or governing type of citizen participation is part of a historic tradition from the oligarchic conceptions of

Athenian democracy through the broadening of the franchise arising out of the French and American revolutions to the emerging conceptions of "participatory" and "anticipatory" democracy. The long-held aim is a governing system in society in which the citizen shares in community and nation decision-making, or, in other words, sharing in *political power*. Because it typifies citizen and community control, the New England open town meeting is frequently held up as the ideal.

The ideal, however, has tended to be elusive, even in New England. Distrust of the masses and clear-cut prejudices have been persistent obstacles. In addition, the growing size and complexity of mass society has made the open town meeting concept difficult to fulfill.

The movement toward community control in the late 1960s arose out of the aim to share political power. Community control is primarily a mechanism for decentralizing political decision-making. It is the exercise of authority by a democratically organized government of a neighborhood jurisdiction.[13]

Alvin Toffler has argued for a variation of community control because of both the growing size of societies and the increased specialism of technology. Toffler proposes the development of constituent assemblies of nation, city, and neighborhood levels charged with social stocktaking and with defining and assigning priorities to specific goals. Toffler terms this *anticipatory* democracy. Equal representation cannot be guaranteed, but it does widen the base of participation in decision-making.[14]

Nevertheless, the governed under Toffler's new society, or under community control or under existing mechanisms of government are ruled by *representatives* (elected or chosen). The representative acts as the decision-maker. Political science textbooks cover this in adequate detail. It is the essential characteristics of the process that is of primary interest here.

First, of course, the constituency does not participate directly in the decision-making process. Each citizen supposedly has the capacity to influence the process. Some constituents have more influence than others, either through control of resources, institutions, knowledge, other constituents, or their own charisma. Decision-making frequently tends to respond to influential interests.

Admittedly, some legislators rise above interests and some indeed make decisions contrary both to influential constituents and their own constituency. These instances occur so rarely, however, that John F. Kennedy could only describe a dozen or so in his book *Profiles of Courage*.[15]

Despite the tendency to frame decisions around the interests of individual groups, the legislative decision-making process itself is designed to serve the "public interest." Indeed legislation is always propagandized as serving the public or national interest regardless of how shallow the piece of legislation. Oil depletion allowances are consistently upheld as serving the national interest. Welfare measures are advanced in terms of the public good. Obviously, the public interest is not often served if only because it is not always possible, if possible at all, to determine the public interest. But what is of importance here is that the legislative decision-making process is *not* intended to serve the "private" interest.

Secondly, decision-making is determined by a voting preference. That is, a simple majority determines a legislative issue. Certainly an executive can veto a piece of legislation. But even in overriding a veto unanimity is not required. The essential issue is that consensus is *not* a characteristic of legislative decision-making.

Indeed, consensus is rare. Conflict, bargaining, negotiation, persuasion, and horse trading are the techniques of the legislative decision-making process. None of these techniques, incidentally, destroys the effectiveness of the legislative body's functioning. Conflict, and at times heated argument, rarely if ever impair the relationship of the members with one another. Dispute is not just common, but viewed as healthy.

Thirdly, except in rare instances and only in instances affecting its own rules of conduct, the legislative body is not responsible for implementing the decision it makes. Once legislation is passed, whether by 51 per cent or 98 per cent of the body, the responsibility for implementing the decision falls to an administrative or executive group. An existing agency or a newly created agency is charged with carrying out the requirements of the decision.

Interest Group Decision-Making

If a public interest orientation and the absence of consensus are essential to the legislative process of participation, quite the opposite is necessary for the interest groups process of participation. Indeed, it operates for different purposes. First it seeks to secure or protect a "private" interest, not a public interest. In its simplest form, it can be described as follows: A group of citizens come together around a common cause. They recruit others and persuade them to identify with their interest. They may even try to make their group "representative"[16] of the total population. But this is a technique, and a technique only, to provide sanction and legitimacy. The group, however, is still an interest group organized to achieve a cause that it alone feels is desirable.

Whether the cause is in the public interest or not is irrelevant. Sometimes it may be. Surely child labor laws and public education for the retarded, both of which arose out of the activities of interest groups, appear to have redounded to the interests of all. The inability to achieve gun registration laws and the continued support of oil depletion allowances on the other hand, appear not to have. The important point, however, is that in this context citizen participation is seen as a means for a group of citizens to obtain its own interests.

A second characteristic is the need for consensus in decision-making. An interest group is a means for organizing opinion and action either to achieve a specific goal or to protect an existing goal. In that sense, then, two functions are necessary. One is decision-making, the second is devising a course of action that will bring about the adoption of the decision. The latter is frequently the more formidable; and it is the latter that demands consensus and agreement during the decision-making phase.

Unlike a legislative body, which can delegate implementation, an interest group must rely on its own membership to achieve action. Members who are in disagreement with a course of action will be unwilling to assist in achieving the goal: the more disagreement, the more impotent the group becomes. Even though 60 or 70 or 80 per cent of a group may vote in favor of a decision, they may still be unable to implement the decision. Those in opposition may have the influence necessary to achieve action.

An interest group, consequently, struggles to achieve consensus and agreement. It is not, incidentally, a Quaker-like consensus that is sought. Some members may be cajoled into agreeing with a decision. Others may be pressured. There may even be conflict. But continued conflict destroys the process. It leads to splintering, and, therefore, frustrating the goals of the groups.

A third characteristic is that interest groups have no authority. Despite the boastful tradition of interest groups in America, they are provided no special privileges of power. Indeed, even a commission appointed by a legislature must depend upon the persuasiveness of its case to commit legislators to agree with its recommendations. In the early 1960s, for example, a half dozen commissions and study groups were established by Congress to study the nation's public welfare system. None of the study groups' or commissions' major findings was implemented by Congress. The power of an interest group is the conviction of its case and the influence of its members.

For voluntary community planning agencies, the interest group process of decision-making is required. The absence of authority or positional legitimacy has required voluntary agencies to rely upon organizing individuals and groups to support planning activities. A basic principle of practice in the voluntary planning field, citizen housing agencies, conservation associations, settlement houses, and community welfare councils is that the planner and the agency are powerless. Planning goals, in other words, cannot be imposed on groups and communities merely for any value reason, but simply because it would be unwise strategically.

Voluntary planning organizations, moreover, serve on behalf of a specified interest group. They may claim they serve the community at large, but this is a symbolic pronouncement; the function of which is to create a wider base of legitimacy for its actions.

In the voluntary social planning literature, a distinction is made between a "functional" community and a "geographical" community. The geographical community is defined, as the term implies, by its geographical boundaries—neighborhood, city, metropolitan region, state, etc. A functional community, on the other hand, is composed of individuals and groups who share a common interest.[17]

This is a useful distinction, despite its obviousness. The voluntary planning agency emphasizes one set of objectives with its common interest group and another set with the geographical community. In working with the functional community, the objectives are to recruit and organize individuals to become a part of the common interest group, develop plans meeting the specific needs of the interest group and the general needs of the geographical community, to win support of such plans from the geographical community.

In relation to the geographical community, the objective is to identify specific needs of the geographical community, develop plans to meet these needs, and to enlist support in the geographical community for implementation of these plans. In working with the functional community, the planning agency uses a community organization and planning method. In working with the geographical community, the agency uses a "community relations" or "public relations" method.[18]

Traditionally, an interest group orientation toward planning has been questionable for governmental planning agencies. Organizing interest groups to support a governmental agency is inconsistent with the public interest objective of government. Altshuler's case studies of planning in the Twin Cities provides an interesting example. In one instance, the Minneapolis city planner established a citizen committee of business people to act as a sounding board for a master plan. The city council resented this tactic and interpreted it as a device to bring outside pressure on the council. This action, the council concluded, was alien to the practice of a planning professional whose primary function is to serve the public, or community-wide, interests.[19]

This conception of planning has been seriously questioned and is no longer considered valid. A number of studies, including the previously cited Altshuler study, report that however conscientiously planning agencies may try, they have considerable difficulty in defining the public interest. Given the diversity of interests in local communities, the search for a public, or community-wide, interest may be an elusive quest. It was this issue that served as a basis for Paul Davidoff's criticism of city planning in the mid-1960s and served as one of his premises for advocacy planning.[20]

Indeed advocacy planning essentially is interest group planning. Davidoff's suggestion that planners act on behalf of such groups as the Chamber of Commerce, labor organizations, antipoverty councils, and neighborhood organizations is a private-interest as opposed to a public-interest approach to planning. In Cleveland they have gone a step further and announced that the city planning agency is not only serving the physical development interests of the city (one development interest among others), but also serving the expressed interest of a singular group—the poor.[21]

Since the mid-1960s the growth in the number of specialized planning agencies further constrains the possibility of planning serving the public interest. Each planning agency is mandated to serve the interests of its own constituency. Community planning, it can be concluded, serves not the public interest, but the private interest of a group, or what Michael Fagence has identified as a "group interest."[22]

Assumption of Pluralism

To suggest that the function of a planning agency is to serve not the public interest but its own particular functional or group interest is not also to suggest that the public interest is achieved through the resolution of competing interests. This is the traditional conception of the private interest approach to governing and decision-making; that is, the interests of all are achieved through the free interplay of interests in the market place of ideas.[23]

However appealing this doctrine may be, it just does not seem to be consistently true. It assumes, obviously, that all interests are represented in the resolution process. It assumes, further, that all interests have equal information and equal access to information.

Even more significantly, the doctrine assumes that all interests have equal resources for influencing decisions. It would be simplistic to assume that all interest groups from bankers to neighborhood organizations have equal capacity to articulate issues, to utilize financial resources, and to organize constituencies. Some groups, in other words, are more equal than others.

Mazziotti has suggested that the assumptions of pluralism question not only the effectiveness of planning serving the interests of the powerless, but also the efficacy of advocacy planning. Advocacy planning, he argues, is premised on the conceptions of pluralism in decision-making. He suggests that the assumption of pluralism is a social myth designed to provide a rationale for instituting social programs that placate the politically and economically disenfranchised. The solution is a radical conception of planning that challenges not only current assumptions of planning but also the assumptions of the way power is structured in local communities.[24]

We are not so pessimistic as Mazziotti. Certainly the powerless are not always represented in the center of decision-making. And certainly there is need for improvement. At the moment, however, the broader interests of a community, including the interests of the powerless, tend to be served over time by means of competing constituencies. The development of issue centered organizations and groups in the 1970s is an excellent example. Issue-centered organizations have broadened the base of community decision-making, as we noted earlier. They act as watchdogs over planning agencies' activities.

We would argue, too, that the *probability* of the public, or community-wide, interest being approximately served is achieved through citizen participation. Indeed, this is the essential function of citizen participation. It sets up the process for dialogue and thereby broadens the base of decision-making.[25]

Summary

Planning is axiomatically participatory. Historically, however, the base of participation in public planning has changed from a small informal elite to a formal broad base of constituents. The aims of citizen participation have also changed. Citizens now can serve three functions in planning. One is to serve as a constituency of support for the planning agency and its activities. The second is to serve as a means of wisdom and knowledge in the development of a plan and in identifying the mission of the planning agency. The third and emerging function is to act as a watchdog over one's own as well as others' rights in the design and delivery of policies.

There are five roles citizens can plan in planning: review and comment, consultation, advisory, shared decision-making and controlled decision-making. Citizens can be enacting more than one of these roles in an organization.

The emergence of a citizen role in planning, as well as the increasing specialized planning agencies, has changed the decision-making base of community planning from purely a public interest orientation to a private interest orientation. Planning agencies function on behalf of a substantive issue and a defined constituency.

NOTES

1. Alan A. Altshuler, *The City Planning Process,* (Ithaca, N.Y.: Cornell University Press, 1965), p. 55.

2. Edmund M. Burke, "Citizen Participation in Renewal" *Journal of Housing,* Vol. 23, No. 1, (January 1966), p. 20.

3. Ibid., pp. 19–21.

4. Ibid., p. 19.

5. Urban Renewal Administration, *Neighborhood Organization in Conservation Areas, Technical Guide 8,* (Washington, D.C.: U.S. Government Printing Office, March 1961), p. 3.

6. Quoted in Edmund M. Burke, "Have the Poor Wrecked Johnson's War on Poverty?" *The Antioch Review,* Vol. XXVI, No. 4, (Winter 1966–67), p. 443.

7. Ibid., pp. 443–458; and Daniel P. Moynihan, *Maximum Feasible Misunderstanding* (New York: Free Press, 1969), pp. 128–166.

8. Moynihan, op. cit., pp. 141–158.

9. Ibid., p. 158–159.

10. Zbigniew Brzezinski, *Between Two Ages,* (New York: Viking, 1970), pp. 262–263.

11. Sherry R. Arnstein, "A Ladder of Citizen Participation," *Journal of the American Institute of Planners,* Vol. 35, No. 4 (July 1969), pp. 216–224.

12. Ibid., p. 223.

13. Alan A. Altshuler, *Community Control* (New York: Pegasus, 1970), p. 64.

14. Alvin Toffler, *Future Shock* (New York: Bantam, 1970), pp. 416, 430.

15. John F. Kennedy, *Profiles in Courage* (New York: Harper & Row, 1956).

16. The concept of "representativeness" is thoroughly explained in Michael Fagence's book on citizen participation. He outlines the various forms and types of representativeness. Michael Fagence, *Citizen Participation in Planning,* (New York: Pergamon, 1977), pp. 50–69.

17. Murray G. Ross, *Community Organization* (New York: Harper & Row, 1955), pp. 40–44.

18. Ibid., p. 43.

19. Altshuler, *The City Planning Process,* op. cit., pp. 242–244, 267–270.

20. Paul Davidoff, "Advocacy and Pluralism in Planning," *Journal of the American Institute of Planners,* Vol. XXXI, No. 4, (November 1965) pp. 331–338.

21. Norman Krumholz, Janice M. Cogger, and John H. Linner, "The Cleveland Policy Planning Report," *Journal of the American Institute of Planners,* Vol. 41, No. 5 (September 1975), pp. 298–304.

22. Fagence, op. cit., pp. 84–91.

23. G. David Garson, "On the Origins of Interest Group Theory: A Critique of a Process," *The American Political Science Review,* Vol. LXVIII, No. 4, (December 1974) pp. 1505–1519.

24. Donald F. Mazziotti, "The Underlying Assumptions of Advocacy Planning: Pluralism and Reform," *Journal of the American Institute of Planners,* Vol. 40, No. 1 (January 1974), pp. 38–47. See also Stephen Grabow and Alan Heskin, "Foundations for a Radical Concept of Planning,"

Journal of American Institute of Planners, Vol. 39, No. 2 (March 1973), pp. 106–114.

25. See also John Friedmann, "The Public Interest and Community Participation: Toward a Reconstruction of Public Philosophy" *Journal of the American Institute of Planners,* Vol. 39, No. 1 (January 1973) pp. 2–7.

Chapter 4

THE STRATEGIES OF CITIZEN PARTICIPATION*

In the previous chapter we identified three essential purposes of citizen participation. One is that it is a source of wisdom and information and thus improves the effectiveness of planning decisions. Second, it is a device to organize approval and support for planning and program goals. Third, it is a way in which individual and collective rights can be protected. How these purposes are put into practice is the objective of this chapter.

Citizen participation is a means to an end. It is a strategy for bringing about the achievement of organizational objectives, whether the organization is composed of citizens and planners or whether it is composed entirely of citizens.

To suggest, however, that citizen participation is a single strategy is misleading. There are several strategies. Each is

---

*Much of this chapter appeared originally in an article published by the *Journal of the American Institute of Planners* and has been used with their permission. See Edmund M. Burke, "Citizen Participation Strategies" *Journal of the American Institute of Planners,* Vol. XXXIV, No. 5 (September 1968), pp. 287–294.

defined in terms of specific objectives. The objectives, in turn, will be determined by resources and the organizational character of the planning agency. Because planning operates through formal organizations, any strategy will be influenced by organizational demands—the necessity for coordinated efforts, the orientation toward purposeful (ideally, rational) action, and the demands of the environment, which, for public agencies, are often the requirements of extragovernmental jurisdictions. Thus, the relevancy of a strategy depends both on an organization's abilities to fulfill the requirements necessary for the strategy's effectiveness, and on the adaptability of the strategy to an organizational environment.

The objective of this chapter is to describe citizen participation on the basis of strategies for achieving planning objectives. The more common uses of citizen participation will be reviewed, indicating the assumptions, conditions, and organizational requirements of each. Six strategies will be identified: *education-therapy, behavioral change, staff supplement, cooptation, community power,* and *advocacy.*

EDUCATION-THERAPY STRATEGY

A frequently proclaimed but rarely viable strategy of citizen participation focuses upon the presumed need for improvement of the individual participants. Accomplishing a specific task is irrelevant; rather, the participants become clients who are the objects of treatment. Consequently, this strategy has often been defined as an end in itself.

One objective of the strategy is increased competency in civic affairs. In this context the act of the participation is held to be a form of citizenship training, in which citizens working together to solve community problems not only learn how democracy works but also learn to value and appreciate cooperation as a problem solving method. This would strengthen local government, spur community development, and create a sense of community or community identification.[1]

Utilizing participation in community affairs as an educational device has had a profound and controversial impact on the practice of community organization employed by social workers. Early writers advocated participation not as the means but as the goal of community organization. At this stage there was a strong social reform orientation attached to community organization, and one of the pioneers in the field, Eduard Lindeman, termed it the Community Movement.[2] Later writers continued this emphasis but referred to participation as the "process goal" of community organization. Murray Ross, one of the principal spokesmen of this school of thought, explains that the aim of community organization is to help communities develop their own capacities to solve problems. Achievement of planning goals is secondary.[3]

In his analysis of voluntary community planning activities, Roland Warren found that expediency vitiates the use of this objective. The process goal becomes abandoned as the demands of achieving specific tasks become dominant.[4]

Another objective of this strategy is to use participation therapeutically as a means for developing self-confidence, and, indeed, self-reliance—an underlying theme, incidentally, of the citizen participation objectives of both urban renewal and poverty programs. Individuals, according to this logic, will discover that by cooperating with their neighbors they can bring about changes affecting their community. More significantly, they will inspire each other, communicating an élan of hope and self-confidence. The participants will learn that they can reform their own lives; or, according to the hopes of the Office of Economic Opportunity they will turn away from the self-defeating and despairing culture of poverty; or, according to the Department of Housing and Urban Development, they will increase their sense of responsibility for their dwelling unit.

However meritorious the aim, there appears to be considerable difficulty in implementing this strategy. Admittedly, social group workers use participation as a device to achieve therapeutic or educational objectives. Then, too, those working with citizen groups report that positive changes do occur among individuals participating in community projects. Oscar

Lewis, the anthropologist, has suggested that organizing the poor and giving them a sense of power and leadership through participation has been one method for abolishing the subculture of poverty, in certain countries, notably Cuba.[5] Black Power advocates, as well, adopt as one of their premises that the organization of the black community will bring about the self-confidence and hope that American society has consistently denied its black citizens. But the formal and deliberate organization of citizens for this purpose has rarely been tried, and if so, seldom for any appreciable time.

What frustrates the use of this strategy in planning is two-fold. First, it is difficult to accommodate it to organizational demands. The focus is on the means; participation is the overriding objective, not the accomplishment of goals or group tasks. Planning organizations are of necessity task oriented. Their function is to accomplish, to achieve, to bring about the attainment of ends. To focus primarily on the maintenance needs of one class of organizational members would be dysfunctional.

Secondly, the citizen participants are themselves oriented to task accomplishment. They would implicitly resist a methodology focused on their educational needs.

Indeed, there has been much criticism about the use of participation as a therapeutic technique for community groups.[6] It is misleading and it functions as a palliative rather than as an honest attempt at seeking planned solutions to community problems. The accusations have merit particularly if the participants are unaware that the principal aim of the participatory process is to educate the participants to the exclusion of planning.

BEHAVIORAL CHANGE STRATEGY

Group participation has been found to be a major force for changing individual behavior. Individuals tend to be influenced by the groups to which they belong and will more readily accept group-made decisions than lectures or individual exhortations to change. This has led to a strategy of participation that, although similar to the education-therapy strategy, is sufficiently different to require a separate classification. The strategy is deliberately change-oriented and is aimed at influencing individual behavior through group membership. It is a strategy commonly associated with community organization practice and more recently with increasing importance in certain schools of management science.[7] Moreover, it is a strategy reflected in much of the urban renewal literature on citizen participation, and, in fact, is even enunciated in a President's Housing Message to Congress.[8]

Briefly, the objective is to induce change in a system or subsystem by changing the behavior of either the system's members or influential representatives of the system. The group is seen as a source of influence over its members. Therefore, by focusing on group standards—its style of leadership or its emotional atmosphere—it is considered possible to change the behavior of the individual members. The group itself becomes a target of change even though the goal may be to change individual behavior.[9] This particular emphasis distinguishes this strategy from the education-therapy strategy, for although many of the techniques may be similar, the objective is different. Whether an individual personally benefits from participating in the process is not necessarily relevant. The focus is on the task and on helping the group accomplish the task goal. It is important to emphasize this distinction so as not to confuse it with the education-therapy strategy.

Two major premises underlie the behavioral change strategy. First, it has been found that it is easier to change the behavior of individuals when they are members of a group than to change any one of them separately. Second, individuals and groups resist decisions that are imposed upon them. They are more likely to support a decision and, more important, more likely to assist in carrying it out if they have had a part in discovering the need for change and if they share in the decision-making process. Participation in the decision-making process, in other words, can create commitment to new objectives.

The effectiveness of this strategy, however, depends on the existence of certain conditions. In the first place, the participants must have a strong sense of identification with the group, and feel assured that their contributions and activities are meaningful both to themselves and to the group. There must, too, be some satisfactions or gains from participation, either through personal and group accomplishments or from the mere fact of the association with other members. The awareness of the need for change, and consequent pressure for change, must come from within the group as a shared perception. Facts, data, and persuasion are not enough.

There is a necessity, too, for participants to be actively involved in the decision-making process. The making of the decisions, the working through of the problem, so to speak, are the dynamic factors that change behavior. Communication channels, consequently, need to be open and undistorted. "Information relating to the need for change, plans for change, and consequences of change must be shared by all relevant people in the group."[10]

Even though committed to the strategy, as many often are, intra- and extra-organizational demands often dictate a change in strategy. The complexity of many planning projects, and more important, the commitment of planners themselves, obstruct the citizen from becoming actively involved in decision-making. Citizens frequently complain that they are unable to understand the planners and consequently unable to become committed to a policy or goal they do not understand.

Extra-organizational demands have the effect of creating barriers to communication channels. Organizations faced with adhering to performance norms, such as budget deadlines, discover that they are unable to apply the strategy. The demands for submission of program proposals or the priority demands emanating from a national agency, such as the Department of Housing and Urban Development or Health, Education, and Welfare, precludes the possibility of involving citizens for the purpose of changing their behavior. Local poverty agencies' staff complain that their time is spent in selling proposals to citizens to gain their support. They have neither the time nor the sanction to effectively foster group deliberation and initiative, however much they would like to.

A further difficulty is relating the participant group to other influential or decision-making centers of the community. It is rarely possible to include all members of a system in a community planning project. Frequently, then, the planning organization is dealing with system representatives. The group becomes not merely a medium of change, but also an agent of change—an action group designed to influence much larger systems. One example would be a representative neighborhood renewal committee attempting to influence other residents and city officials to improve its neighborhood area. But it is not always possible to assume that those involved are in a position to carry out the group's intentions. For the strategy to be effective in community planning, therefore, the participant must not only commit himself or herself to a course of action, but also be in a position to commit others. This has been a vexing problem in community planning. It is not uncommon to involve someone who has little or no influence in the group he or she represents, or who may not be truly representative of his or her group.

If on the other hand, there is a planned attempt to relate system representatives to their own organization and reference groups, this strategy is a highly effective model for planned change. Experiments in industry with this strategy have been quite persuasive.[11] Moreover, a group highly committed to a change objective has proven to be a more effective change agent than an equivalent number of individuals.

STAFF SUPPLEMENT STRATEGY

Probably one of the oldest and certainly one of the most prevalent reasons for citizen participation is the simple principle of voluntarism—the recruitment of citizens to carry out tasks for an organization that does not have the staff resources to carry them out itself. This is a strategy basic to voluntary associations. Hospitals, family casework agencies, recreation services such as the YMCA and the Scouts, and fund-raising agencies rely on citizen volunteers to perform many essential agency functions. In some instances, agencies depend entirely on citizens to achieve their objectives. The clearest example is the voluntary fund-raising agency.

In community planning this strategy has been used to supplement the expertise of the planning agency's staff with the expertise of particular citizens. Basically, this is what Nash and Durden proposed in their suggestion to replace the planning commission with citizen task forces,[12] and what later writers have identified as the basic purpose of citizen participation.[13] The strategy is based on the assumption that the planner is a limited expert. He or she has knowledge that is conceptual and analytic, but he or she is not necessarily an expert in all substantive issues in which planning is engaged. Moreover, the planner lacks what is called *wisdom,* that is, the intimate knowledge of the context of planning within a specific community. Friedmann calls this personal or experiential knowledge.[14]

The strategy is not limited to using only the experiential knowledge of the citizen. The aim is to exploit the wisdom, abilities, free time, and expert knowledge of the citizen volunteer. The citizen is viewed as a staff member fulfilling roles and responsibilities necessary for achieving the objectives of a planning task and the mission of the agency. Interestingly, some agencies actually write up detailed job descriptions for volunteer roles. Much attention, therefore, has to be given to perfecting techniques for recruiting and holding volunteers. Incentives to stimulate willingness to participate become crucial because of the desire to recruit specific individuals.

The particular supplementary staff responsibility may be expert knowledge in a substantive area—a juvenile court judge in a study of delinquency, a public welfare recipient in a study of social welfare issues, a public health doctor in an air pollution study. Or it may be a mundane task—making speeches, writing news releases, designing brochures, stuffing envelopes. Then again, it may be providing the framework and background within which issues and priorities become identified. The strategy is easily compatible with the requirements of community planning agencies.

Cooptation

Another citizen participation practice is to involve citizens in an organization in order to prevent anticipated obstructionism. In this sense citizens are not seen as a means to achieve better planning goals nor are they seen as partners in assisting an organization in achieving its goal; rather, they are viewed as potential elements of obstruction or frustration whose cooperation and sanction are found necessary. This strategy, cooptation, has been defined as "the process of absorbing new elements into the leadership or policy-determining structure of an organization as a means of averting threats to its stability and existence."[15]

Cooptation is neither a new technique nor does it apply only to voluntary or government agencies. Corporations, for example, elect representatives of banking institutions to their boards of directors to provide access to financial resources. Politicians have been notably imaginative in this art. For instance, in order to ward off predictions that his administration would be fiscally irresponsible, President Kennedy appointed a highly respected Republican as secretary of the Treasury.

Cooptation can take two forms, both of which are applicable to organizations involving citizens. One is employed in response to specific power forces. Certain individuals are considered to have sufficient resources or influence—financial, decision-making, legislative—to affect vitally the operation of the organization. It is to capture this influence or at least neutralize it that they are brought into the organization; but, more significantly, they are included at the policy-making level because their influence is crucial to the continuation of current organizational policy. This has been termed "informal" cooptation, and its key characteristic is that it is a technique "of meeting the pressure of specific demands."[16]

Although informal cooptation has obvious advantages, it also exerts its own toll. Choice becomes constrained. Those coopted will want to share in influencing policy, and thus become one more definer of organization policy. Stability and security may be gained by cooptation, but frequently at a price. An organization will have to weigh the benefits against the costs.

A more prevalent practice is to rely upon what has been termed "formal" cooptation. It is a device for winning consent and legitimacy from the citizenry at large. The underlying belief is that the need the organization purports to serve is not in itself sufficiently persuasive to gain community support. Thus, groups who reflect the sentiments of the community are absorbed into the organization in order to gain legitimacy. Clergymen, for example, are inevitably involved in community projects because they bestow credibility upon the projects. Other groups reflecting community sentiments, who consequently are invariably involved, are representatives of labor, business, the professions, and women's organizations.

Formal cooptation also describes the practice of setting up and maintaining communication networks in a community. Any organization needs to establish reliable and readily accessible channels of communication through which information and requests may be transmitted to all relevant segments and participants. An organization depending on community support and sanction is obliged to relate itself to the community as a participant. A common method is to tap into already existing citizen groups—neighborhood organizations or block clubs, for instance. In this way the local citizens, through their voluntary associations or committees, become identified and committed to the program and, ideally, the apparatus of the operating agency.[17]

The participants' ability to affect policy, according to Philip Selznick, is the basis for the distinction between informal and formal cooptation. Informal cooptation implies a sharing of power in response to specific or potential pressures. Formal cooptation, on the other hand, merely seeks public acknowledgement of the agency-constituency relationship, since it is not anticipated that organizational policies will be put in jeopardy. What is shared "is the *responsibility* for power," explains Selznick, "not the power itself."[18]

It is not possible to assume, however, that voluntary groups formally coopted by an organization will be willing to remain passive with respect to policy. Where citizen groups are in general agreement with the goals of the host agency, as may have been the case in Selznick's analysis of the Tennessee Valley Authority, the observation may be applicable. But with changing conditions and possible disagreement on goals, the citizen group may endeavor to capture or at least influence the policymaking centers to insure that policies are made in their interest.

The problem with cooptation is that the term is used so extensively that it suffers from misuse. All citizen groups, for example, need legitimacy and sanction either from the community at large or from the community of interest in which they are involved. Indeed, the principle behind the notion to make a citizen group "representative" of the community is precisely to gain sanction or legitimacy. Are individuals recruited for such purposes coopted?

There is some implication that opponents, not disinterested citizens, become the coopted citizens when they are recruited by an organization. Yet it is traditional technique to recruit individuals who are opposed to an issue not for any quid pro quo basis, but in the belief that the opponent will see the "light" once he or she is exposed to the "facts." Indeed, this is a principle of citizen participation—which was outlined earlier—that the participatory process is designed to create a committed constituency.

A further implication is that if a disinterested individual becomes a part of a citizen group and during the participation becomes an advocate, he or she has been coopted, or in other words, an unwitting supporter. Again, the recruitment of citizens to organizations is designed to do just that—develop an organized constituency on behalf of a particular objective. Example: A neighbor active on behalf of a mental health association recruits her next door neighbor, who happens to be a teacher, to assist the mental health association in developing teaching materials for social studies classes in the primary schools. The teacher is recruited because of his knowledge of teaching materials and curriculum building. The association also recognizes that if a teacher develops the materials, the school system would more readily adopt the material than if it were developed by a nonteacher. The next-door-neighbor-teacher now becomes, in addition to an expert, a sanctioning agent.

In the course of working on the teaching materials and by interaction with other citizens active in the association, the teacher becomes more knowledgeable about mental health needs. Ignorance turns to enlightenment. Now the next-door-neighbor-teacher becomes a very active supporter of the association and its aims. Should the teacher be accused—using the term in its common pejorative sense—of being coopted? Not at all.

The strategy of cooptation should not be confused with techniques of recruiting individuals to work for and support organizational objectives (staff supplement and behavioral change strategy). It should be reserved for describing a technique of recruitment in which the exchange is for the benefit of the organization exclusively.

COMMUNITY POWER STRATEGIES

Power may be defined as the ability to exercise one's will even over the opposition of others. Individuals are capable of obtaining power and influence through the control of wealth or institutions. Whether such power can be exercised in all instances, or whether a small group can control all community decisions is a matter of dispute as was indicated in Chapter 1. Not disputed, however, is the fact that centers of power do exist outside the formal political structure of a community and such centers are influential in shaping community decisions.

Most community organizations are interested in exerting influence. Frequently, organizations come into being exclusively for the purpose of bringing their will to bear on community decisions. There are two strategies of citizen participation based on theories of community power, both designed to exploit community power.

The first is to recruit influentials who can bestow power and influence on the organization. Of course, this is more easily announced than accomplished. People participate in organizations primarily for the satisfactions they receive out of that participation. Any organization then has to think of the satisfactions or incentives it can offer.

Influentials are eagerly recruited by all kinds of citizen organizations. But by the very definition they are scarce. Thus, there is considerable competition for influentials.

Influentials, moreover, participate primarily in organizations that can maintain or enhance their status as an influential. One of the conundrums of citizen action is that there are only two ways in which an organization can confer status on its members. One is by *successful* and well publicized action. Some United Ways are examples; a foreign policy council is another.

A second is through the status of the individuals themselves. The president of a bank is more likely to participate in an organization in which presidents of other prestigious business and industries are involved. Hospital boards recruit individuals on the basis of the status of existing members. This explains why influentials are clustered among very few organizations.

Organizations interested in utilizing a strategy of community power have to view it as a long-term goal. Successful actions produce incentives for recruitment. Then begins the building block process of continued recruitment, continued successful activities that may eventually lead to the recruitment of one influential who may thereby attract other influentials.

ADVOCACY STRATEGY

Another significantly different strategy accepts the premises of community power theories but not the conclusions. Change, it is suggested, can be caused by confronting existing power centers with the power of numbers—an organized and committed mass of citizenry. In effect, a new center of power is created, based not on control of wealth and institutions but on size and dedication.[19] This type of organization has the ability to obtain accommodation from existing power centers, both from its inherent strength and from its choice of tactics.

One set of tactics is demonstrations, boycotts, and picketing. Negotiation on issues is inevitable, but negotiation from strength is a prerequisite. The power structure must first be put into a position of willingness to negotiate and this occurs only after they have been pushed to do so. "When those prominent in the status quo turn and label you an agitator," says Saul Alinsky, the chief ideologist of the conflict-oriented strategists, to his organizers, "they are completely correct, for that is, in one word, your function—to agitate to the point of conflict."[20]

The conflict technique works best for organizations committed to a cause rather than to specific issues or services. In securing the involvement of individuals indentified with the basic cause, the organization serves as the unifying vehicle for achievement of individual aims. There is, then little necessity to include the participants in the goal-defining process. Agreement is assumed. But on specific means to achieve the goal, disagreement may arise. Because the participants are emotionally involved in the ends, detached, pragmatic analysis of alternatives is difficult. Concerns are immediate and give rise to impatience, which, coupled with emotional involvement, can often lead to internal squabbling and dissension. Such conflict over means can immobilize an organization and lead to schisms. Certain race relations agencies have exhibited this difficulty.

Moreover, the effectiveness of the strategy appears limited in duration. Maintaining citizen interest appears to be the chief difficulty. The organization has only its goal, its idealized purpose, to sustain interest and create satisfactions. It is difficult to maintain interest in idealized goals over long periods of time. The emotional commitment required is too personally enervating. Often the leader of the organization is forced to depend on exhortations or the manufacturing of crises to recharge interest. Membership dwindles or frequently the organization changes, tending to rely less on conflict tactics and more on cooperation. New classes of participants, reflecting community sentiments or power forces, are invited to join. Goals are modified and the organization becomes indistinguishable from other service-oriented organizations.

Another and more recent tactic of the advocacy strategy is to use legal and regulatory procedures to achieve action. Organization and agency operations are monitored. Where violations are found, a suit or regulatory hearing is initiated. This tactic appears to be less onerous than the picketing and demonstration tactics and, therefore, becomes more and more popular by advocacy planning agencies.

One characteristic of the tactic is that citizens tend to play a limited role. They act primarily in supportive functions to the staff, paying dues and attending hearings and meetings. The staff, many with legal backgrounds, see themselves as representing the citizen members much like lawyers representing clients.[21] In policy-making or planning, the role would appear to be inappropriate and dysfunctional for identifying and supporting planning objectives.

SUMMARY

We have identified six strategies of citizen participation. The appropriateness and effectiveness of these strategies depend upon two conditions.

One is the organizational condition; that is, the mission, auspices, and resources of an organization. Not all strategies are appropriate for all organizations. Conflict-oriented strategies that depend on public protest, as local antipoverty agencies demonstrated, are inappropriate for public planning agencies.

A strategy of conflict appears best suited to social reform organizations that are privately supported, or, even more advantageous, self-supporting. Most disadvantaged groups seeking social change have had to depend upon either their own resources or the resources of groups highly sympathetic to their cause. The civil rights struggle is one good example; organized labor is another.

The appropriate strategies for public planning agencies and most community-wide planning agencies are the *behavioral change* and the *staff supplement* strategies. The function of the staff supplement strategy is to provide resources, legitimacy, and support for planning decisions and the planning organization. Such resources, legitimacy and support, however, cannot be obtained without the acceptance and involvement of the participants in the organizational activities.

In this respect the citizen participant can be compared to a staff member of the planning organization. The specific skills of the participants are viewed as having value in assisting the organization in achieving its objectives. The organization clearly recognizes that the specific skills and knowledge are important as premises for decision-making. Final authority for decision-making rests with those higher up in the organizational structure—board of directors, authority board, legislative constituency. If, on the other hand, the organization continually refuses to heed the suggestions and advice of the participant, the relationship will be terminated. The expectations of the participant will not be met and the participant will withdraw his or her support.

The behavioral change strategy appears to be useful in overcoming what is commonly referred to as the "politics" of the planning process. Given the debatable preference characteristics of planning goals and the free-market concept of competing community organizations, it is advisable to employ a strategy of participation aimed at accommodating various interests. The behavioral change strategy has the advantage of subjecting value preferences to a dialogue, allowing them to be aired within the context of the planning process. Other involved organizations are also encouraged to participate in order to allay their fears, gain their advice, and seek their cooperation.

The second condition that determines the effectiveness and appropriateness of a citizen participation strategy is the specified role that citizens are given in a planning organization. If the role of the citizen is to provide a *review and comment* function (See Chapter 3.), then a strategy of supplementing staff or the behavioral change strategy are clearly inappropriate. The appropriate role or roles for staff supplement strategy are *advisory* or *shared decision-making*.

It should be emphasized that the strategy of citizen participation will determine the structural role of citizens in the planning organization.

NOTES

1. In this context citizen participation can be defined as part of exchange theory. See David R. Godschalk, *Participation, Planning and Exchange in Old and New Communities: A Collaborative Paradigm* (Chapel Hill: Center for Urban and Regional Studies, University of North Carolina, 1972).
2. Eduard C. Lindeman, *The Community* (New York: Association Press, 1921), pp. 58–76.
3. Murray G. Ross, *Case Histories in Community Organization* (New York: Harper, 1958), pp. 10–11; and Murray G. Ross, *Community Organization* (New York: Harper, 1955), pp. 13, 21–22, 48–53.
4. Roland L. Warren, *The Community in America* (Chicago: Rand McNally, 1963), pp. 329–330.
5. Oscar Lewis, *La Vida* (New York: Random House, 1966), pp. xlii–lii.
6. Sherry R. Arnstein, "A Ladder of Citizen Participation," *Journal of the American Institute of Planners,* Vol. 35, No. 4 (July 1969), pp. 216–224.
7. See, for example, Douglas McGregor, *The Human Side of Enterprise* (New York: McGraw-Hill, 1960).
8. John F. Kennedy, *Housing Message to Congress,* March 1961.

9. Dorwin Cartwright, "Achieving Change in People: Some Applications of Group Dynamics Theory," *Human Relations,* IV (1951), p. 387.

10. Ibid., p. 390.

11. See L. Coch and J. R. P. French, Jr., "Overcoming Resistance to Change," *Human Relations,* 1:4 (1948), 512–532.

12. Peter Nash and Dennis Durden, "A Task Force Approach to Replace the Planning Board," *Journal of the American Institute of Planners,* XXX (February 1964), pp. 10–22.

13. Robert A. Aleshire, "Planning and Citizen Participation: Costs, Benefits, and Approaches," *Urban Affairs Quarterly,* Vol. 5, No. 4 (June 1970) pp. 369–393 and John Friedmann, *Retracking America: A Theory of Transactive Planning,* Garden City, N.Y.: Anchor Doubleday, 1973).

14. Friedmann, op. cit., pp. 172–185.

15. Philip Selznick, "Foundations of the Theory of Organization," *American Sociological Review,* 13 (February 1948), p. 34.

16. Ibid., p. 35.

17. Philip Selznick, *TVA and the Grassroots* (Berkeley: University of California Press, 1953), pp. 224–225.

18. Ibid., pp. 34–35 (his emphasis).

19. Advocacy planning appears also to stress the concept of community power as a strategy of change. The power the advocate planner is stressing, however, is the power of knowledge—the technical apparatus that he or she can offer local interest groups, which thus enables them to gain concessions from City Hall. See Lisa R. Peattie, "Reflections on Advocacy Planning," *Journal of the American Institute of Planners,* XXXIV (March 1968), pp. 80–88.

20. Quoted in Charles E. Silberman, *Crisis in Black and White* (New York: Vintage Books, 1965), p. 335.

21. A complete study of participation in rule making is by Michael Asimow. See Michael Asimow, "Public Participation in the Adoption of Interpretive Rules and Policy Statements" *Michigan Law Review,* Vol. 75, No. 3 (January 1977) pp. 520–584.

Chapter 5

PLANNING AND SOCIAL CHANGE

To suggest, as in Chapter 2, that planning intervenes into and attempts to influence the process of decision-making is to suggest that planning is also part of a change process. It is necessary to add that planning is part of a *social* change process; and this for three reasons.

First, planning is initiated, sustained, and implemented by individuals. The individuals are organized—formally or informally—around a common purpose. As a consequence of that organization, networks of interactions are established that influence both the process and the outcome of planning.

Secondly, the tools of planning are social in character. Admittedly data gathering and factual analysis are *a* social. But it is individuals who determine which data are to be gathered, the way they are to be gathered, how they are to be interpreted. And they are determined not by individuals in isolation, but by individuals interacting with one another.

Thirdly, the effects of the planning-change endeavor are institutions and organizations. Some may be highly formalized, others less so. The change may involve restructuring institutions, coordinating organizational activities, and refashioning the physical artifacts of institutions. Nonetheless the willingness to accept or reject the change rests with specific individuals within organizations and institutions affected by the planning. Oftentimes, too, the acceptance or rejection of change rests with individuals at a variety of different levels within the institutions and organizations.

Planning and social change, it must be concluded, are interrelated activities. To understand planning, therefore, it is necessary to understand social change: how it is initiated, how it is maintained, and how the change objective is achieved—if it is achieved. The purpose of this chapter is to outline types of social change applicable to community planning. The types of social change, in turn, serve as a basis for describing strategies of decision-making outlined in Chapters 10 and 11.

Preliminary Considerations of Social Change

Before beginning a discussion of social change, it will be helpful to outline some preliminary considerations. This will provide a focus for analysis and a frame of reference for the reader.

Exclusionary Considerations

There are any number of theories and explanations of social change. Some, for example, are based on philosophical premises, others on economic factors, and still others are based on knowledge of human behavior. Certainly it is not possible to cover all the explanations of social change in a book of this size. Nor is that necessary for purpose of this text. It is necessary, therefore, to be exclusive rather than inclusive.

There are two bases for exclusion. First, inasmuch as it has already been postulated that planning is an interventionist process, then, by definition, it will be necessary to focus on theories related to enacted as opposed to crescive or evolutionary change.[1] The emphasis is on change efforts that are deliberately initiated either by an individual or group or a combination of both. Excluded, as a result, are theories or explanations deterministic in character; or, in other words, theories that view change and development as part of a natural evolutionary or cyclical law.

Secondly, it is necessary to focus on social change explanations that have a relationship to planning at the community and interorganizational level. This is not to say that some explanations discussed in this chapter are not applicable to societal level planning or to work with individuals or groups. Indeed, some theorists discussed in the chapter would insist they are. But our interest is in social change hypotheses or explanations that have relevance for *community* planners.

Excluded, consequently, are theories on the one hand that are related to individual change or the enhancement of individual social functioning. Psychotherapy, group therapy, and most normative re-educative explanations of change[2] are included in this category. Excluded at the other extreme are grant theories of societal change, such as those postulated by Sir Thomas Maine, Lewis Mumford, or Walt Rostow.

On the basis of these two premises, five explanations of social change related to the social process of planning have been identified. Two are theories as defined both by their proponents and by the commonly accepted definition of theory. The two are field theory and learning theory.

The other three are interorganizational behavior, diffusion of innovation, and conflict. It is conceivable that each of these explanations of social change can be subsumed under a general theory of social change, such as field theory or learning theory. The preference, however, is to classify them separately, and the reason, quite simply, is for clarity and emphasis. The objective is to identify and signify for the purpose of the planner a typology of social change methods applicable to the planning process.

Framework Considerations

When examining social change it is helpful to view it in three distinct, yet interrelated ways. First is the initiation of change. How does it emerge and under what circumstances? Equally important are questions related to the agent of change. Does the change emerge internally, arising out of the interests of a group (if it is a group-initiated change) or an individual? Or is it externally induced by some identifiable agent? What function does such an agent serve?

Secondly, there are issues related to the technology of change. What methods or techniques are used to initiate and bring about the change? And thirdly, there is the direction of the change. Towards what entity or system is the change directed? What, in other words, is the target of change?[3]

Although distinct, each of these aspects of change need not reside in different systems. By identifying that there is a target system of change does not imply that the initiator of the change is a separate system. An informal group, for example, that decides to repair and "fix up" its neighborhood, may concentrate on their own properties. They are, consequently, the initiators and target of change. At the same time there can be two different systems: the neighborhood group organizes and attempts to persuade others to fix up their properties.

The technology of change can also be part of or separate from the system undergoing change. To return to our neighborhood group: the group can use educational meetings to raise their own consciousness about the need to fix up the neighborhood, they can invite specialists in to educate them about the need for change, or they can hire an organizer-planner to stimulate them about the need to fix up the neighborhood.

Whether separate or singular, it is important for planners to identify each of these aspects if he or she is going to understand planning as a process of social change. In some theories they are explicitly considered. In others they are implicit. The task here is to make them explicit.

Field Theory

Field theory is one of the classical theories of social change. Developed by Kurt Lewin, the theory posits that all social systems are governed by a force field containing driving and restraining forces. Driving forces are directed towards change and development. They are in response to needs, ambition, hopes, and values. Restraining forces, such as habit, conflictual driving forces, energy levels, and coercion, are obstacles to change.[4]

Further, social systems tend towards equilibrium. Driving and restraining forces act as a balance to maintain a steady state. The process, however, is not a static one. Social systems are in what Lewin maintains a "quasi stationary equilibria," which can be likened to a river that is constantly flowing, yet basically unchanging in direction.

Change, nonetheless, is not ruled out. Indeed, the theory is directed toward explaining change. But change occurs when the balance or equilibrium is altered. Any increase in driving forces—new needs, developmental changes (physical and social), changed values—or a reduction in restraining forces brought about by new learning, new rewards and punishments, new experiences, and new group values and attitudes is necessary for change to occur.[5]

Lewin suggests that it is the restraining forces that give direction to change, because the direction of change is a result of what restraining forces can be modified. Moreover, increasing the driving forces tends to increase tension within the system. While it is possible for a system to increase its driving forces (such as ambitions or values) to bring about change, the tension produced may make the change shortlived. Diminishing restraining forces, then, appear to be a more powerful force for change.[6]

Restraining forces not only give direction to change but also serve as an influence in the initiation of change. Social systems, suggest Lewin, respond to change less in terms of moving to an ideal goal than in response to dissatisfactions or pain. It is the dissatisfactions or pain that most often serve as the impetus for change. Without these conditions, or the ability to create or stimulate them, initiating change efforts are problematic.[7]

Analysis of change efforts with groups by field theorists has been an important contribution to social change theories. Their studies of groups reveal that group values have a significant effect on individual human behavior. The greater the value of a group standard, the greater the resistance of the individual to move away from that standard.[8]

But this suggests, too, that resistance to change is lower within group-carried changes than in individual change efforts. Lewin's studies of groups undergoing change reveal, "it is usually easier to change individuals formed into a group than to change any one of them separately. As long as group values are unchanged, the individual will resist changes more strongly the further he is to depart from group standards. If the group standard itself is changed, the resistance which is due to the relation between individual and group standard is eliminated."[9]

Furthermore, the change is more likely to be permanent in group-change efforts in comparison to nongroup efforts. So often the difficulty in any change efforts is not so much initiating the change, but that of maintaining the change once it occurs. In group-change efforts, group members tend to support each other through the change activity. The group, in other words, acts as a stabilizing and support mechanism for the individual members. The change, therefore, will more likely be permanent.[10]

An ambitious application of field theory to social change activities was conducted by Ronald Lippitt and his associates.[11] Lippitt's interest was in *planned* change; that is, change that was a deliberate attempt to improve a social system, and, moreover, made use of an outside agent in helping to make that improvement. Four different kinds of social systems were analyzed: individuals, groups, organizations, and communities.[12]

Lippitt's findings, which were obtained by analyzing case studies, are instructive for our purposes. He refines and clarifies the construct of driving and restraining forces. Forces toward change can include pain or dissatisfaction with the present situation or an external pressure forcing the system to change. The dissatisfaction can also arise from a perceived discrepancy between what is and what might be. In other words, an individual or group might be satisfied with a current situation but when compared with another more favorable situation, a dissatisfaction and thus force for change arises.[13]

But Lippitt further suggests that change cannot begin unless there is an awareness that improvement is possible. Dissatisfactions alone, in other words, are not sufficient, because a specification of the change is required. The change becomes specified when the direction of the change is clearly identified, and the problem defined.[14]

Once the change effort is begun, support for it can be generated from among forces other than dissatisfaction or the desire for improvement. Neighboring or other subsystems that can benefit from an identified change may emerge to provide support. A second likely sustaining force for change may merely be the need to complete a task once it has begun. The change activity itself often creates a commitment that acts as a driving force for change.[15]

In clarifying the resistance forces, Lippitt helps to identify specific obstacles to change efforts. Some resistance may be quite general—other satisfactions, for example. Some may be quite specific to the change itself—despite the awareness of a problem, ideological preferences or belief systems can inhibit change. For a number of years, as an illustration, individuals who could benefit from a nationalized health program opposed it because it was simply "wrong."

A further obstacle may merely be the lack of energy once the change process begins. Change requires endurance and patience. If these cannot be sustained the change effort breaks down.[16]

Lippitt indicates as well that resistance may not be the only obstacle to change. Forces not specifically resistant to the change may interfere, and in effect become obstacles to change. Interference, for example, can result from competing preferences—one change effort or project is preferred over another. A second type of interference can be the lack of resources, such as the loss of funds. Frequently even conflicting interpersonal relationships can interfere with a change effort that is desired and needed. Opposition, for example, can emerge out of fear, distrust, or dislike of the individual or group proposing the change.[17]

A further contribution of Lippitt is his expansion of the change model to seven stages. Lewin postulated a three-stage change model; viz., unfreezing at the present level; moving toward a new level; and freezing the change at the new level.[18] The Lippitt model is:

Phase 1. *Development of a need for change.* Comparable to the unfreezing stage of Lewin, Lippitt suggests that a process of planned change can begin only when the stress or pain within the system is translated into a desire to change and a desire to seek help.

Phase 2. *Establishment of a change relationship.* Given the concept of "change agent" the assumption of a client-agent relationship is necessary. Further, the relationship must be accepted with mutuality of expectations.

Phases 3, 4, 5. *Classification or diagnosis of the client system's problem—the examination of alternative routes or goals; establishing goals and intentions of action—the transformation of intentions into actual change efforts.* These phases are similar to Lewin's second stage of moving from one level of performance or functioning to another level. Phases 3, 4, and 5 are the process of working toward change. Although similar to planning stages, the emphasis is placed on the client system taking responsibility for diagnosis, goal setting and reality testing.

Phase 6. *Generalization and stabilization of change.* Similar to Lewin's freezing stage, the focus in this stage is the development of procedures, structures, or subsystem connections to maintain the change once it is achieved.

Phase 7. *Achieving a terminal relationship.* A derivative of the change-agent relationship phase, the focus is on providing a means to end the agent-system relationship.[19]

As an explanation of change, field theory is useful in understanding some of the basic characteristics of bringing about and sustaining social change efforts. There are some limitations in the theory, however. Generalizations applying to the group effects on individual attitudes and behavior are sometimes questionable. Group norms do have an effect on attitudes, but this may be due to an initial self-selection process. Individuals may choose to associate with groups that are more likely to support their individual standards. Also, although it is true that a group change is likely to be more permanent than an individual change, the point is that it is only "likely" not certainly. This limits the theory's precision.[20]

Secondly, field theory studies are limited to the analysis of change within small groups. Admittedly, the Lippitt study attempts to go beyond this limitation. Yet the case analysis of community change efforts is small in comparison to the analysis of individual and group change efforts. Even the community analysis is less a study of communities undergoing change than a small segment of the community. Moreover, the segment members are identified as the unit undergoing change.

The theory's explanation of change, consequently, is based on an assumption that the initiator and target of change are one and the same entity or system. The client system—using field theory terminology—whether it be an individual, a group, or a segment of a community are the only ones to be affected by the change. A derivative assumption is the client system has the power and capacity to bring about the change. In this sense the change model is a clinical model and can be depicted as shown in Figure 5-1.

The model also defines the relationship of a "change agent" to the client system. Although the change agent can act as a catalyst in stimulating change, the change process cannot proceed without an agreed upon relationship between the system and the agent. Furthermore, the system has to agree to accept the need for assistance. The change agent uses a technology of group processes to bring about an agreement for change among all members. The group, then, is the medium through which the change takes place. The change agent is both part of but not a member of the group undergoing change.

Despite these limitations, field theory provides a set of principles of use to planning.

First, of course, is the premise that social change is initiated as the consequence of pain or dissatisfaction. This principle appears to support the observations of Braybrooke and Lindblom that policy-making is remedial.[21]

Secondly, change can begin only after the dissatisfaction is translated into a desire or a willingness to change.

Thirdly, because desire or willingness has to precede the change effort, it is necessary to create an environment that positively supports the initiation of change efforts. Awareness of the need for change presupposes the initiation of change.

Fourth, social change implies a modifying of existing attitudes and behavior. For social change to occur, behavior has to

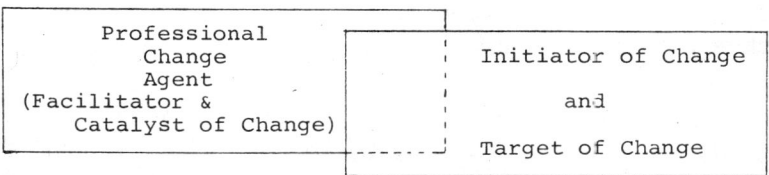

Figure 5-1 Model of change appropriate to field theory.

change. It is necessary, therefore, to employ a technology designed to change attitudes. Field theory suggests that the technology is one in which individuals formed into groups can bring about the behavioral change.

Fifth, obstacles to change can include not only direct opposition but also elements that have no direct bearing on the change activity or objective, which are defined as interference forces.

Sixth, social change involves a staging process. For change to occur, there must be not only movement to the desired change level, but also a level of permanence must be reached. Without devising means for making the change permanent, individuals tend to revert to preexisting levels of attitude and behavior.

LEARNING THEORY

Learning theory is one of the earliest explanations of behavior and change. Based initially on the works of the Russian psychologist Ivan Pavlov, it suggests that individual growth and change (the elemental factors of behavior) are conditioned responses to drives, stimuli, and rewards. Change is a function of adapting to the environment. It is an attempt on the part of individuals to move from dissatisfactory states to ones that are more satisfactory as a process of *learning*.

More recent work, particularly on the part of B. F. Skinner,[22] has refined the theory. Similarly to field theorists, learning theorists accept the premise that individuals move away from pain or harmful contacts. Unlike the field theorists, however, there is no necessity for willing a change or desiring a change before it occurs. In fact, learning theorists deny the concept of will.[23]

The theory states further that behavior is acquired as a result of continuing satisfying consequence. "When a bit of behavior," explains Skinner, "is followed by a certain kind of consequence, it is more likely to occur again, and a consequence having this effect is called a reinforcer."[24]

Consequences—or contingencies, in Skinner's terminology—can as a result be reinforced. Praise and credit, for example, condition approved behavior. Awards, in fact, are "established reinforcers," and are used by groups and societies to denote approved behavior patterns. Equally significant, praise also influences the one giving praise, because anyone who praises a person or approves of what a person has done is inclined to reinforce the person in other ways.[25]

Behavior, therefore, is shaped by the consequences of action, which in turn leads to change. The consequences are external, or environmental—$B=f(E)$. (Field theorists, on the other hand, suggest that behavior is a function both of the person and the environment—$B=f[P+E]$). Punishment is one example. Punishment is nothing more than arranging contingencies to manage certain kinds of behavior.

Yet, punishment as a behavior-controlling technique is limited. It tells how *not* to behave; it does not tell how *to* behave.[26]

It is possible to reinforce behavior positively by the use of a technique called operant conditioning. Learning theorists maintain that this is a more effective technique than punishment, because it is based on the assumption that a person acts intentionally "not in the sense that he possesses an intention which he then carries out, but in the sense that his behavior has been strengthened by the consequences."[27] Therefore, by arranging contingencies, which act to reinforce wanted or desired behavior, a specific change can be achieved.

Learning theory is a much more ambitious explanation of social change than field theory. It describes a theory of behavior, and, as a consequence, a set of principles and techniques for changing behavior much more precisely than field theory. Field theory suggests that a change is likely to occur given the operation of a certain set of conditions. Learning theorists suggest that it *will* occur.

The techniques of operant conditioning have given rise to a whole new school of psychology—behavior modification. With the retarded, the mentally ill, delinquents, school children, and even with workers in industry, behavior modification methods are being used with remarkable results. It lay behind a New York City plan in late 1971 to provide rewards for welfare clients who utilized resources to become self-sufficient. The plan was aborted because of public controversy. It was criticized for being too manipulative and demeaning to the welfare recipients.

And this suggests one of the limitations in applying the theory. Ideological obstacles may be insurmountable, regardless of the theory's validity.

A further limitation is its applicability to large groups such as communities or regions. Skinner insists that it can be and describes its possibility in *Walden Two*.[28] Nonetheless, religious organizations, for example, have used the techniques of operant conditioning and established reinforcers to mold and control behavior. Yet schisms occur, and they occur because of competing consequences of action. This may suggest that individuals *choose* as well as learn sets of behavior.

Another limitation is defining the function, role and legitimacy of the change agent in applying the theory to planning. In defining the role in therapeutic situations, the role problem appears clarified. The therapist is called upon to provide a specific type of treatment by the client or the client surrogate. In this instance, the initiation of change is presumed to come from the client. This relationship legitimizes the therapist's role.

When the theory is applied to a planning situation, the change agent assumes the role not just as the agent of change, but also the initiation of the change. (See Figure 5–2.) How that role is legitimized is not explained, or at least not clearly.

Despite the limitations, learning theory provides a set of principles that may be useful in planning.

First, change is initiated in response to dissatisfactions—"harmful contacts" in the terminology of Skinner.

Secondly, change can be initiated also in response to satisfactory consequences of action.

Thirdly, pain or satisfactions serve to give direction to change and provide a mode for learning how to adapt.

Fourth, social change implies the modification of behavior. The most effective technique for modifying behavior is operant conditioning. Operant conditioning is the management of contingencies of behavior to secure desired behavioral objectives.

Fifth, awards, praise, model behavior can be used to positively reinforce and direct desired behavior.

INTER-ORGANIZATION BEHAVIOR EXPLANATION OF CHANGE

One of the principal limitations of the social-psychological explanations of change is that social change is defined as a resultant force related to a specific problem or area of dysfunctioning. But is this the only explanation of how change is initiated? Roland Warren, after an analysis of community action activities, suggests otherwise. While not refuting the

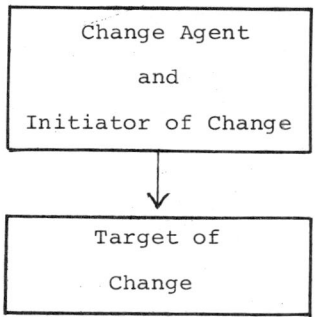

Figure 5–2 Model of change appropriate to learning theory.

premises of field theory, Warren explains that change also can be initiated as a consequence of previously successful change efforts. For those involved, the change effort produces an enjoyment that is translated into an attitude that says, "Well, we got that one going. What's next boys?"[29]

What Warren uncovered is the role satisfactions play in influencing behavior—specifically satisfactions accrued through cooperative activity. Cooperation is a method used by individuals to overcome limitations to individual activity. In addition to its central purpose—attaining an objective—cooperation produces benefits to the individuals engaged in the cooperative activity. Chief of these is the satisfaction that may be derived through the association of the members with one another. This satisfaction, as well as the satisfaction derived from the achievement of the objective, can produce further cooperative efforts.

Learning theorists will say that this is precisely what they mean when they say that satisfying consequences of an action reinforce continuance of that action. And this is true. But the consequences produce further consequences, and that is the necessity to maintain the cooperative group that serves to induce and achieve social change objectives. Let us explain.

Chester I. Barnard suggests that cooperation depends upon two conditions. One is effectiveness—the accomplishment of recognized objectives. Without any recognizable objectives, individuals will not come together around a cooperative task. The second is efficiency—which is related to the satisfactions of individual motives. If an individual's motives cannot be satisfied, either through sharing in the benefits of securing the objective or personal association or previous obligations, cooperative activity cannot occur.[30]

Equally significant: The satisfactions themselves are derived by the changes the cooperative effort is able to secure from its ability to change the environment.[31]

Efficiency, as the term is defined here, is also a condition for the existence of formal organizations. Formal organizations are simply a subset of a class of entities called cooperative systems. An essential element of organizations is the willingness of the members to contribute their individual efforts to achieving organizational objectives. The efforts are secured through incentives; that is, the inducements the organization can hold out to individuals for their contributions.[32]

Incentives, explains Barnard, are critical to the existence of organizations:

> The individual is always the basic strategic factor in organization. Regardless of his history or his obligations he must be induced to cooperate, or there can be no cooperation. It needs no further introduction to suggest that the subject of incentives is fundamental in formal organizations and conscious efforts to organize. Inadequate incentives means dissolution or failure of cooperation. Hence, in all sorts of organizations the affording of adequate incentives becomes the most definitely emphasized task in their existence.[33]

Barnard catalogues a number of inducements that an organization might be able to proffer to secure willingness to cooperate:

1. Material incentives, such as salaries, wages, opportunity for personal gain.
2. Opportunities for distinction, prestige, and power.
3. Desirable physical conditions for work or other activities.
4. The opportunity to satisfy personal ideals.
5. Associational attractiveness; that is, the satisfactions gained through work with group members or other employees.
6. The opportunity to be engaged in an important and prestigeful activity or event.

Although not an inducement, but a method of persuasion, are techniques for inculcating motives such as training. Training is a method of socializing individuals to engage in cooperative activities.[34]

Significantly, the source of inducements is derived from the contributions of the participants themselves. It is their activities that generate inducements.[35] This borders on the tautological, but an example may help.

An effective way for an organization to develop influence in community decision-making is to include in its membership individuals of status and influence.[36] Yet individuals with status and influence tend not to participate in organizations unless the organization itself has status. For an organization to attract individuals with status and influence, it must engage in activities that are status producing and successful.[37] But the organization's success is related to the proportion of high status membership as stated in the opening sentence of the paragraph. Organizations, as a result, must engage in a building-block process of activities designed to attract higher and higher people with status and influence.

It is theory of incentives that creates a condition in which the maintenance of the organization dominates the ends and also provides a focal point for social change. Banfield states the thesis this way:

> Civic controversies in Chicago are not generated by the efforts of politicians to win votes, by differences of ideology or group interests, or by the behind-the-source effort of a power elite. They arise, instead, out of the maintenance and enhancement needs of large and formal organizations. The heads of an organization see some advantage to be gained by changing the situation. They propose changes. Other large organizations are threatened. They oppose, and a civic controversy takes place.[38]

While organizational enhancement can be an initiating force for change, both the achievement of change and the type of change achieved is determined by the interplay of a variety of organizations with an interest or stake in the specific change. (See Figure 5-3.) The change target itself exerts considerable influence in the change outcome. This conception of the change

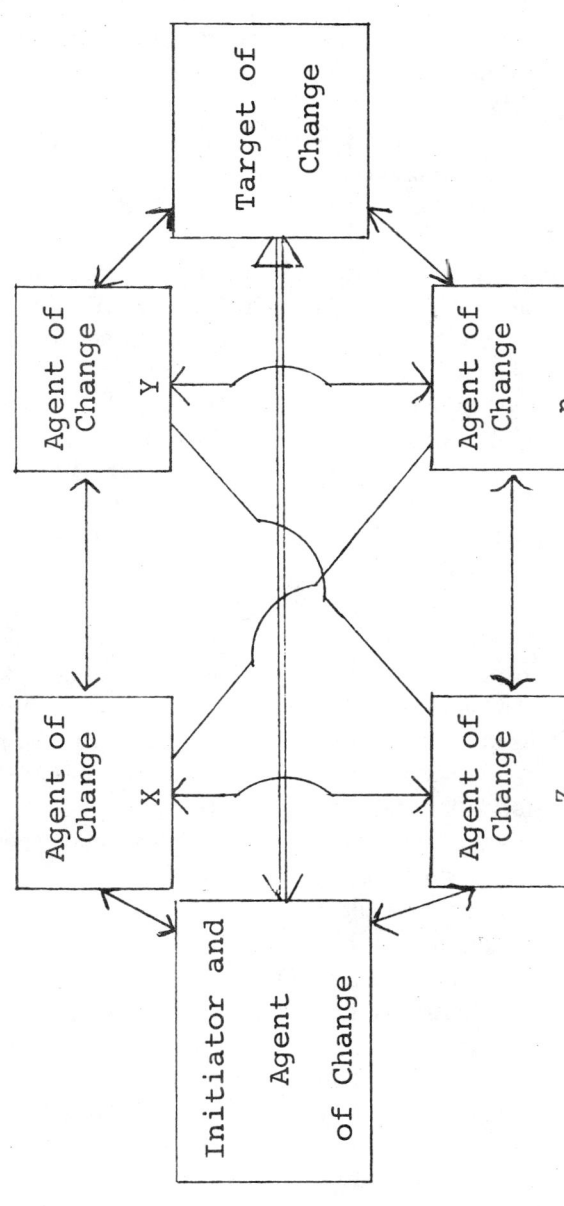

Figure 5-3 Model of change appropriate to inter-organizational behavior explanation of change.

process determines the medium through which the change takes place. The technology of change is defined as the "politics of decision-making."

Organizations, in other words, vie with one another to influence the specific change once the initiation process has begun. Specific actors and organizations are identified in terms of their influence over other actors and decision centers.[39] Techniques such as coalitions, conflict, cooptation, and bargaining may be used to achieve the desired change. The primary objective is to persuade or compel the change target to accept the change.

A major advantage of the inter-organization behavior explanation of social change is that it focuses attention on the relationship between the organization as a change agent and the change target. Field theory and learning theory assume that the change target can become involved in the change process as an active participant. The technology, therefore, is directed toward modifying the behavior of the target.

Inter-organization behavior explanation assumes just the contrary. The target is always external to the agent, and the change agent is not an individual but an organization. No attempt is made to involve the target in the process for the purpose of modifying its behavior. The implicit assumption is that there is no functional relationship between behavior and change. Change is achieved and sustained by bringing about a change in policy or law governing the operations of the change target. The desired change becomes mandated.

A further advantage is that the type of change activity that can be initiated is broadened. Field and learning theory accept an assumption that change is related to need. An organizational theory of social change accepts this assumption but is not restricted to it. Organizations tend to seek out change activities that can generate widespread support. The more likely that the need is widespread, or "felt" in the terms of the social psychologist, the more likely the success in achieving the change objective.

Yet it is also true that organizations initiate change efforts that do not at the outset have widespread support. Many are unsuccessful, a fact that supports the "feasibility" thesis. But some are successful. Two conditions appear to be necessary for success.

The first is the amount of influence and power the organization has. The greater the amount of influence an organization has over decision centers, the greater the likelihood it will have to achieve its objectives. This was discussed in Chapter 2 under the concept of legitimacy.

The second is the campaigning strategy of the organization. The more an organization develops strategies for winning support for its objective through publicity, organizing citizens and groups, and developing coalitions with other organizations, the more likely it will be successful. The organization, in other words, *creates* the need for change. There is evidence to suggest that the campaigning strategy as a technology of social change is as important, if not more so, than the amount of community influence an organization has.[40] Once the initiation phase has begun, therefore, a planned campaign is necessary to influence the change target and other contending organizations.

A principal limitation of the organizational theory of social change is that it neglects the influence of attitudes and behavior in sustaining a change once it is achieved. The assumption that a change in policy or law is all that is required to sustain a desired change is questionable. If the system is such that decision centers can control or disregard the behaviors of the members, then the assumption may be valid. President Truman's desegregation order for the armed forces in 1945 is a classic example of how a policy change can bring about the desired effect without regard for attitudes and behavior.

On the other hand, where there is an absence of control, a change in policy may not bring about the desired effect. The desegregation policies and laws of the 1950s are a case in point. While desegregation was mandated, desegregation practices remain unchanged. Similar examples can be pointed out in housing and welfare. While this does not negate the thesis, it does suggest a severe limitation.

Another limitation is that the role of an individual change agent or planner in the process is not specified. This is not a criticism. The literature examined focused on the behavior of organizations in influencing change, and assumed:

1. That the organization had gone through a process of commitment to the objective.
2. That the planner or change agent is a member of and acting in behalf of the organization.

The planner, however, does play a significant role in creating commitment to the change objective both within the organization and among and between other organizational entities.

Despite these limitations, an inter-organization behavior explanation of social change provides the following principles for planning:

1. Organization enhancement is an initiation force for social change.
2. Negotiations among competing organizations is the major force for determining the direction of change.
3. Power and influence over decision centers is a principal variable in achieving change objectives.
4. To achieve change objectives, strategies are necessary that will compel or influence a change target to accept the change.
5. The technology of change is similar to the politics of decision-making.

DIFFUSION OF INNOVATION

Of all the explanations and theories of social change one of the most rigorously studied and oddly the least well known in the planning field is diffusion of innovation.[41] Rural sociologists, anthropologists, medical sociologists, and industrial economists have engaged in explorations on how an idea becomes diffused among groups and becomes eventually adopted. The results of the studies are instructive.

First, it will be helpful to start with a definition of terms. An *innovation* is an idea perceived as new by the individual (whether it is new or not). *Diffusion* is the process by which an innovation spreads. The *diffusion process* is the spread of a new idea from its source of invention or creation to its ultimate users or adopters. *Adoption* is a decision to continue full use of an innovation.[42]

Everett Rogers, a major synthesizer of diffusion research, identifies five stages in the process of an adoption of an innovation. They are:

1. *Awareness stage.* At this stage the individual has some awareness of the innovation, but is not yet motivated to seek further information. This is also considered the initiation phase.
2. *Interest stage.* At this stage the individual purposively seeks more information about the innovation.
3. *Evaluation stage.* At this point the individual determines whether or not the innovation is worth a trial.
4. *Trial stage.* Following evaluation, the individual may decide to test the innovation on a probationary basis. The object is to determine the utility of the innovation in his or her own situation.
5. *Adoption stage.* Adoption means continued use of the innovation in the future. The functions of the adoption stage are consideration of the trial results and the decision to ratify sustained use of the innovation.[43]

There is some similarity between Rogers's adoption of an innovation model and the previously outlined seven-stage change model of Lippitt. Both recognize the development of an awareness about a change before a change process begins. Both, too, stress the need for a trial of an innovation, or as Lippitt terms it, the need for reality testing, before the change can be adopted.[44]

The differences, however, are based on basic assumptions regarding change that each has made. The Lippitt model presumes a clinical working relationship between a client and a change agent in which the client is directly involved in seeking help. The change agent, moreover, is seen as a professional helper with skills in diagnosis and in helping the client develop a plan of action for change. Secondly, the initiation to change is in response to a defined need for change. It is the client's motivation for change that initiates the change effort. And, finally, the Lippitt problem-solving method is directed toward helping a client gain insight into the nature of the problem or difficulty. It is important for the client to gain a diagnostic understanding of the problem before establishing goals and intentions of action can begin.

The Rogers model, on the other hand, is based on a different set of assumptions. The client is a target system external to the change agent. The function of the change agent is to influence adoption of a decision in a direction that the change agent feels is desirable.[45] The client does not seek help. Change, moreover, is in response to an innovation that will provide increased satisfactions or benefits to an individual; for example, a new strain of corn, a more efficacious drug, or increased productivity.

In comparison, the Rogers model is a more goal-directed process than the Lippitt model. The target system does not become involved in diagnosing the nature of a problem but is involved in a means-end schema of arriving at a decision. The decision-making process is related to learning theory rather than field theory.[46]

A major contribution of diffusion research is the analyses of target system behavior. Why does one target system adopt an innovation while another does not? Who tends to adopt innovations more rapidly than others? What forces contribute to a target system adopting an innovation?

One likely and expected finding is that where an innovation is response to the felt need of the target system, it is more readily adopted. "Discontented target systems generally are more innovative than contented ones," is the way it is described.[47] This supports the findings of field and learning theories.

Based on diffusion studies, Rogers has developed a classification of five adopter categories. The distinctions are not arbitrary but based on the relative time of adoption of an innovation. They are, however, as Rogers warns, descriptions of ideal types. Nonetheless they provide information on the characteristics of target systems.[48]

> *Innovators.* Innovators are venturesome, quick to try new ideas. They are risk takers, and as risk takers they have sufficient resources to withstand occasional failures.
>
> *Early adopters.* Early adopters, as distinct from innovators, are integrated members of a local social system. They have the highest degree of opinion leadership; and opinion leaders, it is important to note, play an important role in the diffusion and adoption of innovations. The opinion leader provides a primary source of influence for the initiation and ultimate acceptance of innovations. A principal function of opinion leaders is to provide a face-to-face communication exchange in influencing adoption of an innovation. Others in the social system tend to look to early adopters before using an idea.
>
> *Early majority.* The early majority adopts a new idea just prior to the average person. They are participators in innovating activities but not leaders. They provide an important link in legitimizing innovations.
>
> *Late majority.* The late majority adopts innovations in response to necessity or pressure. They respond to public opinion.

Laggards. The last to adopt an innovation, and they do so reluctantly, are laggards. They are tradition-oriented in contrast to early adopters. Laggards are generally from lower socio-economic groups, again in contrast to early adopters who are from high socioeconomic groups.[49]

The change process in diffusion of innovation involves a sequence of change targets. The objective is to spread the base of support by using the influence characteristics of individual change targets to influence other change targets. This is particularly true in the relationship of early adopters and the early majority change targets. (See Figure 5–4.)

Innovators, incidentally, are generally unrelated to a change process that involves other groups. They are less interested in influencing other groups to adopt innovations than in adopting an innovation for its own sake. Where, however, the innovation may be of personal benefit, innovators will assume the role of change agent.

The change agent's relationship to the targets is to act as a catalyst for change and an influence for the innovation. He or she plays a direct role in influencing the change and outcome. Change targets can modify the innovation and, as well, influence the role of the change agent. The purpose of the change agent is to inject a cosmopolitan influence into a client social system. He or she initiates the adoption process by identifying opinion leaders early in the change process.

One of the problems of diffusion of innovation is determining its applicability to planning. Few, if any, studies can be found in planning. Therefore, it is difficult to say whether or not the principles can be applied to a complex process involving competing organizational interests or a process involving conflicting innovations.

Nevertheless, research on diffusion of innovations does provide generalizations that are useful for planning.

1. Adoption of an innovation is more likely where the innovation has a perceived and felt need. This further

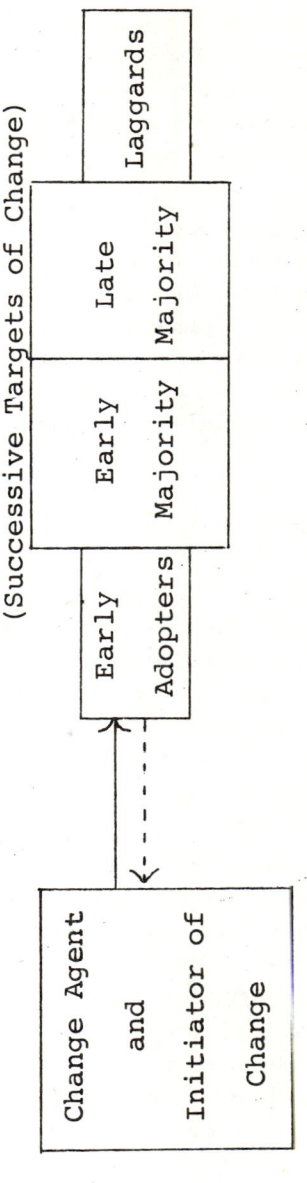

Figure 5–4 Model of change appropriate to diffusion of innovation explanation of change.

supports the generalization that pain or dissatisfaction is an initiating force for change.
2. Adoption of innovations requires a process of change involving five stages. In each stage, different sets of behavioral responses, as well as influence sources, come into play.
3. In the adoption process, actors involved can be categorized. Early adopters of innovations share common attributes; e.g., they are more cosmopolitan than late adopters. Early adopters, moreover, serve as important source of influence for the adoption of innovations. As sources of influence, consequently, early adopters serve to direct the focuses of change.

CONFLICT AS AN EXPLANATION OF SOCIAL CHANGE

That conflict may produce change is not often disputed. That it is an explanation or a theory for explaining change may be open to dispute. It is a conceptual explanation of change that is difficult to categorize. Some view it as a cause for change. Others depict it as a strategy for bringing about change. And still others define conflict as a consequence of change; that is, that rapid social change creates conflict.[50]

A further difficulty is that analysts of conflict have tended to focus on the utility of conflict to social systems. Some have taken a social Darwinist viewpoint that conflict is an inevitable part of system growth. Some insist, further, that conflict contributes to the maintenance, adjustment, or adaptation of social relationships and social structures.[51]

Others follow the reasoning of Kropotkin who viewed cooperation as the essential element of social system growth. Conflict exists, they would insist, but like Parsons they consider conflict as disruptive and producing negative consequences for social systems.[52]

These differing viewpoints tend to obscure an understanding of conflict in relation to social change. Yet it is generally agreed that conflict can produce change; and it is further agreed that conflict, whether functionally or dysfunctionally, is a means by which individuals and groups interact with one another to achieve change objectives. For our purposes, therefore, we will accept the assumption that conflict is an explanation of social change.

Conflict brings about change principally because of the function it may serve. One function of conflict, for example, is that it provides a means for preserving and maintaining the identity of groups.[53] The initiation of the conflict may act as a consciousness-raising mechanism. The conflict stimulates an awareness of group identity. Marxists, for example, insisted that humanitarian offers on the part of the governing class have to be rejected because it will vitiate class conflict and thereby lead to a weakening of class identity.[54]

A derivative function is the use of conflict to maintain an organizational entity. Conflict acts as a force for creating group cohesion, and, as was seen, for developing class identity. The disappearance of the conflict, consequently, can destroy the cohesion and identity of the members to the group organization. It is not unlikely, therefore, for organizations to "search for enemies."[55]

Alinsky, a technician of conflict, uses the expression "keeping a fight in the bank." As he explains, it is necessary to provide an emotional stimulus to help organizational members engage in a conflict situation. If victory is easily achieved, the aggression that has been created may be displaced inward and threaten the existence of the organization. The objective, therefore, is to search for enemies to maintain the membership and to keep the membership's focus outwardly directed.[56]

In each of these instances, change emerges as a resultant, to use Banfield's term. Conflict serves the purpose of organizational survival, and change is the by-product. In this sense, conflict is a *means* that can more appropriately be included under the inter-organizational behavior explanation of change.

Conflict, however, may bring about change independent of organizational survival or the development of class identity. Conflict may emerge in response to the way scarce status, power, and resources are allocated. When the customary procedures or institutions are unavailable to resolve allocative problems, conflict can be a result. The conflict arises when individuals and groups "clash in the pursuit of claims based upon frustrations of demands and expectancies of gain."[57]

Note, however, that two concepts are identified. One is "frustration." The persistent inability to redress the unequal distribution of status, power, or resources creates a force for change and, as a result, conflict is the only reasonable method to effect that change. This presupposes an awareness of the inequality. Hostility alone is not sufficient. There must be an awareness that there is a legitimate claim to redress the wrongs.[58]

Alinsky points out, for example, that a crisis alone is not enough to bring about change through conflict. The crisis, or series of crises, must first be turned into problems. The problems are the mechanism for operationalizing the issue and creating an awareness on the part of the group that change can result.[59]

The second concept is the "expectation of gain." Groups will not engage in conflict unless there is some belief that the goal they seek can be attained. It is not that the goal can be achieved, but the *belief* that it can be achieved that is crucial. Without that expectation there can be no conflict and therefore no change.

Conflict may emerge and lead to change or a means of testing the relative strengths of antagonistic interests. When two parties are contesting an issue, the strengths of one of the parties in terms of resources and power may be the prevailing variable. When the strength of either party, however, is unknown there is no way to determine which party will prevail. Accommodation, that is the willingness to resolve the issue between the two parties, is possible only if each is aware of the relative strength of each other. Without such knowledge, conflict is a means of resolving the relative strength issue.[60]

Strikes are frequently a manifestation of the relative strength principle in conflict. The strike is a weapon of last resort. It is, too, a test of economic endurance. The final outcome is determined by relative resources of the parties. Once the relative strength has been determined, it may be easier for the parties to arrive at new accommodation with each other.[61]

Of all the theories and explanations of change, conflict is the most explicit about the structure of group and organizational leadership. Groups engaged in conflict require a high degree of cohesion. Conflict, as indicated previously, serves a group-binding function. At the same time, unity is a condition for groups engaged in continued struggle. Dissension cannot be tolerated, because it destroys the unity and reveals a weakness in the group's purpose.[62]

To develop and maintain unity, strong leadership is required. The function of the leader is to exercise control, identify the parameters of loyalty, and convince the members of the worthiness of the effort. The control and discipline is legitimated by the followers who invest in the leader a charismatic influence. Alinsky uses the term, "native leader," which means much the same thing, and denotes a position given to a person by a group that is independent of other positions or statuses.[63]

There are two descriptive modes of change in relation to conflict. One is a class-struggle model that does not allow for interaction between the target system and the agent of change. In such instances the agent is attempting to compel the target to accept the change objectives. Compromise is out of the question.

A more common conflict/change model, however, depicts an interactional relation. (See Figure 5–5.) The degree of change that occurs is determined by the interaction of the two groups. It is a transactional process. There is an assumption that the target is implacable. Initially it may be. It does not necessarily remain implacable. If change is achieved, it is

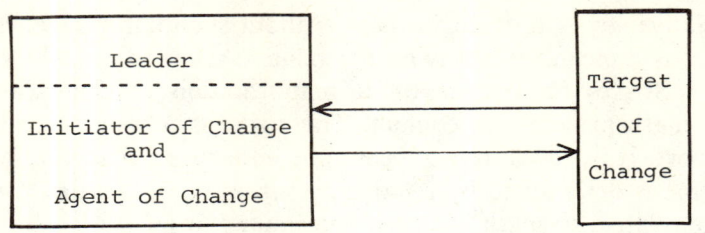

Figure 5–5 Model of change appropriate to conflict.

through an accommodation between the initiator/agent who are one and the same and the change target.

Alinsky adds, however, a further change agent role, and that is the position of the "organizer." The organizer is not part of the group. Yet his or her function is to seek out and recruit "natural leaders," develop and broaden their leadership capabilities, and assist in organizing the followers.[64] The organizer, consequently, becomes a facilitator and a catalyst of change for the development of a "client group." The client group, thus, is a change target for the organizer. Once organized, however, the client group becomes the agent of change. It is a two-staged model. (See Figure 5–6.)

A limitation of conflict as a means of change is that it requires considerable energy and commitment on the part of those engaged in the conflict. Few people are willing to engage in activities that are likely to engender personal hostility.

Individuals, too, whose livelihood depends upon the good will of others, such as merchants or professional people, will not use conflict because it will alienate them from customers.

A second limitation relates to the stabilization of change once it occurs. Conflict is a force that has capacity for initiating change. Yet it is not a means for stabilizing change. Bureaucracies, for example, appear almost impervious to change when conflict is the initiating force.[65]

Despite these limitations, conflict provides a set of principles of use to planning.

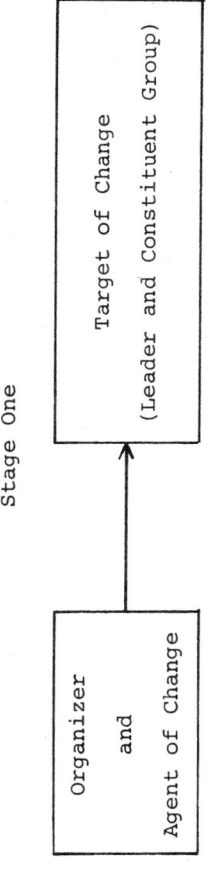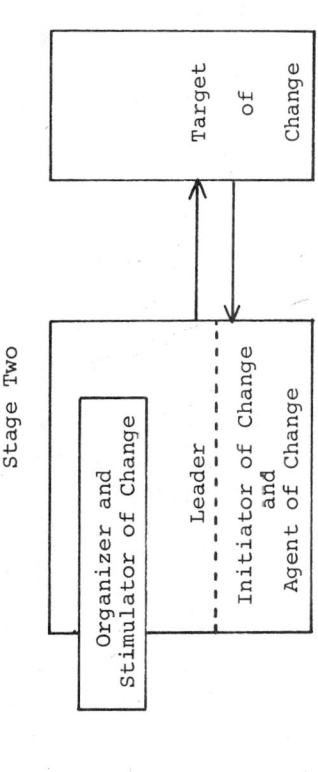

Figure 5–6 Model of change appropriate to conflict when assisted by an organizer (two stages).

1. Supporting the principle set out under organizational behavior, change can be initiated as a consequence of organizational survival. The conflict is used to preserve the organizational membership, as well as to keep their energies outwardly directed.
2. Change can be initiated as a consequence to the distribution of status or power resources.
3. Change can be initiated as a means of testing and identifying the power forces of two competing groups.
4. Leadership and organizational structure may be necessary in change efforts.

Conclusions

Based on the assumption that social change is an elementary characteristic of planning, the objective of this chapter has been to describe strategies of change applicable to planning.

We have indicated that three factors have to be considered in a process of social change; viz., the initiation of change, the medium or technology of change, and the change target.

Five explanations of social change have been described, viz.: field theory, learning theory, inter-organizational behavior, diffusion of innovation, and conflict. If viewed as *strategies,* these change theories, singularly or in combination, can be used as a base for devising the social process means for planning.

NOTES

1. For an overall summary and explanation of social change and the components of social change within the context that we will use here, see: Roland L. Warren, *Social Change and Human Purpose: Toward Understanding and Action* (Chicago: Rand McNally, 1977), pp. 1–61.

2. A helpful typology of social change strategies is outlined in Robert Chin and Kenneth D. Benne, "General Strategies for Effecting Change in Human Systems"; in Warren G. Bennis, Kenneth D. Benne, Robert Chin, and Kenneth E. Corey, *The Planning of Change* (New York: Holt, Rinehart, and Winston, 3rd. ed., 1976), pp. 22–45.

3. Although we use it somewhat differently, this terminology is borrowed from Dorwin Cartwright, "Achieving Change in People: Applications of Group Dynamics Theory," Gerald Zaltman, et al., *Creating Social Change* (New York: Holt, Rinehart and Winston, 1972), pp. 74–82.

4. Kurt Lewin, Field Theory in Social Sciences (New York: Harper and Brothers, 1951), pp. 218, 259–260.

5. Ibid., pp. 217–218.

6. Ibid., pp. 218–220.

7. Ibid., p. 225.

8. Ibid., p. 227.
9. Ibid., p. 228.
10. Ibid., pp. 229–230.
11. Ronald Lippitt, et al., *Dynamics of Planned Change,* (New York: Harcourt, Brace and World, 1958).
12. Ibid., pp. 5–10.
13. Ibid., pp. 73–74.
14. Ibid.
15. Ibid., pp. 74–76.
16. Ibid., pp. 77–86.
17. Ibid., pp. 86–88.
18. Lewin, op. cit., pp. 228–229.
19. Lippitt, op. cit., pp. 129–143.
20. Michael S. Olmstead, *The Small Group* (New York: Random House, 1959), pp. 68–72.
21. David Braybrooke and Charles E. Lindblom, *A Strategy of Decision* (New York: Free Press, 1963), pp. 102–104.
22. B. F. Skinner, *Beyond Freedom and Dignity,* (New York: Knopf, 1971).
23. Ibid., p. 26.
24. Ibid., p. 27.
25. Ibid., pp. 44–45.
26. Ibid., p. 61.
27. Ibid., p. 108.
28. B. F. Skinner, *Walden Two* (New York: Macmillan, 1948)
29. Roland Warren, *Community in America,* (Chicago: Rand McNally, 1963), pp. 316–317.
30. Chester I. Barnard, *The Functions of the Executive* (Cambridge, Mass.: Harvard University Press, 1946), pp. 50–60.
31. Ibid., p. 59.
32. Ibid., p. 139.
33. Ibid.
34. Ibid., pp. 138–153.

35. James G. March and Herbert A. Simon, "The Theory of Organization Equilibrium," in Amitai Etzioni, *Complex Organizations* (New York: Holt, Rinehart and Winston, 1962), pp. 61–71.

36. Peter B. Clark and James Q. Wilson, "Incentive Systems: A Theory of Organizations," *Administrative Science Quarterly*, Vol. 6, No. 2 (September 1961), pp. 141–146.

37. Clark and Wilson, op. cit., pp. 141–146.

38. Edward C. Banfield, *Political Influence* (New York: Free Press, 1965), p. 263.

39. Ibid., pp. 307–323.

40. This was a point made in Chapter 1.

41. There has emerged a beginning recognition of the relationship of discussion and adoption of innovations and planning. See, for example, Jack Rothman, *Planning and Organizing for Social Change* (New York: Columbia University Press, 1974).

42. Everett M. Rogers, *Diffusion of Innovations* (New York: Free Press, 1962), pp. 19–20 (His emphasis). This is the classical work on this subject. For an illustration of research application of diffusion theory, see: Everett M. Rogers, *Communication Strategies for Family Planning* (New York: Free Press, 1973).

43. Ibid., pp. 81–86.

44. Lippitt, op. cit., pp. 204–206.

45. Rogers, *Diffusion of Innovations* op. cit., p. 254.

46. Ibid., pp. 76–78.

47. Rothman, op. cit., p. 433.

48. Rogers, Diffusion . . . op. cit., pp. 168–171.

49. Ibid., pp. 148–192.

50. Alvin Toffler, for example, posits the view that accelerated change can create conflict. Alvin Toffler, *Future Shock* (New York: Random House, 1970), p. 322.

51. Talcott Parsons, *The Structure of Social Action* (New York: McGraw Hill, 1937).

52. Lewis Coser, *The Functions of Social Conflict,* (New York: Free Press, 1956), p. 151.

53. Ibid., pp. 33–37.

54. Ibid., p. 35.
55. Ibid., pp. 104–107.
56. Saul Alinsky, *Revilee for Radicals* (Chicago: University of Chicago Press, 1946), p. 171.
57. Coser, op. cit., p. 54.
58. Ibid., pp. 36–37.
59. Alinsky, op. cit., pp. 62–67.
60. Coser, op. cit., pp. 133–137.
61. Ibid., pp. 136–137.
62. Ibid., pp. 101–103.
63. Alinsky, op. cit., pp. 87–93.
64. Ibid., pp. 94–95.
65. Mobilization for Youth, a New York City poverty agency, used conflict techniques in a number of projects. An account of the system employed by Mobilization for Youth is described by sociologists Peter Marris and Martin Rein. See Peter Marris and Martin Rein, *Dilemmas of Social Reform* (New York: Atherton Press, 1967), pp. 67–70.

Part II

Chapter 6

INTRODUCTION TO PART II

The objective of the first part of this text has been to outline planning from a social process perspective. Planning, we have said:

- Intervenes into and attempts to influence decisions.
- Requires legitimacy to intervene and influence decision-making.
- Is participatory in character.
- Is influenced by the role and strategy of the participation.
- Is part of a process of social change.
- Is an attempt to capture and control the future.

The objective of this part of the text is to apply these characteristics to an overall strategy of planning. That strategy is represented by a planning diagram depicted in Figure 6–1.

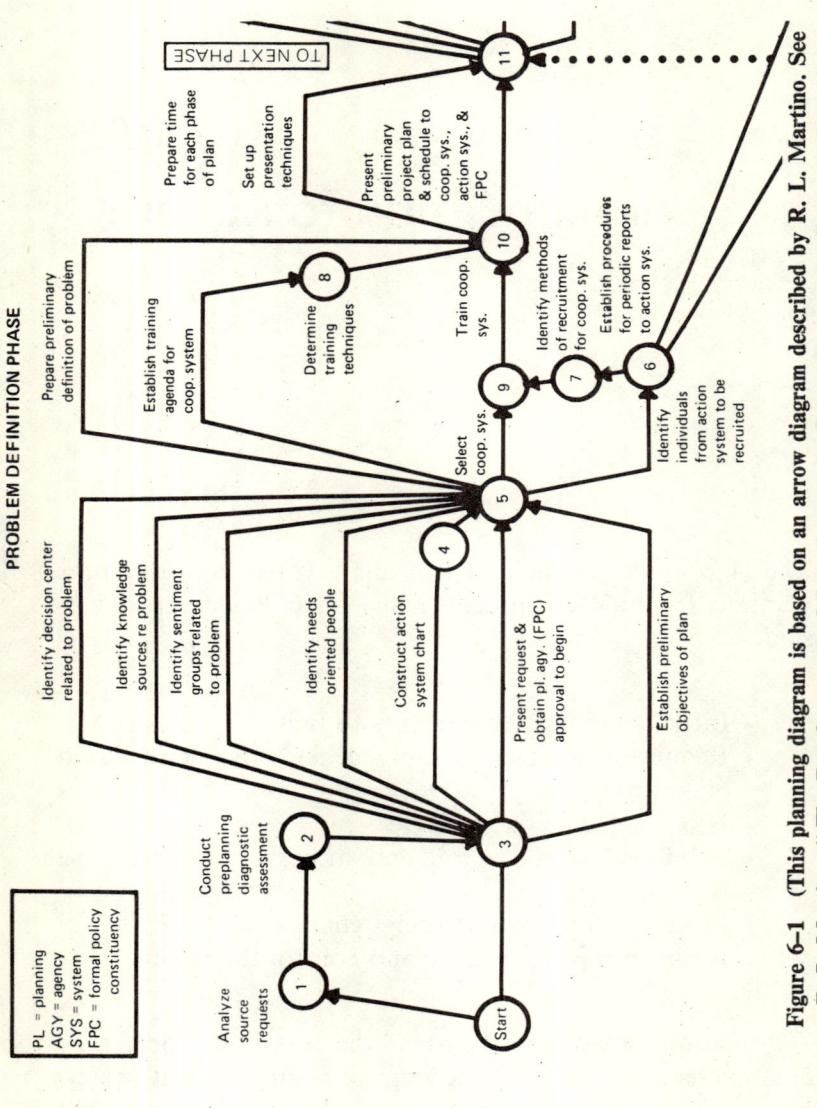

Figure 6–1 (This planning diagram is based on an arrow diagram described by R. L. Martino. See R. L. Martino, "The Development and Installation of a Total Management System," Peter B. Schoderbeck, Ed., *Management Systems*, 2nd Ed.; New York, Wiley, 1967, pp. 369–374.)

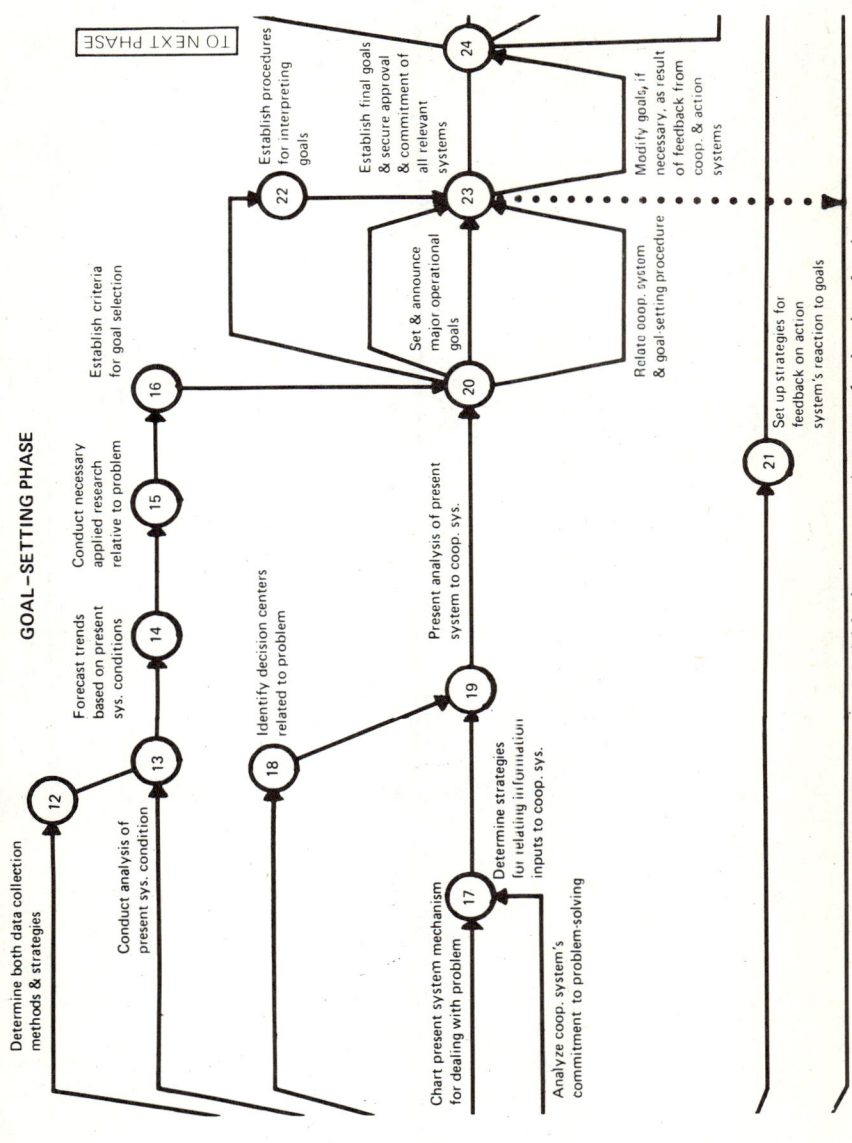

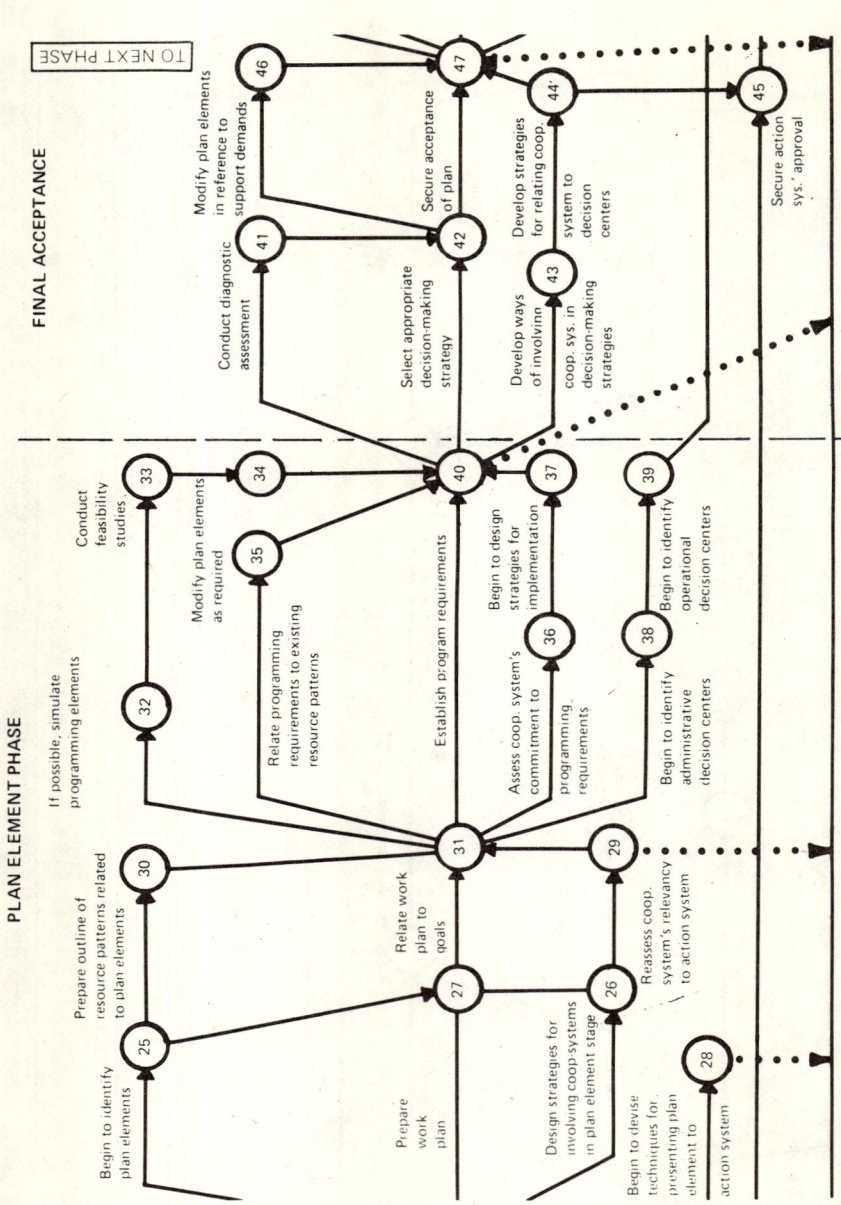

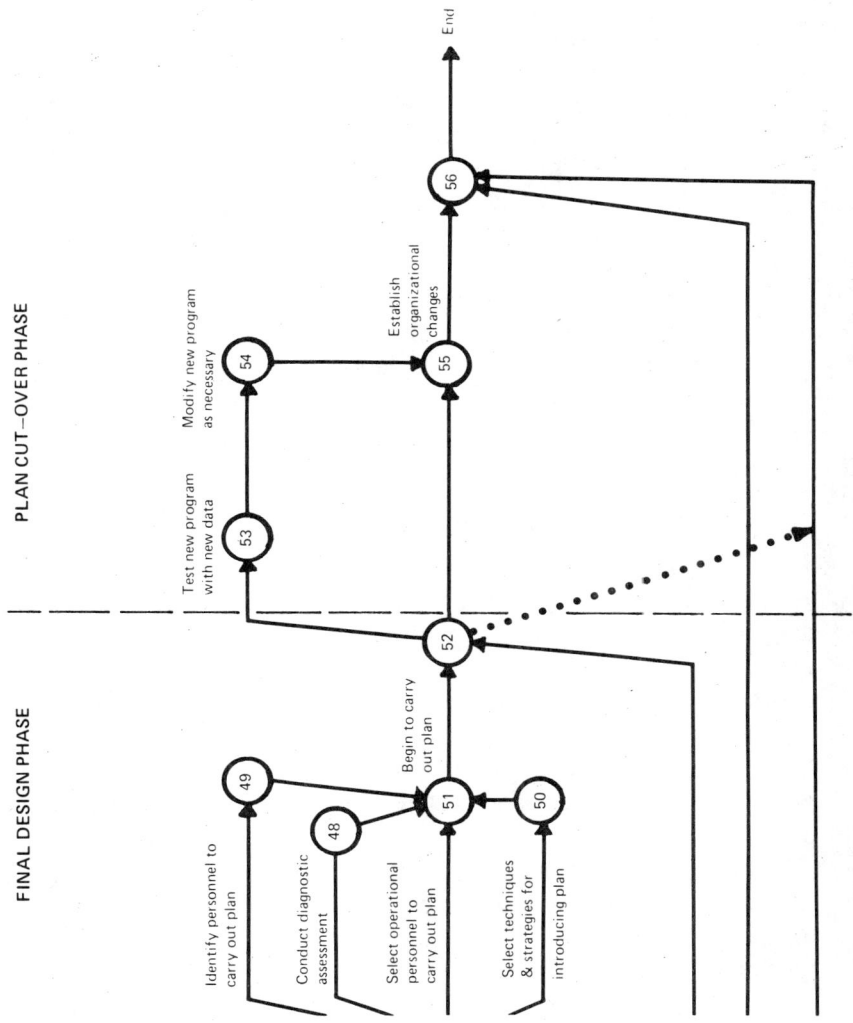

Assumptions of Planning Diagram

The planning diagram is predicated on three assumptions:

1. Planning is a sequence of events in which there are a number of specific decision points along the planning process, from the initial decision to plan to the point where the plan is implemented and carried out.
2. The successful accomplishment of planning objectives depends on the cooperative activities of a number of individuals and groups.
3. The achievement of planning objectives requires both a carefully constructed plan and an organized use of strategies of decision-making.

Characteristics of Planning Diagram

The planning diagram is an adaptation of an arrow diagram. As an adaptation, consequently, it has limitations that an arrow diagram does not have. An arrow diagram, for example, depicts the interrelationship and sequence of events of one activity to another. (On the planning diagram, incidentally, an activity is represented by an arrow; an event is represented by a number.) It assumes no event can be completed or even started until all prior events have been completed. This is not the case in the planning diagram for four reasons.

First, not all the activities listed in the planning diagram on pages 148–151 need to be carried out. The nature, complexity, and composition of a plan determine the number and type of activities for planning. What has been proposed here are suggested activities that can serve as a guide for the planner. The intent, moreover, is to be as inclusive as possible; that is, to include a large number of examples of activities and events.

Second, the sequence of events in the planning diagram is not as rigid as in a customary arrow diagram. It is not uncommon for an event in a later phase of the diagram to be completed before an event in an earlier phase. For example, a diagnostic assessment of forces for and against acceptance of the plan (Event 41) may be accomplished as early as Event 3. Before the phase of final acceptance can be completed, however, the activity for assessing forces for and against change must be done. Whether it is done by Event 41 or earlier is dependent on the characteristics of the actors involved in the planning and the decision-making strategy that has been selected or required. Much of this is explained in Chapter 10.

Some activities may also be carried out simultaneously rather than sequentially. For example, while the planner is identifying training methods for the cooperative system (Events 9 and 10), he or she can begin to prepare preliminary objectives for the plan (Event 5).

Third, activities in a traditional arrow diagram are generally routine. Procedures for carrying out the activities are standard. Most of the activities in the planning diagram, however, are not routine. An activity is noted, but not how the activity can best be carried out. For example: Between Events 2 and 3, the activity is to "present the source request to the planning agency policy group (e.g., the agency board of directors, authority board, agency executive) and obtain approval to begin." How this activity should be accomplished will depend on an assessment by the planner of the best way to achieve commitment from the policy group to initiate the planning endeavor (see Chapter 7). In some instances, this may be routine and, according to customary procedures, is accomplished by a simple report and request by the planner to the policy group.

In other instances, more deliberate strategies related to assumptions of social change may be necessary for the purpose of creating an attitude of commitment on the part of the policy group to initiate the planning activity. One technique based on diffusion of innovation (Chapter 5), is to have someone who has peer influence with the policy group to act as the innovator and bring the plan proposal before the policy group. Another technique (assuming that the source request is external) is to request that the individuals or organizations requesting the plan proposal present it to the policy group. This technique is based on field theory.

In any event, the objective by Event 3 is to create approval and commitment on the part of the policy group to begin planning. What techniques are used will vary according to the planner's assessment of how to accomplish the activity, not upon routine procedures.

Fourth, and finally, an arrow diagram is used primarily for the implementation of a process, procedure, or system. The activities and the sequence of activities from start to finish are all generally known. Planning, however, is more art than science. Not all the activities necessary from the initiation of a plan through acceptance and final implementation are known. Indeed, unanticipated events may intervene and disrupt the sequence of activities. This may require the addition of activities not provided for in the planning diagram, or it may require adjusting the sequence of activities.

The planning diagram, consequently, does *not* specify all the activities nor the correct sequencing of events for planning. As we pointed out earlier, the number and type of activities will differ with each plan. The planner must map out the expected activities that would appear to be necessary for carrying out a specific plan. Two points may be of help.

One is the diagnostic assessment activities that are conducted in various phases of the planning diagram. The first is the preplanning diagnostic assessment in the problem definition phase of planning. This assessment helps to identify the conditions and forces for planning as well as the obstacles for initiating a plan. The function of this assessment is to suggest what activities may be necessary to overcome obstacles, or indeed, even to indicate whether or not a plan should be initiated.

The second assessment is conducted during the final acceptance phase. This diagnostic assessment leads to identifying the activities necessary for relating a plan to a decision center. The final assessment is conducted during the implementation phase where the need is to identify the activities required for carrying out the objectives of a plan.

Another point is that the phases of planning can be defined as decision events. The concluding activity in each phase is a *critical* decision point. It can be interpreted as a "go ahead" signal for the planner. At the conclusion of each phase, the planner must decide the feasibility and advisability of continuing on to the subsequent planning phase.

Phases in the Planning Diagram

There are six discrete and identifiable phases in the planning process. These phases are:

1. The identification of a problem. This is a critical phase in the planning process. On the one hand, the nature of the problem has to be diagnosed. How is it defined and by whom? Is it capable of being resolved and, if so, capable of being implemented?

On the other hand, the capability of the organization and planning team has to be considered. Does it have the resources and the desire to resolve the planning problem? What kind of momentum can be generated to achieve the implementation of a planning solution?

The planner, therefore, has two main objectives during the first phase. One is a clear understanding of the problem and the second is the development of an organized effort to resolve the problem. It is during this phase that the planner organizes the planning team.

2. Establishing planning goals. Goals are statements of wants. They emerge from an understanding of a problem and they identify particular end states. The objective during the goal-setting phase is to establish desirable and feasible end states. The judgments of desirability and feasibility are made by the planner, the planning organization, and the planning team as they move through this phase of planning. These judgments are also conditioned by assessing the forces for accepting planning goals on the part of the public and specific decision centers.

3. Determining the elements of a plan. Plan elements are basically operational definitions of a plan. They describe the means necessary for achieving goals and thus emerge as the concrete description of a plan.

This is the point at which opposition is likely to occur, because it is during this phase that the consequences of a plan become clear. An objective during this phase, then, is to initiate the process of gaining acceptance of a plan.

4. Achieving acceptance of a plan. This is the decision phase of planning. Decision-making, however, is not an isolated event occurring in some automatic sequence of events. It is a complex activity related less to any one phase in planning than to a process of social change. It is the function of the planner to make an assessment of the social change properties of the plan and to relate these to a strategy or strategies of decision-making.

5. Implementing a plan. What determines the success of a plan is whether it is carried out as designed—not whether it has been accepted or not by a decision center. The implementation of a plan, therefore, cannot be left to chance. It requires the planning of methods and procedures to ensure that the plan is carried out.

6. Evaluating a plan. Before a plan is institutionalized, steps are necessary to evaluate the effectiveness and efficiency of a plan over a previously specified period of time. This is an extension of the final design or implementation phase of planning. The objective is to plan for introducing necessary modifications before the plan solution is finally put into practice.

ORGANIZATION OF PART II

The planning diagram is used as a guide for organizing the chapters in the second part of this text. The phases and chapters related to the phases are as follows:

Problem identification phase: Chapters 7 and 8
Goal setting the plan element phases: Chapter 9
Final acceptance phase: Chapters 10 and 11
Final design and plan cut-over phases: Chapter 12

Chapter 7

DEVELOPING LEGITIMACY FOR PLANNING

As the planner begins to identify and define the focus of a planning problem, he or she is confronted with two difficulties. One is motivation; that is, the willingness of individuals and groups to engage in planning and become committed to achieving a plan's objectives. The second is legitimacy; the sanction both to plan and to influence decisions. Both legitimacy and the willingness of individuals to commit themselves to planning are necessary functions for planning. It is the responsibility of the planner to develop these functions.

The way in which the planner develops motivation for planning is explained in Chapter 8. The objective in this chapter is to explain the means by which a planning activity is legitimated.

In Chapter 2, the principle of legitimacy was defined as a sanction that allows the planner and planning agency to intervene into and influence decision-making. Three forms of legitimacy were identified: positional, organizational, and role. Positional and organizational will be explained in this chapter.

The techniques of role legitimacy will be outlined in a later chapter.

Improving Positional Legitimacy

Positional legitimacy applies only to governmentally sponsored planning agencies or planning projects. It is derived from a legislative mandate that defines the scope, function, and purpose of the agency or project.

The legislative mandate, moreover, defines the relationship between the planning agency and a legislative or administrative decision center. Urban renewal agencies, for example, seek approval for projects from city councils or their counterparts and the Department of Housing and Urban Development. Planning units of public welfare departments relate primarily to administrators—division chiefs and commissioners, who in turn receive their mandate from governors.

The effectiveness of a planning agency's positional legitimacy will depend on the nature of the relationship between the agency and the legislative or administrative decision center. The more positive the relationship, the more likely the legislative or administrative unit will continue to legitimate the planning agency's activities—that is, allow its behavior to be influenced by the planning agency. The objective, therefore, is not to develop positional legitimacy, but to *improve* it.

There are three techniques for improving positional legitimacy. The first, strictly speaking, is not a technique. It is to practice competency and is the most effective means of improving positional legitimacy. A planning agency that exhibits technical competence, measured by its successful performance in implementing planning objectives, develops credibility and trust with its legislative or administrative entity.

A second technique is to strengthen relationships with the legislative and administrative units that sanction the planning agency's activities. This is done in a number of ways—reports, meetings, informal contacts, participation in other activities, personal relationships, and the like. The intention is to keep communication open and groups appraised of agency operations.

The same type of open relationships should exist between the planning agency and other governmental agencies in the community. This is not meant to imply that agreement and consensus between the planning agency and other governmental groups and agencies within the same community is not uncommon. Nonetheless, decision-making strategies that rely on surprise and the withholding of information are inappropriate for *public planning* agencies. (See Chapters 10 and 11). This destroys trust and, therefore, weakens the agency's positional legitimacy.

The third technique is to involve members who have leadership roles in the agency for purposes of relating to legislative or administrative units. This is generally limited to citizen members of the agency presenting reports at public meetings or hearings before legislative committees. Where possible, this is an extremely effective means for strengthening positional legitimacy. It broadens the credibility of the agency beyond that of merely the staff.

A secondary effect of the technique, by the way, is that it also strengthens the agency's relationship with citizens. The involvement in a strategic agency function increases citizen identification with the agency and its programs.

DEVELOPING ORGANIZATIONAL LEGITIMACY

Positional legitimacy exists and the objective is to increase its effectiveness. Organizational legitimacy, which is a necessary function of all planning agencies, on the other hand, has to be created. To develop organizational legitimacy, the planning agency has to establish and work with constituencies that will provide the sanction to intervene into and influence community decision-making.

It must be remembered that except in extreme crisis situations, few organizations are willing to give up their decision-making to another individual or organization. Before an organization allows its decision-making to be influenced by another, it must be convinced, persuaded, or compelled to do so. The capacity of the planning agency to convince, persuade, or compel other organizations to accept planning decisions depends on its ability to obtain trust or power. Trust and power come from individuals, and in the case of the planning agency, it comes from individuals who are associated with the planning agency. These individuals form the basis for developing constituencies to work on behalf of and in support of the activities of the planning agency. It is the organization of constituencies that is the means for developing organizational legitimacy.

There are three possible types of constituencies that can serve to legitimate a planning agency's activities: *organizational constituency, formal policy constituency,* and the *planning constituency.*

Organizational Constituency

The organizational constituency is composed of individuals and organizations who are or have been associated with the agency, and as well, individuals and organizations who share an interest in the aims or mission of the planning agency. This constituency may include, for example, current and previous board and committee members, political officials, coalitions of other like organizations, and any interested citizens.

The organizational constituency serves two purposes for the planning agency:

1. It acts as a functional interest group on behalf of the goals of the agency. Its function is to promote the aims of the agency among other organizations and interest groups.
2. It serves as a pool of citizen resources for the recruitment of individuals to assist the agency in its planning functions.

The planning agency should endeavor to expand this constituency. It is a broad-based mechanism of support. Generally, however, it is not formally organized. It is a loose association of individuals and groups. The planning agency relates to it through annual meetings, newsletters, or periodic community-wide meetings.

Formal Policy Constituency

A second type of constituency, the formal policy constituency (FPC), is an organized part of the agency's formal structure. Some writers define it as the client group that engages the planner's services.[1] We see it as also the policy making constituency of the agency. It can be a board of directors, authority board, commission, or a board of trustees. Where the planning agency or function is responsible to an individual, such as the director of a direct service agency or a mayor, city manager, or county executive office, that individual or office serves as the FPC.

The purpose of the FPC is threefold:[2]

1. It serves as the authorized and primary sanctioning agent of the planning agency or function.
2. It acts as the initial legitimating agent for any and all planning activities. Its approval is necessary before any planning activity can commence.
3. It assumes responsibility for any planning decision made by committees, groups, or personnel of the planning agency.

It is important to underscore the role of the FPC as the initial legitimating agent for planning. By giving approval to begin planning, the FPC implicitly agrees to commit its resources and its influence to the entire planning activity—from initiation to acceptance and implementation. The FPC, in other words, agrees to stand behind and support the planning activity.

This is not meant to imply that the FPC cannot withdraw its support once the planning activity has begun. But if it does so, it is done consciously and deliberately. The important point is that the FPC both recognizes and accepts responsibility for initiating and sustaining planning activities.

At the very outset, therefore, the FPC should have as full an understanding as possible of the planning problem and the consequences of engaging in the planning process. This is effectively accomplished with a formal report. It is identified as Event 2 on the planning diagram. The way in which the report is prepared is described in Chapter 9.

In large planning agencies it is true that tacit approval of the FPC may be assumed. The approval process is a function of the planning director. It is wiser, however, to seek approval from the FPC in all instances. The reason, again, is that the FPC, not the professional staff, has the mandate for intervening into the process of community decision-making.

Planning Constituency

While the FPC can provide initial legitimation and some organizational support for an ongoing plan, it cannot provide all the legitimation necessary for the acceptance and implementation of a plan once the process has begun. Planning issues, as indicated in Chapter 1, move through a number of decision phases. Planning itself, moreover, requires the application of specific skills in the development of a plan. A number of individuals, therefore, are required for a particular plan to be developed, accepted, and implemented. Each plan, in other words, requires its own base of legitimation, and as a consequence, its own constituency. This constituency is called the planning constituency.

The planning constituency has three purposes:

1. To be involved in or assist in the development of a plan;

2. To advocate for the acceptance of a plan once it is produced.
3. To achieve implementation of a plan once it has been accepted.

Theoretically, the planning constituency can be made up of any number of individuals. It could be composed only of the professional staff, or it could include, also, members of the FPC and the professional staff. The assumption of this text, however, is that wherever possible the planning constituency should be much broader. It should be composed of citizens and groups recruited by the planning agency to be specifically involved in the development of a plan. There are, as we pointed out earlier,[3] two reasons for this:

1. It increases the likelihood that the plan outcome will reflect the needs and aims of the community.
2. It increases the likelihood that the plan will be accepted and implemented.

What will be described here, therefore, is the development of a planning constituency composed of citizens recruited for the purpose of developing and supporting a plan. This is, of course, compatible with the general thesis of the text; that is, that planning is a participatory activity.

Before individuals can be recruited for a planning constituency, it is necessary to know which individuals *could* be involved, and whether or not they *can* or *should* be involved. The first question—which individuals *could* be involved—is answered by preparing what is called an action system chart.

Action System

An action system[4] is defined as a social system comprising those actors who have the capacity to agree to or withhold action necessary for the acceptance and implementation of a planning decision.[5] Capacity is meant to include the complete range of influence: viz., manifest, potential, or reputed influence.[6] An action system, therefore is an influence system, and it is composed of individuals and organizations sharing one or more characteristics of influence. The characteristics are represented by four distinct categories of influence. They are power, sentiment, knowledge, and needs.

Power

A description of power was outlined in Chapter 1. The point here is to acknowledge that individuals who possess power through the control of or access to resources can play a significant role in shaping community decisions. Acknowledged further is the point that within any community or institution there are a number of power structures each related to different issue areas. This does not preclude that an individual may be a member of more than one power structure.

Within any structure of power, there are various hierarchies of influence. Some may have control over a decision center; others may be able to utilize persuasion with someone in authority; others may be able to withhold resources (votes, for example) to gain control but are able to act as intermediaries between decision centers and those wishing to exercise control. Each of these sources of power has to be identified.

A useful analytical device for identifying actors with power is Banfield's model of concerting influence, which was explained in Chapter 1. It bears a summary repeating here. Actions necessary for the adoption of a proposal are termed *requisite actions.* An actor who can perform a requisite action is said to have *authority* over that action. An actor who has power over an individual having authority over requisite actions is defined as an actor having *control.*[7] Figure 7–1 depicts the relationships.

Using the Banfield typology as a framework, the planner

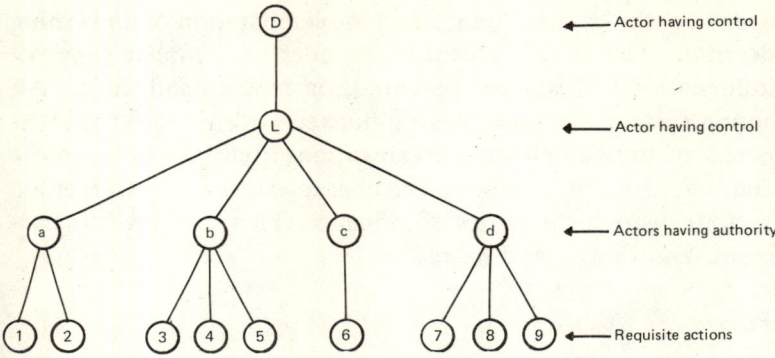

Figure 7-1 Relationship of requisite actions to actors having authority and control. (From Edward C. Banfield, *Political Influence;* New York, Free Press, 1961, p. 311.)

first identifies the potential requisite actions necessary for the adoption of a particular plan proposal or elements of a plan. He or she next identifies the actors having authority over those requisite actions. The final step is identifying the actors having control over actors with authority. This forms the basis for identifying actors in the power category of an action system.

Sentiment

Although the "power" people are necessary in influencing decisions, a second category of individuals associated with what is termed community or institutional sentiment groups is also important.

Identified by Charles Willie, after analyzing health planning activities in Syracuse, sentiment groups are those groups or organizations that have widespread membership and support.[8] Examples are civic associations, labor organizations, ethnic groups, and religious organizations.

Sentiment groups are characterized within the decision-making framework as generally powerless by themselves to initiate and achieve community action. Opposition from a sentiment group, on the other hand, is usually sufficient to hinder acceptance of a planning decision. The opposition, however, must be voiced. Unlike a power person who can successfully oppose acceptance of an issue by merely withholding support, sentiment groups must state their opposition in order to veto an issue.

Sentiment groups serve two functions. The first is that they are able to generate broad support for an issue. The second is that they are able to reflect community information and feelings on issues and proposals. Thus, they serve as a means of communication in framing planning decisions.

Expertise

Surprisingly, facts often have little and sometimes marginal influence in decision-making. Yet facts are necessary and they are a necessary influence on achieving acceptance of a decision. This may appear to be contradictory, but it is not. The issue is not the influence facts play in *making* a decision, but the influence facts play in achieving *acceptance* of a decision.

Decision-makers react primarily to influence. They have to in order to maintain their position. Nonetheless, a decision-maker needs a factual rationale to support or make a decision. The facts may be inconsistent, or even unsupportable, but they are required. The facts are supplied by experts.[9]

Experts include government officials; technicians, and professionals in functional fields (such as doctors, lawyers, judges, and university professors). Consumers of a service or those directly affected by a planning proposal are also defined as experts. Welfare clients, tenants of housing projects, or health consumers, for example, would be classified under the expertise category.

The experts, however, are not a random category. They are identified as experts in relation to the particular planning problem. If, for example, the planning issue was housing, the experts would be chosen from the housing issue area.

Needs-Oriented

A final category, which has less force in assuring acceptance of a decision than in providing an integrative function for a planning constituency is composed of individuals and organizations who may personally benefit from the resolution of a particular planning proposal. Homeowners in an upgrading renewal area (in an urban renewal project) or parents of children with learning problems in an educational planning project are examples.

Because of their self-interest in resolving the issue, needs-oriented individuals or groups have a stake in the planning outcome. This stake in the outcome creates a steadfast commitment to a planning proposal. If such individuals or organizations can be identified, they can act as a force to maintain interest and commitment to resolving an issue.

CONSENSUS/DISSENSUS ACTION SYSTEMS

The action system chart is one step in the development of the planning constituency. The action system itself is too large obviously to be involved directly in planning with the agency. A second step, then, is the recruitment of individuals from the action system to serve as members of a planning constituency.

Before a constituency can be recruited, however, two questions raised previously need to be answered: *Can* all categories of the action system be represented? *Should* all categories be represented?

Whether or not all categories *can* be represented relates to the planning agency's ability to recruit from all categories. Power people, for example, may be identified who could be effective in assisting the planning agency in achieving its planning goals, but the agency itself may not have sufficient inducements to attract such people to the agency. That category, consequently, may not be able to be involved.

The answer to the question of *should* all categories be represented relates to the planning agency's own objectives.

The inclusion of some individuals in the planning group may compromise the agency's overall goals. An advocacy planning group of low income residents, for example, may wish deliberately to exclude certain power figures or sentiment groups because they would not necessarily identify with the agency's objectives, and thus, would thwart the agency in achieving some of its goals. The organization, therefore, would deliberately exclude certain categories from the makeup of its planning constituency.

If it is possible to involve representatives from each of the four categories of influence, then an assumption can be made that the planning activity is operating within a *consensus* decision environment. There is, in other words, likelihood that an agreement on a planning decision can be achieved.

On the other hand, if it is neither possible nor desirable to include the four categories of influence on a planning constituency, then it should be assumed that the decision environment will be unresponsive or antagonistic to the planning issue and, thus, unlikely to accept the planning decision. This is a *dissensus* decision environment.[10]

The action system, nonetheless, is still a reference group for planning. It provides the framework for identifying those individuals and decision centers—such as politicians, administrators, influential persons, "gatekeepers," representatives of interest groups, technical staffs from competitive institutions, and many more—who may have an effect on achieving planning objectives. As Friedmann has noted: "This cast of characters produces an 'action'."[11] And the manner in which this cast of characters is represented will affect the agency's strategies for planning and decision-making. (See Chapters 10 and 11.)

Cooperative System

The planning constituency is a subdivision of the action system. This subdivision is termed a "cooperative system." Others have used the term "cooperating group."[12]

A cooperative system is basically nothing more than a planning committee, a planning task force, or a planning team. The term "cooperative system" is used because it typifies the basic behavior required of a planning group. This is more fully explained in the next chapter where the behavioral characteristics are described. At this point, the intention is to describe the function of the cooperative system as a legitimating agent for planning. The reader's indulgence is begged for resorting to what appears at this juncture to be jargon.

The cooperative system is the basic unit for legitimating the acceptance of a planning proposal. Its effectiveness as an agent of legitimacy depends, however, on its own capacity for creating sanctions for its decisions. It cannot presume acceptance of any decision it makes regardless of how "representative" a cooperative system may be, either of the total community or of the action system. It must secure acceptance and implementation of a plan through its own actions. There are three methods the cooperative system uses to develop sanctions for the acceptance of a planning proposal.

The first is the relationship of the cooperative system to the action system. The cooperative system is a derivative unit of the action system. Cooperative system members are recruited on the basis that:

- They can act as representatives of their action system reference group.
- They can influence or persuade their action system reference group to accept planning decisions.

The relationship of the cooperative system to the action system, consequently, has to be maintained throughout the planning activity.

Periodically, progress reports should be given to action system groups. At specific stages, moreover, the cooperative system needs to seek agreement to continue either through collaboration or negotiation from the major action system reference groups. The planning diagram identifies events at which this activity should take place.

This procedure assumes a collaborative relationship between the cooperative system and the action system. Where this is not possible or desirable because not all categories of the action system are represented on the cooperative system, or if the cooperative system's relationship to the action system is not fully tenable, different strategies of relating to the action system are required. Examples of such strategies can be found in Chapters 11 and 12.

The second method for sanctioning planning is the role of the cooperative system as an advocacy group. A group, of course, is a more effective agent for the adoption of a proposal than a single individual. It is, for one thing, more efficient. An organized group has the capacity to deploy manpower resources to spread both the need for change and the acceptance of a proposal. In this respect, the cooperative system acts as a *change agent.*

As a representative entity, the cooperative system also can symbolize a broad base of support for a proposal. Decision centers are more willing to act positively if the request for change emerges from a group rather than from an individual. The broader the representativeness of the group, the more likely the proposal will be accepted.

Its effectiveness as a change agent, however, will depend on its own commitment and unity of action. To arrive at this commitment, consensus and agreement on decisions are necessary before the cooperative system acts to advocate for a decision. This does not preclude debate, but it does require unity once the debate is over. If only half the members of a cooperative system are in agreement on a decision, only half will be willing to work for its acceptance. Furthermore, when a group is divided, it has little chance for negotiating or winning acceptance from other groups. Techniques for consensus type decision-making are outlined in Chapter 10.

A third means by which a cooperative system creates sanctions for its activities is by developing a plan that is reasonable, coherent, and a conscious and deliberate attempt to use rational means for solving a problem.

A plan that is reasonable is one that reflects the needs of the community, the acknowledged goals for community development, and the sentiments of the community. The more widespread a plan responds to the needs of a community, the more the plan will act as its own sanctioning force. This does not exclude the possibility of a plan generating controversy. This is frequently possible. A controversial plan, however, may reflect a response to a genuine community need. A plan that is a controversial answer to a need, however, will require more effort in organizing support for its adoption.

A plan that is coherent is one that is understood. It is, therefore, a plan that can be communicated to a variety of individuals and groups in a community. A plan that is technical and replete with jargon loses its acceptability and consequently diminishes in force as a sanction for acceptance.

A conscious attempt to apply intelligence to the solution of a problem should be the base of any plan. As Alan Altshuler notes, "Planning is, in the final analysis, simply the effort to infuse activity with consistency and conscious purpose."[13] A cooperative system seeks, therefore, two goals: (1) an intelligent and systematic response to a need; and (2) an organized effort to secure adoption of the response. These goals are not mutually exclusive. They are interactional. Each has to be balanced for a cooperative system to accomplish the mandate of the planning agency that appointed it.

PLANNING DIAGRAM ACTIVITIES RELATED TO CHAPTER

Both this and the next chapter are related to the problem definition phase of the planning process. The underlying premise is that planning begins with a recognition of a problem and a desire or opportunity to resolve the problem.[14]

In relation to the legitimacy issues in planning the following events need emphasizing:

> *Event 3:* presenting request and obtaining approval of FPC to initiate planning. First legitimating step.
>
> *Events 4 and 5:* identifying action system members and constructing action chart. Chart is simple listing of influence categories and individuals associated with each category.
>
> *Events 6 and 7:* identify individuals from action system who will be recruited for the cooperative system. Determine how and who will recruit cooperative system members.
>
> *Event 12:* the actions system is brought into the planning process at this point by means of a report. The report can be a simple news release of who is involved or a description of the planning problem.

Note that there is an activity running from event 6 to 54 related to publicity activities for the duration of the planning project. The planning staff should prepare a schedule of news releases and meetings or media events that will take place to support the planning activity.

During this phase, of course, the planner is also initiating activities related to the cognitive function of planning. The emphasis of this book, however, is upon the social processes of planning. The cognitive activities which are indicated on the diagram are suggestive and not exclusive. At this phase, for example, the planner is establishing preliminary objectives of the plan (5) and preparing a preliminary definition of the problem (10). The planner may also be reviewing similar reports related to the problem, examining the literature, or developing the beginning design of a quantitative model.

Summary

To improve positional legitimacy, a planning organization works through and with the legislative and administrative units which have authority over the organization's functions. The objective is to maintain and strengthen positive relationships with these entities.

To secure organizational legitimacy, the planning organization develops constituencies to assist it in its activities and support its efforts. There are three types of constituencies, each serving a specialized purpose. They are the organizational constituency, the formal policy constituency, and the planning constituency.

The organizational constituency provides a broad base of support for the organization's general activities.

The formal policy constituency provides both a base of support and a mandate for the initiation of a particular planning proposal.

The planning constituency is responsible for developing a plan and securing its acceptance. It is composed of an action system and a cooperative system related to a specific planning problem. The cooperative system is derived from the action system and is the basic participatory unit for planning.

NOTES

1. Richard S. Bolan, "The Social Relations of the Planner," *Journal of the American Institute of Planners,* Vol. XXXVII, No. 6 (November 1971), p. 388.

2. These should not be confused with the purposes of a board or mission. The functions of an organization board are much broader and relate to the total operation of the organization. An excellent description of the functions of a board are contained in Peter F. Drucker, *Management* (New York: Harper and Row, 1973), pp. 631–634.

3. The principles underlying these assumptions are contained in Chapters 3 and 4. For a theoretical perspective on this assumption see Andreas Faludi, *Planning Theory* (New York: Pergamon Press, 1973), pp. 248–252, pp. 288–290.

4. Roland Warren uses the term "action system" to denote actors who initiate a community action or planning episode. The term as used here has been changed and broadened. For a comparison, see Roland Warren, *The Community in America* (Chicago: Rand McNally, 1963), p. 317. See also Bolan, op. cit., p. 393.

5. This is a variation of Banfield's definition of power. See Chapter 1.

6. See Chapter 1 for a description of these terms.

7. Edward C. Banfield, *Political Influence,* (New York: Free Press, 1961), pp. 309–312.
8. Charles V. Willie, "A Success Story of Community Action," *Nursing Outlook,* Vol. 9, No. 1 (January 1961), pp. 19–20.
9. See the Syracuse decision-making study for an explanation of the role of experts in sustaining and implementing an issue; Roscoe C. Martin, Frank J. Munger, et al., *Decisions in Syracuse,* (Garden City, N.Y.: Doubleday, 1965), pp. 325–326.
10. See Chapter 10 where this is more fully discussed. The terms are from Roland L. Warren, *Social Change & Human Purpose: Toward Understanding and Action* (Chicago: Rand McNally, 1977), pp. 126–129.
11. John Friedmann, "Notes on Societal Action," *Journal of the American Institute of Planners,* Vol. XXXV, No. 5, (September 1969), pp. 316–317.
12. Bolan, op. cit., pp. 393–394.
13. Alan A. Altshuler, *The City Planning Process,* (Ithaca, N.Y.: Cornell University Press, 1965), p. 409.
14. This is similar to Faludi's conception of defining a problem. Faludi, op. cit., pp. 84–88.

Chapter 8

DEVELOPING THE MOTIVATION TO PLAN

For a planning agency to be effective, it requires not just legitimacy but also the willingness of individuals and groups to commit themselves to a course of action. In this case action is the complete process of planning—from identification of the problem; through its resolution, decision, and the seeking of acceptance; to the final implementation of the planning decision. Without a willingness, or motivation to plan, planning becomes a ritualistic exercise. There is no commitment to the planning objective, and, thus, no interest in influencing the acceptance of a plan. Developing the willingness to plan is an essential feature of effective planning.

In a participatory planning activity the issue of motivation is complex. Not only does the planner have to be able to develop the motivation to plan among the staff but also among citizens and groups associated with the agency and the planning activity.

Developing the willingness to plan calls for two skills on the part of the planner: one is a diagnostic skill and the other is an administrative skill. The diagnostic skill refers to the planner's ability to assess the planning motivation of individuals and groups who become involved in the planning process. The administrative skill refers to the planner's ability to develop incentives, environmentally and structurally, that bring people together to become committed to a course of action. It is, further, the ability to develop in people the willingness to work together for collective action.

The objective of this chapter is to explain how motivation is analyzed and developed.

Systems Involved in Planning

In community planning there are six distinct systems that become involved in the resolution of a planning problem:

1. Initiating set
2. Formal policy constituency
3. Action system
4. Cooperative system
5. Decision center system
6. Implementation system

Each of these systems has a distinct and influential role in the planning process, and the planner is engaged in varying degrees with each one. The principal functions of the planner are to identify the members of the system; develop procedures for relating the system to the planning activity; to assess the motivation of the system for planning; and to develop the motivation of the system to plan and achieve acceptance of the plan.

In this chapter, four of the six systems—initiating set, the formal policy constituency, the action system, and the cooperative system—will be explained. (The decision center and implementation systems will be discussed in succeeding chapters.) The focus of the chapter will be on the particular relationship of the system to a planning activity, and the means used for assessing *and* developing motivation for planning.

INITIATING SET

An initiating set is the initial sponsor of a plan or community action project. The concept was developed by Christopher Sower from his analysis of community development and community health planning activities.[1] In Sower's terms, an initiating set is an individual, a small group, or an organization which has a socially defined right, or what we have labelled, "legitimacy," to propose an action to bring about community change.[2]

For the planner the concept of initiating set provides a diagnostic base point for a planning activity. At the outset of planning, two questions need to be asked: Who is proposing the plan? and, What are the reasons or forces generating the planning activity? In other words, Why is the plan being proposed?

Plan Proposers

There are two sources of a plan. One is from a planning agency. This is the most common source of planning in a community. This planning source is defined as arising from an *internal initiating set*.

A second source of planning is from an individual or group outside a planning agency, such as a community organization. A neighborhood group, for example, may request the urban renewal agency to assist it in preparing a neighborhood rehabilitation plan. The planning agency's help is sought for its knowledge and technical assistance. In such cases the planning agency enters into a collaborative relationship with the group seeking assistance, and the source of planning is defined as an *external initiating set*.

In both instances the planner should analyze the legitimacy of the source request. If the plan is internally proposed, does it emerge as part of the agency's mandate? Is it routine function? If it is routine, the planning organization should have normal procedures for initiating the plan, and an analysis of the source request is not necessary.

If the plan, however, is initiated as a *proactive* response to a community problem, additional analytical techniques should be invoked. Who in the organization is initiating the plan? What is the authority of the source? What role has or will the formal policy constituency play in the authorization of the plan? These questions help to provide a consistent management focus for the initiation of a plan.

When a plan, however, emerges from an external initiating set there is a further task, and that is analyzing the nature of the set itself. The planner should determine who the initiating set represents. What interests or groups does it purport to represent? Does it have credibility with the group it represents? Does it have decision-making power or influence in the issue area of the planning problem? And, most important, what commitment does the initiating set have in participating with the planning agency in resolving the planning problem?

Following the analysis of the initiating set, the planner next conducts a *preplanning diagnostic assessment.*

Preplanning Diagnostic Assessment

A diagnosis is a hypothesis. It is a judgment about a problem situation on which tentative plans of action may be devised for solving that problem, and a description of the forces or conditions for and against achieving a solution to the problem.

The objective of the preplanning diagnostic assessment, therefore, is to identify the forces that contribute to the initiation of a plan. There are four forces that can bring about the initiation of a plan.

The first is an organizational *mandate.* The planning organization is required to initiate a plan because of legislation or administrative regulations. A good example is the social service planning requirement of the Social Security legislation (Title XX).

Annually the state-designated social services agency must prepare a comprehensive social services plan. The elements of the plan, the role of participants, and the dates for submission of the plan are all prescribed by regulations. The initiation of the plan, therefore, is a legislative mandate.

A second force that can initiate a plan is a *felt need*. A felt need is a state of discontentedness or dissatisfaction in an individual or group strong enough to impel a desire for change. The dissatisfaction can arise or be stimulated in a number of ways. One is a recognized dissatisfaction with a particular state of being or situation. Inadequate health services, deteriorating neighborhoods, and environmental pollution are a few examples.

Dissatisfaction can arise also out of a comparison between what is and what can be. The discontent, in other words, emerges not from an inherent dissatisfaction but from an awareness that a potential improvement in an existing state is possible. The results of a planning activity in Community X, for example, may serve as a stimulus to engage in a similar planning activity for Community Y.

Felt needs are probably the most compelling forces for initiating planning activities. This tends to explain the critical observation that planning appears only to arise once a crisis has emerged. This is not always the case, yet a crisis or a recognized state of dissatisfaction is a persuasive prerequisite to initiating planning. Its strength, however, is based on how wide the dissatisfaction is spread. The more the discontent is shared by the potential target system, the more likely the force for planning is viable.

In this respect it is useful to test the extent of dissatisfaction before initiating planning. If the basis for planning is a felt need, yet it is not widely shared, it may be prudent to delay planning and to stimulate an awareness of the need prior to engaging in planning. Successful examples of environmental planning are usually preceded and accompanied by a campaign that creates an awareness of need.[3]

A third force for initiating planning is the likelihood of a *reward or benefit* which can be received either for initiating the planning or for the potential results. A planning activity may increase the competitive condition of an organization or community. Examples are broadening the base of organizational support, increasing the tax base of a community, and attracting newer sources of resources. Federal grant-in-aid programs are examples of the "carrot" that can stimulate planning activities.

The planner, however, should be cautious when analyzing the potential rewards for initiating planning. A reward system is based on an individual cost/benefit analysis. For some the cost, although not tangible, may outweigh the benefits. Urban renewal agencies, for example, are often unable to estimate the values that residents place on a neighborhood environment. Organizations, to offer another example, frequently cannot predict the satisfactions being derived by employees for current norms of practice. Planning is viewed as a threat to these values, a greater threat than the potential benefits, which in turn creates resistance to planning.

The obverse of rewards—penalties—can also stimulate planning activities. The setting of minimum codes or ordinances is an example of a threat that has stimulated urban renewal planning. Judicial decisions have proved to be another force for planning. The courts stimulated a wide variety of planning activities in the 1970s.

Organizational enhancement is the fourth force that can initiate a planning activity. The planning activity is a means used by the organization to protect, maintain, and increase its stock of status and influence. All organizations, as noted previously, need to offer incentives to participants in exchange for their participation. Community and civic organizations rely heavily on status incentives. Planning presents an opportunity to increase an organization's status incentives.

Indeed, in some instances an organization may initiate a planning activity to protect its status position. This is a defensive response. Again, however, the initiation of the planning is a means to provide incentives in exchange for membership and contributions of work.

It should also be pointed out that individuals stimulate planning to enhance their own personal image. Mayors and planning officials sometimes use planning as a vehicle for increasing their status.

Organizational enhancement is a common force for planning. Even if it is not the prime force, it is frequently an ancillary force. Organizations generally condition their involvement in planning on the effect the activity may have on the position of the agency. It is a function of the planner to weigh this influence in order to see that it does not unduly affect the planning outcome.

FORMAL POLICY CONSTITUENCY

The planner uses the analysis of the initiating set and the preplanning diagnostic assessment for two reasons. One, it helps the planner understand the preliminary motive of the problem. Secondly, it is used as part of the guidance to the formal policy constituency (FPC) in its initial decision phases.

The role of the FPC at this stage is to make a decision either to initiate or not to initiate planning. This is a critical decision and should be based on as full a knowledge of the planning proposal as possible. The issues the FPC should consider in making this decision are:

1. Knowledge of the initiating set and its reason for proposing the plan.
2. The preplanning diagnostic assessment.
3. A historical assessment of the issue, what actions, if any, in the past have been taken to resolve the planning issue, and what has been the result of such actions.

4. An assessment of the feasibility of the plan, and does the organization have the capability of carrying out the plan.
5. A preliminary identification of the potential decision center that would affect the outcome of a plan.
6. An outline of probable planning solutions.

The issues are presented to the FPC by the planner or member of the planning staff. The planners, however, are not disinterested observers. It is both necessary and desirable for them to contribute their judgment to the decision.

It would, moreover, be impossible for the planners to maintain a neutral stance. Their own involvement in the preliminary phases creates a commitment to a decision one way or the other. This bias should be acknowledged.

It should be remembered, however, that the ultimate decision to begin or not begin a planning study is the responsibility of the FPC. Only the FPC can commit the resources and status of the agency to planning. The planning staff should be sensitive to the FPC judgement. If it is reluctant to initiate a planning study, it would be unwise to convince it to do otherwise.

In working with the FPC, the planner uses both diagnostic and administrative skills. The diagnostic skills are used to assess the degree of commitment on the part of the FPC to planning. The administrative skills are used to help the FPC arrive at an initial decision—whether or not to begin planning—and, if the decision to plan is made, how planning should be initiated.

ACTION SYSTEM

The action system comprises those individuals or actors who have the capacity to agree to or withhold action necessary for the acceptance and implementation of a planning decision. An action system, consequently, comprises a large number of individuals, groups, and organizations. This makes it impossible for the planner to work directly with the action system. It must be accomplished indirectly.

The planner relies primarily on administrative skills in working with the action system. He or she attempts to maintain structural relationships with action system entities. Publicity skills are the most often required.

Consensus Action System

A consensus action system assumes the likelihood that agreement on a planning decision is possible. (See Chapter 7.) The intention in working with a consensus action system is to further the development of an atmosphere or environment that allows the planning agency's decision to be accepted. This can be accomplished by periodic reports during the planning process. (See events suggested on planning diagram.) The techniques can include:

- Providing opportunities for cooperative system members to report to their action system constituencies.
- Open meeting to which action system members are invited.
- Newsletters and information reports sent to action system members.
- News releases to community media.

Antagonistic or Unresponsive Action System

When it is not possible or desirable to assume a consensus environment then the above techniques are inappropriate for use by the planning constituency or cooperative system. The task, consequently, will be to rely on strategies that will compel or negotiate a decision from the action system. Techniques based on such strategies are explained in Chapters 10 and 11.

COOPERATIVE SYSTEM

The cooperative system is the basic planning team and it is the one with which the planner works most directly. Both diagnostic and administrative skills are required of the planner in working with the cooperative system. (It is implicitly assumed, of course, that planning skills are also required. These are explained in the next chapter.)

The planner uses *diagnostic skills* continually throughout the planning process. He or she must regularly assess the motivation of the cooperative system to carry out the planning and decision-making requirements. He or she must be careful to move with the cooperative system, not against it. Their pace of movement, not the planner's, is the guide.

The accomplishment of this task requires diagnostic insight. There are few prescriptions to guide the planner. He or she, however, must have a sensitive understanding of individuals and groups in order to gauge the level of motivation of cooperative system members. A capacity to listen, to analyze communication patterns, and a willingness to subsume the planner's own needs for recognition and status in deference to the needs of the cooperative system members are also required.

Administrative skills are necessary for the purpose of coordinating and managing the activities of the cooperative system. The cooperative system, it will be remembered, is an advocacy group—an agent of change for the planning proposal. It is, in effect, a *formal organization*.

It is organized to achieve a specific objective. A leadership pattern, albeit quite simple, emerges or is selected. Roles are defined and a division of labor is required. As a planning team, it is designed to utilize cooperative behavior in order to attain its ends—hence, the meaning of the term "cooperative system."

The effectiveness of a formal organization depends on three requirements: (1) a commonly accepted and achievable purpose; (2) a system of internal communication; and (3) the willingness of the participants to contribute their activities to achieve the purpose.[4]

The purpose of a formal organization is related to the characteristic of cooperation. Individuals come together to achieve an objective that none of them could achieve if each acted individually. The purpose, in other words, is of such complexity or magnitude that its achievement demands the activities of two or more people working cooperatively with one another.

Whether or not, incidentally, the objective is actually accomplishable is not the issue. It may prove not to be. But the participants must *believe* it to be accomplishable. Individuals will not engage or continue to engage in a cooperative activity if there is no hope of achieving the purpose.

The effectiveness of a formal organization depends, too, on a common understanding of the purpose. Differences of opinion regarding the purpose frustrate cooperative activity. Agreement on joint tasks will not be possible.

There is less likelihood for differences of opinion when the purpose is vague or defined generally. Once, however, the purpose becomes clearly defined, divergencies of opinion tend to become evident.[5] This, of course, becomes an obstacle to cooperation.

A principal function of the planner is to assist the cooperative system in attaining a unity of purpose. It is critical at the outset, therefore, that the purpose of the planning activity be clear and understood. This is accomplished by developing a precise preliminary description of the planning problem.

A second technique is to conduct a training or orientation program for the cooperative system. The training program is defined to achieve three objectives:

1. An understanding of the planning problem.
2. A belief that the planning activity is accomplishable.
3. A common understanding of the purpose.

In order for the members of a group to work with one another in the achievement of an objective, a conscious system of communication is required. In fact communication is the *process* by which an organization achieves its objectives.[6] It is the means by which the necessary tasks for achieving a common purpose become known.

Because of its voluntary nature, communication patterns are difficult to systematize and coordinate when working with citizens in planning activity. The cooperative system meets periodically rather than regularly on a day-to-day basis. Cooperative system members, moreover, have relationships with individuals external to the planning agency who may have an interest in the planning agency's activities. Communication patterns of this type cannot be known, let alone coordinated.

The method of communication with the cooperative system is limited. Meetings, memoranda, and reports are the only techniques available to the planner. As a consequence, the planner must give considerable attention to the way meetings are conducted and the way memoranda and reports are written and distributed.

Meetings of the cooperative system are the basic tool by which decisions are made in participatory planning. The success of a meeting depends on the contributions of the members and function of the chairperson.

Meetings should be conducted in an atmosphere that contributes to joint problem solving. This requires a mutuality of trust and respect among the members. Any member should feel free to participate in the proceedings. It requires, moreover, a full sharing of information by the members of the committee and the staff of the agency.

The chairperson's role is critical to the functioning of the cooperative system. He or she must be able to encourage full participation, yet lead the group. The chairperson provides leadership through advance planning for meetings, stimulating discussion, and moving the committee efficiently toward decision-making.

The planner obviously plays a role equally as critical and as important as that of the chairperson. The planner acts as the staff person for the cooperative system. He or she meets regularly with the chairperson to plan agenda for the meetings and to provide resource materials for the chairperson and the cooperative system.

The third condition of a formal organization—willingness of individuals to contribute their activities to achieving the organizational goal—is the most difficult to sustain in planning. The willingness is related to the satisfaction of individual motives; the satisfactions, in turn, are the consequences of incentives. An individual, in other words, is willing to engage in a cooperative task and contribute his or her energies in achieving the task, if he or she receives benefits in return. The benefits take the form of specific inducements.

Chester Barnard catalogues a number of inducements or incentives (see Chapter 5) for satisfying individual motives. It is only necessary here to focus on three which appear to be most useful for planning.

The first is material inducements: "money, things or physical conditions. . . ."[7] For employees of a business firm, this is considered an essential inducement. For activities of a voluntary nature, material inducements, at least in the way Barnard considers them, are not applicable.

Nonetheless participants may be guided by the potential for personal gain. In certain planning activities—urban renewal, land use zoning, for example—individuals can materially benefit as a result of their participation.

This, of course, raises the question of conflicting interests. The personal reward can become the primary objective of participation. The planner should be cautious and recognize that this inducement may serve to frustrate or interfere with the planning objectives.

Another type of material inducement for participating in community planning ventures is the indirect opportunity for personal gain through community recognition. Small businessmen and professionals (realtors, lawyers, and the like) are able to publicize themselves through community activities.

There is less opportunity for conflicting interests in this

reason for participating than in the former. Those who participate for recognition reasons can identify with the group effort. The inducement is external to the group's objectives.

The one hazard is that an individual may agree to participate induced by this motive, but not contribute his or her activities. The joining alone may be sufficient to satisfying the individual's motives. Such individuals are frequently referred to as "letterhead participants."

The expectation of personal gain as an employee of a business firm is also related to this type of material inducement. Large corporations, for example, encourage employees to become involved in community activities. From the corporation standpoint, this is seen as a means of creating community goodwill. From the employees' viewpoint, it is a means for advancement within the firm.

The orientation of the class of participants is generally toward the group objectives. Although the inducement is external, it is related to success in achieving the objectives.

A second category of incentives is *personal* or *nonmaterial opportunities.* These are related to opportunities for distinction, prestige, and personal power.[8] This is the most common inducement used by community organizations for the recruitment of individuals in participatory activities. Status incentives are developed in two ways.

One is through the association itself. Individuals achieve status, or a feeling of status, by the act of participating in civic or community activities. The higher the status of the organization, of course, the more status it has to confer on the participants.

A second way is for the organization to manufacture status through publicizing the activities of the organization. Press releases, feature news articles, television appearance of participants, and awards to participants are ways used to generate status incentives. Organizations with minimal status have to rely heavily on news stories and press releases to create status for the membership in addition to the reason of press releases to communicate the activities of the organization.

A third type of inducement is what Barnard refers to as *ideal* benefactions; that is, the capacity of the organization to satisfy the personal ideals of individual members.[9] These may include altruism and loyalty to the organization's purpose. This is a purposive incentive that generates willingness to participate because of the organization's purpose alone.

Issue-oriented organizations rely on this type of incentive almost exclusively. It is a powerful motivating force, but it is difficult to sustain over time. Moreover, it requires a strong leader who has the ability to exhort the membership to continue to devote their energies to the organization's activities.

Organizations do not or should not rely on a single set of incentives. Incentives are merely a method of exchange. In exchange for the cooperative system members' activities and support, the planning organization provides satisfactions. The more satisfaction individuals receive—in the form of status, or accomplishment, or benefits—the more likely they will contribute their energies and influence to the planning activity. It is the function of the planner to develop and manage the incentives necessary for the voluntary contribution of support from the cooperative system members.

PLANNING DIAGRAM ACTIVITIES RELATED TO CHAPTER

The purpose of this chapter has been to explain the motivational factors necessary for planning. In relation to motivation or developing a willingness to plan the following events need emphasizing.

> *Event 1*: Analyze source request for planning. Determine the motivation of the initiating set.
>
> *Event 2*: Conduct a preplanning diagnostic assessment and determine way in which diagnostic assessment will be presented to the formal policy constituency.

> *Events 9 and 10*: Determine methods for orienting cooperative system to planning problem and issues. It is at this point that the problem is not only clarified and defined, but also the point at which the purpose of the planning activity is defined for the cooperative system. The aim is to achieve a common understanding of the planning purpose.
>
> *Event 11*: This is an important decision event in the planning diagram. It is a "go-ahead" signal. The planner has to determine if there is sufficient clarity about the planning problem and sufficient understanding about the purpose of the planning activity to move into the next phase (goal setting).

The problem-definition phase is critical. An inadequate problem definition presents difficulties not only for planning but also for implementation later on.[10] It also interferes with the ability of the cooperative system to work together. There are just too many uncertainties to develop a unity of purpose. It is sometimes advisable to delay moving into a goal-setting phase until the problem-definition difficulties are resolved.

> *Activities 11–17*: As the planning program moves into the goal-setting phase the planner should assess the cooperative system's commitment to the solving of the planning problem. Is the need still evident and is the cooperative system still committed to solving the problem?
>
> *Events 20 and 45*: At both these events a planned program of assessing the action system's relevance to the planning activity should be conducted. If the action system is to be involved, techniques such as newsletters or meetings should be introduced at these points. If the action system is antagonistic to the potential planning outcome, techniques for overcoming this antagonism should be planned at these points.

Events 28 and 35: Diagnostic points during the planning activity. It is important that the planner continually assess the cooperative system's commitment to planning and carrying out the planning decision.

Summary

A major task of the planner involved in a participatory planning activity is to create the willingness of a variety of participants to commit themselves to a planning course of action. To accomplish this requires the planner to analyze:

- The source of the plan proposal.
- The reasons for the plan proposal.
- The motivation of the plan proposers.

This analysis culminates in a preplanning diagnostic assessment. The preplanning diagnostic assessment is used as a means for making the decision by the formal policy constituency of the agency to initiate, or conversely, not to initiate planning.

If the decision to plan is positive, the planner must create a willingness on the part of the planning team (cooperative system) to engage in the planning activity. Willingness is achieved by developing a unity of purpose, a conscious system of communication, and the manipulation of incentives. Incentives are satisfactions the planning organization offers in exchange for the voluntary contributions of individuals to work together for the achievement of a common goal.

The planner also attempts to structure the decision environment (action system) to permit the establishment of a relationship between the cooperative system and decision centers. The relationship may be collaborative or antagonistic, depending upon the ability or desires of the planning agency.

NOTES

1. Christopher Sower, et al., *Community Involvement,* (New York; Free Press, 1957).
2. Ibid., pp. 66–69.
3. One well-explained example is E. Jack Schoop and John E. Hirten, "The San Francisco Bay Plan; Combining Policy with Police Power," *Journal of the American Institute of Planners,* Vol. XXXVII, No. 1 (January 1971), pp. 2–10.
4. Chester I. Barnard, *The Functions of the Executive* (Cambridge, Mass.: Harvard University Press, 1946), p. 82.
5. Ibid., pp. 86–88.
6. Ibid., p. 89.
7. Ibid., pp. 142.
8. Ibid., pp. 145–146.
9. Ibid., p. 146.
10. Andreas Faludi, *Planning Theory* (New York: Pergamon Press, 1973), pp. 87–98.

Chapter 9

GOAL SETTING AND PLAN ELEMENTS

The terms *planning* and *goal* are interrelated. They are in one sense correlatives of one another. Although it is possible to have a goal without planning, it is not possible to have planning without a goal. Indeed that is what distinguishes planning as a rational activity. Planning is, or at least purports to be, a conscious and deliberate means for achieving a particular objective or goal.

Yet the task of goal setting, along with operationalizing goals through the establishment of plan elements are conceivably the most difficult and most frustrating in planning.

As we explained earlier, the planner's own knowledge limitations, the value assumptions underlying goal selection, and the politics of community decision-making serve to frustrate planning activities that proceed from a goal-oriented premise. Indeed, it has been a consequence of this frustration that has served to move planning away from a goal-oriented procedure to a process sensitive to the political implications of decision-making. For some theorists planning is a process of "muddling through"[1] toward a design of "feasible solutions."[2] The emphasis sometimes is on acceptability at the expense of analysis and design. Planning, however, should not be a search only for solutions that are acceptable. That is a contradiction of the meaning of planning. Planning is both a way of achieving the future and a *way of imagining the future.*

IMAGINING THE FUTURE AND ACHIEVING THE FUTURE

A paradigm outlining the domain of planning theory has been devised by Richard Bolan, which is helpful at this point.[3] Bolan has developed a classification scheme that depicts both the cognitive and social perspectives of planning as two main axes of a matrix of planning theory. (See Figure 9-1.) The horizontal axis lists a set of coordinates outlining the social perspectives of planning. The social framework is characterized by its depiction of different contexts of social relations.[4]

The vertical axis presents planning as taking place within three different cognitive frameworks. It is this set of coordinates that is pertinent here. Not only does it identify the scope of planning as one glances across the social framework perspective, but also it specifies the knowledge and time dimension of planning.[5]

The first category, *ways of understanding the past and present,* contains the core knowledge and disciplinary methods for understanding the world. This is the knowledge armament of the planner. It is clear, as one views the horizontal axis, that there is a breadth of knowledge that can help the planner understand a problem, as well as help the planner to begin to understand the ways in which the problem can be resolved.[6]

Imagining the Future

In the introductory chapter, planning was defined as a means for capturing the future. It follows, therefore, that a distinguishing characteristic of planning is determining *ways of ima-*

TIME COGNITIVE PERSPECTIVE \ SOCIAL PERSPECTIVE	SUBSTANTIVE FRAMEWORK OF THINGS AND RELATIONS	CULTURAL FRAMEWORK OF IDEAS AND NORMS	INSTITUTIONAL FRAMEWORK OF CONTROL AND ORDER	PSYCHOLOGICAL FRAMEWORK OF BEHAVIOR AND BEHAVIORAL STIMULI
WAYS OF UNDERSTANDING THE PAST AND PRESENT	Basic physical and social sciences Architecture Engineering Economics Demography Geography Sociology	History Ethics Jurisprudence Theology Culture Fashion	Political theory Administrative theory Institutional structure Judicial precedent Administrative rules and regulations	Personality development Conditioning Transactional analysis Small group behavior Political behavior Environmental psychology
WAYS OF IMAGINING THE FUTURE	Straight-line extrapolation Incremental-marginal analysis Predictive modeling Systems theory Game theory Decision theory	Utopian constructs Master planning Futuristics	Organizational development Allocative planning Innovative planning Scientific management Temporary society	Behavior modification Market research Political voting research Behavioral technology
WAYS OF ACHIEVING THE FUTURE	Persuasion by force of reason and rationality	Ideological indoctrination Ideological revolution	Coercion Regulation and rule-making Power elite strategies Institutional change strategies Conflict strategies	Communication and diffusion strategies Education and learning strategies Participation and exchange strategies

Figure 9–1 Outline of mapping categories for planning theory terrain. (From Richard S. Bolan, "Mapping the Planning Theory Terrain," David R. Godschalk, Ed., *Planning in America: Learning from Turbulence;* Washington, D. C.: American Institute of Planners, 1974, pp. 20–21.)

gining the future. It is this process of thinking that leads to examining alternatives and selecting preferred objectives—the essence of planning.

The future, however, is not imagined in isolation. The knowledge of the past and present influences not only the image of the future, but the ways by which the future itself can be imagined. The storehouse of knowledge, as well as the planner's own understanding of that knowledge, define the scope of the future.

The scope of the future is determined also by the exigencies of the present, the values, and hopes of the planner,[7] and the issues surrounding the planning problem itself. In some instances this may limit the planner's image of the future. Competing issues, for example, may limit the time that can be spent on exploring alternative images of the future. In other instances these determining factors may expand the planner's image of the future. The planner's own values, his or her own hopes may act as a stimulus to creativity.

The way in which the future can be imagined is determined, as well, by the way that future can be achieved. This is not true in all instances, but in most. Utopian writers or futurists, for example, need not be burdened with achieving their own imagined ideal. Their objective is to stretch our imagination of the future. In this respect they serve to explore alternative images of the future.

The practicing planner, however, is forced to construct his or her image of the future always with a view to how that image can be achieved. There is a continuing interaction to this aspect of the cognitive process. The image of the future affects its achievement, and the achievement of the future affects the image. It is necessary to design specific events in the planning process to allow for these interactions to take place. (See below.)

A theme of this text is that planning is a participatory process. Individuals and groups external to the staff and formal policy constituency are involved in defining planning objectives.

They may be involved formally, as in the capacity of a cooperative system, or they may be involved informally through the medium of public hearings or meetings. They provide not just a value orientation to planning choice (that is, interpreting their desires and hopes); but citizen participants are often able to provide also a source of wisdom and knowledge that helps to frame alternative ways of solving problems.[8] However they may be involved, they do act as one further definer of the scope of the future.

The planner should view the cognitive process of ways of imagining the future as a methodological category. We depend on the present state of technologies to fashion choices for the future. The nature of the plan, also, will influence the method or methods used.

The means for imagining the future are less certain and less factual than our knowledge of the past and present. The lack of accumulated wisdom to help understand the future is one reason for this deficiency. It has been only recently that attention has been given to exploring *means* for capturing the future. This signals a caution to the planner. The image that is constructed of the future may be faulty and go astray.

These two categories (understanding the past and the present and imagining the future) underly the thinking process necessary for the formulation of a plan. It is on the basis of these two ways of thinking that planning goals and plan elements are developed. A plan, for example, related in part to population changes and population trends would require knowledge of demography. Using demographic information as a base, the planner may use extrapolation methods as a guide to imagining the future.

Another and more complex example: A plan designed to provide a variety of treatment programs for the mentally ill would necessitate an understanding of human growth and behavior, personality theory, treatment techniques, subcultural definitions of mental illness, and judicial precedents, to name a few knowledge areas and disciplines.

There are a number of methodologies the planner can make use of in applying his or her understanding of the past and present for the purpose of designing alternative choices of treatment programs for the mentally ill. A simple straight-line extrapolation might provide gross client population estimates. More advanced and sophisticated techniques, such as predictive modeling and system theory, might provide additional and different client population estimates. Market research techniques might be useful in targeting areas for program developments. Both treatment technologies and organizational development methods would provide the bases for imagining the types of mental health organizations that can be designed.

Achieving the Future

It is by using this framework of thinking that a plan becomes a statement for solving a problem or designing an ideal future state. Achieving that future, however, requires a different mental process. What is required in *ways of achieving the future* is a planned change perspective. It denotes the engagement of the planner and the planning organization with individuals, groups and organizations for the purpose of bringing about planning objectives.[9]

In achieving the future, the planner emphasizes the *social process* characteristics of planning. The social process characteristics are the interactional activities of planning; that is, the recruiting and organizing of those who contribute skills and knowledge to the development of a plan. The social process characteristics are also related to strategies for achieving planning objectives. The focus in this respect is diagnosing obstacles to plan implementation.

The time dimension of the cognitive perspective is significant from the point of view that it is possible to identify those phases in the planning process where one mode of thinking is more relied upon than another. If the categories of understanding the past and present, and imagining the future are combined and termed a planning-decision mode of thinking and the third category is identified as a *social process* mode of thinking, this distinction becomes more apparent.[10]

During the problem identification phase of planning, for example, the planner relies on a social process mode of thinking. The objective at this point is to develop the initial means for achieving the future. The focus is on providing legitimation to begin and to diagnose the commitment of the planning agency constituencies both to planning and to achieving the implementation of the planning objective.

In this phase, too, the planner is anticipating the future. Can the problem be defined realistically and consciously acknowledged *before* the planning process can and should be initiated? Is there sufficient force for change based on a recognized need, or the enhancement needs of an organization, or the influence of the planning agency and its constituency to achieve the future? The previous two chapters considered these aspects of planning.

During the final acceptance phase the emphasis is also on the social process mode of thinking. The aim is to identify those strategies that will achieve acceptance of planning goals. In this respect it is a way of imagining how to achieve the future.

The emphasis in the goal-setting and plan-element phases, however, is on the planning-decision mode of thinking. These phases can be compared to the traditional model of "rational" planning. Goals are identified, alternatives are explored and analyzed, and solutions are determined by the relationship between alternatives and goals. The reader should be aware, however, that this is an *analogous* conception of planning, and not the conception of planning described in this text.

To suggest that one mode of thinking is relied on in one phase of the planning process and not in another is not to suggest it is an exclusive reliance. Rarely, if ever, is it possible for the planner to imagine the future without considering almost simultaneously ways of imagining how to achieve that future. None of the categories is independent of the others. The difference in emphasis is one of degree and to illustrate for the planner that there are shifts in focus as the planner proceeds through the planning process.

Goal Setting

Goal setting is a *means* for *choosing* the future. But the future cannot be chosen without an understanding of the past and the present. A beginning step, therefore, is to identify present conditions related to the problem. The planning diagram illustrates events that the planner might use for the analysis and study of present conditions. There are, of course, other analytical techniques the planner might employ to understand the nature of the problem. Bolan's paradigm suggests a few. Others can be found in texts dealing with the substantive process of planning.[11]

Following this analysis the planner identifies assumptions for goals. Goals, it must be remembered, are value preferences. They suggest a desired state one wishes to occupy or attain. They are not then provable or measurable. Certainly it is possible to measure or evaluate whether or not you have achieved a goal. But the selection of the goal itself is a *choice*.

Health care that is both free to the patient and easily accessible are examples of goals. They are choices that a group or a society may desire. Obviously a host of reasons can be assembled to support both goals. But reasonable arguments can also be offered in opposition to these goals. A goal, in other words, represents one person's choice as opposed to another.

Assumptions are the basis for the selection of a goal or goals. Example: Mothers with no prenatal care are likely to give birth to infants with low birth weights. Low birth weight is associated with almost half of all infant deaths and greatly increases the chance of birth defects, including mental retardation. An assumption can be made, therefore, that regular prenatal care will reduce infant mortality. The assumption once made serves as a criterion for the establishment of goals. It is important that the criteria be clearly defined, because it is a standard guiding not only the establishment of goals, but also plan elements. The criteria for goals and plan elements, moreover, are measures for events in the final design and cut-over phases of planning. (See Chapter 12.)

Continuing with the example: The establishment of a health care program at no costs to patients and readily accessible (goals) will make it likely that infant mortality will decrease. Note, however, the word "likely." Even though a criterion has been set against which goals are established, it is still an assumption. It has been assumed that prenatal care will reduce infant mortality. Other factors may be present that influence infant mortality—basic health of the parents, genetic factors of mothers and fathers, and behavioral characteristics of the mother and father are a few examples.

Normally these additional factors would be analyzed as part of a study of the past and present conditions related to the problem. Some would lead to further assumptions that may qualify the goal or require additional sets of plan elements. To return to the example: Easily accessible health care facilities may not be a function only of physical or geographical location. *Acceptability* of the facility may also influence the use. This could lead to the establishment of another goal or to a qualification of the accessibility goal. In turn, this would lead to additional elements of the plan related to the goal, one of which could be the design of a facility from a physical and personnel standpoint that meets value and cultural preferences of potential patients. It could also mean that a program of the facility would be designed to reach out and encourage the use of the facility by potential patients.

It is this process of analysis that is required during the goal setting state; namely:

- Analysis of past and present conditions.
- Identifying assumptions.

- Establishing criteria for selection of goals.
- Operationalizing goals through establishing plan elements. (See below).

One further point about assumptions: They are measurable. They can be tested. Will easily accessible and free health care reduce infant mortality? It may or it may not. Indeed, there is even a further catch; infant mortality may be reduced, but it may not be as a result of easily accessible and free health care. Attitudes may change at the same time as a result of entirely different influences. This does not reject the need for analysis.

The *social process* events during the goal-setting phase are of two kinds. One is the nature and extent of involvement of the cooperative system in the analysis and establishment of goals. Evidence, as we have indicated, suggests that groups involved in planning activities tend to become committed to the goals they have devised, and tend also to be committed to supporting these goals. Equally important, the goals that are devised tend to reflect the needs of the larger community; that is, more so than if devised by a central planner.

The extent of the cooperative system's involvement varies. In some instances the cooperative system's involvement is extensive in all activities, including the collection and the analysis of data. In other instances the cooperative system depends heavily on the planner and planning staff, but reserving the decision rights at the conclusion of the major phases of the planning process. An example of this type of cooperative system involvement can be found in the case study of environmental planning in San Francisco.[12]

In the early 1960s, concern arose regarding the chaotic and reckless filling in of the marshes and shoreline of the San Francisco Bay Area—a nine-county area. A small group of citizens initiated the establishment of a study commission to develop a conservation plan for the bay. A legislatively financed San Francisco Bay Conservation Study Commission was established in 1964 with instructions to report back in six months.

An early decision was made to reject the usual process of preparing a complete and comprehensive plan for public review and discussion in favor of a process involving widespread public involvement during the plan preparation period. This decision, it was recognized, might lead to fragmentation and vitiate the development of a comprehensive plan meeting the needs of the Bay Area. At the same time, it was also recognized that without public understanding of the problem, acceptance of any plan might prove difficult.

The planning process was divided into 25 elements requiring open and public approval of each element. Preliminary reports were tested on interested parties and as many decision-makers as possible (the action system). Consensus on plan elements was the goal. The planning staff, moreover, accepted as many speaking engagements in the nine-county area as possible, which averaged two or three a week.

By the time the plan was completed, the commission (cooperative system) had only four months to complete action on the plan. However, because of the widespread awareness of the emerging plan elements, which served as policies, and extensive involvement of key elements in policy development, the commission was able to move into three public hearings. All interest groups were heard. Subsequently the commission reviewed every page of the plan, made necessary revisions, and formally adopted the document by a 20-to-1 vote.[13]

Whether or not the kind of involvement of citizens and groups in planning should be as extensive as that followed by the San Francisco Bay Conservation Study Commission depends greatly on the nature of the plan and its objectives. Three guidelines can be followed. One is the nature and complexity of the plan. Second is the degree of commitment required for the cooperative system to support the plan. Third is the extent to which the plan adequately represents the interests of the planning agency's constituency. The determination of these factors is made by the planner in his or her diagnostic analyses.

A second kind of social process activity during the planning phase is to assess the reaction of the action and community systems to the planning goals.¹⁴ This can be accomplished in a number of ways: news releases, newsletters to individuals and organizations, meeting with groups and organizations, or a combination of any of these means.

At the conclusion of the goal-setting stage it is preferable to announce these to the wider geographic community. The purpose is informational and to provide an environment positive to the planning objectives of the organization. It can also provide a support for the action and cooperative systems. The only means for announcing such information to the larger community is through the news media.

Once the reaction from the action system is obtained, a decision then has to be made regarding the need to modify the goals. Whether or not it is necessary to modify them will depend on two conditions. One is the reaction to the goals by the action system. The second is the willingness of the cooperative system and the organization to modify the goals. In some cases the modificaiton is slight. In others it may be so extensive that the plan itself becomes seriously compromised. Each of these issues needs to be examined before a decision is made.

Plan Element Phase

Experience tends to show that reaction to planning goals from groups outside the organization is either positive or nonexistent. Goals themselves are desirable alternatives to existing conditions. Indeed, they generally reflect the aspirations of most people in society. Negative reaction to goals then is rare.¹⁵

Once the plan elements are announced, however, negative reaction to a plan can be swift and vociferous. Few people, for example, are opposed to more humane and therapeutically effective treatment for the mentally ill. As a further example, few are opposed to dismantling large impersonal state mental hospitals in favor of small deinstitutionalized facilities, such as halfway houses or residential centers.

But once the plan elements begin to identify *where* the halfway houses or residential centers are to be located, opposition can be expected. The same example can be used for highway planning, housing planning, zoning, and criminal justice planning. The plan elements are the concrete and visible measures of a plan.

As the planner moves into the plan-element stage, therefore, he or she has to be concerned not only with ways of imagining the future, but also with ways of imagining how to achieve the future. A glance at the planning diagram will reveal that the top half of the diagram identifies events that are related to the planning-decision mode of *imagining* the future, while the lower half describes events related to *achieving* the future.

The *planning-decision* objective in this phase is to identify each of the elements necessary for achieving a planning goal. Equally important is the necessity to determine the feasibility of the plan elements. This is accomplished by developing, in detail, the programming and resource requirements for the plan elements—that is, staffing, funding, acquisition requirements, and the like. If possible, simulation and feasiblity studies should be undertaken. These help to reassess the adequacy of program and resource requirements.

One helpful technique at this point in planning is to translate the plan elements into a work plan. Borrowed from the management discipline, a work plan is a device for clearly defining elements, relating them to goals, and to identifying tasks necessary for achieving the elements. A work plan is composed of five activities:[16]

- *Goals:* a statement of an end result that is desired.
- *Elements:* statements of what is necessary to achieve a goal; sometimes referred to as subgoals. Plan elements are stated in terms of action and generally prefaced by the proposition "to" (written or implied); e.g., to provide, to develop, etc. A plan element is one that is attainable and understandable by the people working on it and

the people who would be affected by it. It is also measurable and lends itself to accountability.
- *Work tasks:* the specific tasks, activities, steps, resources, and the like that are needed to be accomplished to reach the plan element. Each work task is listed with estimates of the time needed each will take in sequence leading to final accomplishment of the plan element.
- *Responsibility:* identification of the individual or committee (or combination of both) who has the responsiblility for completing the specific work task(s) leading to the accomplishment of a plan element.
- *Completion date:* the "benchmark" or "target dates" for completion of the specific work tasks in sequence that when completed result in the accomplishment of the plan element. These can be estimates, or more sophisticated scheduling techniques like PERT (program, evaluation, review techniques) may be used.

The *social process* events during the plan-element phase are of three kinds. One is related to the involvement of the action and cooperative systems in committing themselves to the plan elements. It is necessary to diagnose the cooperative system's commitment to the plan elements prior to moving into the decision phase. Do the plan elements represent the interest and needs of the cooperative system? Is the cooperative system willing to support the plan elements? If not, should the planning activity be halted, or can a commitment be brought about?

A second activity is to reanalyze the cooperative system's relationship to the action system. As the process of planning proceeds, a number of original assumptions about the cooperative system's influence with the decision environment may change. An actor, for example, who was thought to have authority over a set of requisite actions may no longer have that authority, because of either the changing character of the plan or a changed decision environment. As a consequence, it may be necessary to recruit additional and more influential members

GOAL SETTING AND PLAN ELEMENTS 209

to the cooperative system. If this is not feasible, alternative decision-making strategies may have to be explored.

A third social process activity is related to the implementation phase of planning. The plan elements represent the character of a plan. Once they are identified—and the tasks necessary to achieve them—the steps required to implement the plan begin to emerge. It is during the plan-element phase, therefore, that preparations should begin for implementation. The identification of administrative decision centers and the design of implementation strategies are examples of preliminary activities related to implementation that should be initiated during the plan-element phase.

Planning Diagram Activities Related to Chapter

In relation to goal setting and developing plan elements, the following events and activities need emphasizing:

Events 12, 13, 14, and 15: These are *suggested* analytical events. They are listed to show the point at which analytical activities should be conducted and also to show the relation of analytical activities to social process activities.

Event 18: This is a preliminary step. As the planning problem is being analyzed the planner should be identifying potential decision centers for future action.

Events 19 and 20, Activities 20–23: These are events and activities designed to indicate the involvement of the cooperative system in goal setting. The nature and the techniques for involvement should be planned in advance.

Event 24: This is the final goal-setting event before moving into the plan-element phase. Goals should be established after discussion and work with the cooperative and action systems.

Event 27: This is the point at which a work plan is prepared. Other events during the plan-element phase are related to operationalizing the work plan.

Events 38 and 39: As the plan elements emerge, decision centers responsible for carrying out a plan can begin to be identified. These are decision centers that will implement a plan once it has been accepted. Administrative decision centers are those with management responsibilities, and operational decision centers are those that will directly carry out a particular aspect of a plan.

Event 40: At this point the plan "ideally" is prepared. Modification of a plan frequently does take place during the decision and implementation phases. Nonetheless, at Event 40 a product called a plan has been readied, the cooperative system is committed to it as a consequence of their involvement, and it is now possible to move into an action or acceptance phase of planning.

SUMMARY

Planning involves three interdependent cognitive processes: ways of understanding the past and present, ways of imagining the future, and ways of achieving the future. During the goal-setting and plan-element phases, the main focus of attention is on understanding the past and present and imagining the future. It is during the goal-setting and plan-element phases that the substantive act of planning takes place. The end result is a plan.

The plan devised represents a response to a recognized problem, is reflective of the planning constituencies' needs, and is feasible of being accepted. The acceptance of a plan by the appropriate decision centers depends on a number of factors, not the least of which is the capability of the plan itself to solve the identified and stated problem.

The planning-decision tasks during the goal-setting and plan-element stages, therefore, are significant and critical factors in the feasibility and acceptability of a plan.

Acceptance of a plan will also depend upon the strategy of decision-making chosen by the planning organization. Strategies for imagining how to achieve the future are contained in the next chapters.

NOTES

1. Charles E. Lindblom, "The Science of 'Muddling Through'," *Public Administration Review,* Vol. XIX No. 2 (Spring 1959), pp. 79–88.
2. Robert Morris and Robert H. Binstock, *Feasible Planning for Social Change* (New York: Columbia University Press, 1966).
3. Richard S. Bolan, "Mapping the Planning Theory Terrain," David R. Godschalk (Ed.), *Planning in America: Learning from Turbulence* (Washington: American Institute of Planners, 1974), pp. 13–34.
4. Ibid., p. 15.
5. Ibid.
6. The reader should be aware that there are weaknesses both in our understanding and use of substantive knowledge. See Ibid., pp. 20–21.
7. Ibid., p. 16.
8. Faludi provides an excellent case history of the value of citizen participation in planning. The knowledge and experience of local citizens in an Austrian village enabled the government planners to avoid a costly and dangerous solution in a highway planning project. Andreas Faludi, *Planning Theory* (New York: Pergamon Press, 1973), pp. 120–121.

9. Bolan, op. cit., p. 16.

10. John Friedmann has made the distinction between decision and action models of planning. Decision models refer to the common notion of planning as the application of scientific technical intelligence in societal action. This is what we mean by the decision-planning mode of thinking. Action, on the other hand, encompasses both the decisions and implementation dimensions of planning. The action planning model, explains Friedmann, "fuses action and planning into a single operation so that the conceptual distinctions of planning—decision—implementation—recycling are worked out." John Friedmann, "Notes on Societal Action," *Journal of the American Institute of Planners,* Vol. XXXV, No. 5. (September 1969), p. 312.

    The fusing of planning—decision—implementation was also made by community organization writers. The emphasis of community organization in relation to planning is the development of a plan that "is feasible, that will be supported." This is what Murray G. Ross writing in the 1950s called "action planning." Murray G. Ross, *Community Organization* (New York: Harper and Row, 1955), p. 134.

    We, too, take the position that *action planning* combines both the planning—decision—implementation—recycling aspects of planning into a single concept of planning. That is a principle of this book. The distinction, however, between the social process and the planning-decision characteristics of planning is made purely for analytical purposes.

11. See, for example, Stuart F. Chapin, Jr., *Urban Land Use Planning,* (Urbana: University of Illinois Press, 1965) and International City Managers Association, *Principles and Practice of Urban Planning* (Washington, D.C.: Author, 1968).

12. Jack Shoop and John Herter, "The San Francisco Bay Area Plan: Combining Policy with Police Power," *Journal of the American Institute of Planners,* Vol. XXXVII, No. 1, January 1971, pp. 2–10.

13. Ibid., pp. 2–7.

14. Whether or not the action and community systems become involved will depend on the type of decision-making strategy that will or can be used. See Chapters 10 and 11. For purposes of illustration we are describing procedures that would be used in strategies in which all systems could become involved.

15. The Bolan-Nuttall study of urban planning cases in Boston, New York, New Jersey, and Pittsburgh bear this out. Of four cases studied, goals were accepted in all and the elements or means to achieving the goals

were rejected in three. See, Richard S. Bolan and Ronald L. Nuttall, *Urban Planning and Politics,* (Lexington, Mass.: Health, 1975), pp. 136–139.

16. A sixth activity, evaluation—whether or not the element for tasks was achieved—is frequently included in a work plan. We have omitted it, although not rejecting its reliance or importance in a work plan.

Chapter 10

THE DECISION PHASE OF PLANNING: PART I

Planning is a seductive activity. Those involved can become so involved in the process and can so identify with the conclusions that they become enamored with the plan itself. A belief begins to emerge that the plan is attractive enough to gain immediate acceptance.

Nothing can be further from the truth. A planning activity that does not take into account ways of achieving the future leads to no solution and no conclusion. Planning can thus become an academic exercise leading to frustrations and disappointment for the planner and the participants. In turn, this will affect future planning activities. Repeated failures are obstacles for future planning activities. Strategies for gaining acceptance of a plan are equally as important as strategies for planning.

It should be noted that the phrase "gaining acceptance" rather than "implementing" is used. The implementation of a plan takes place *after* the plan has been accepted by a decision center. Implementations of planning objectives will be explained in Chapter 12. The intention in this and the next chapter is to outline strategies for gaining acceptance of a plan: that is, the *decision phase of planning.*

A strategy is a means to an end: an organized set of procedures or general scheme used to attain objectives. The procedures are often described as tactics. (Strategy is originally a military concept.) We use the term "techniques" rather than "tactics." By a decision-making strategy, therefore, we mean an organized set of procedures involving techniques used to attain acceptance of a planning outcome.

It is misleading, however, to suggest that there is a particular phase in the planning process during which acceptance takes place. In some cases this may be true. The planning goal, elements, and objectives are identified; a plan prepared; and then a process for gaining acceptance of the plan commences. In other cases, however, the process of gaining support for a plan may emerge as early as the problem-identification stage.

At which point or phase in planning the process of gaining acceptance of a plan begins depends upon three functions:

1. Diagnostic assessment of forces for and against the plan.[1]
2. The particular strategy or strategies of decision-making that is or are chosen.
3. The capacity and willingness of the planning organization to use or select a particular strategy or strategies.

These three functions will be the basis for explaining ways of achieving the future in planning.

DECISION-MAKING DIAGNOSTIC ASSESSMENT

In Chapter 7 we suggested that a diagnostic assessment should be conducted before initiating planning. The purpose of that assessment was to determine the strength of the forces for beginning planning.

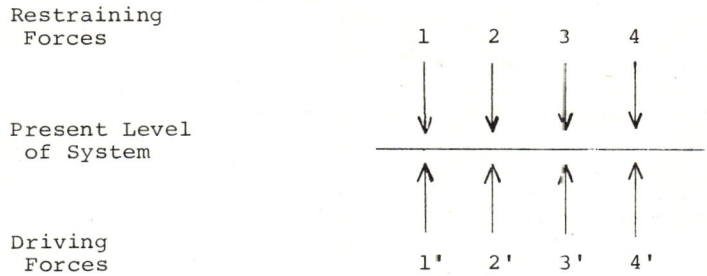

Figure 10–1 Lewin's force field model.

As the process moves into the decision phase, a second diagnostic assessment is necessary. The purpose of this assessment is twofold: one, to analyze the forces for and against the plan, and, two, to select the most appropriate strategy for achieving acceptance of the plan. A practical and effective diagnostic tool for making this assessment is Lewin's force field paradigm,[2] the theoretical framework of which was explained in Chapter 5.

To review briefly: Lewin postulates that all social systems are kept in balance by a combination of driving and restraining forces as depicted in Figure 10–1.

The top and bottom of the figure represents the outer boundaries of the system. The driving forces are toward change or new directions for the system. The restraining forces act as barriers to change (or, in our case, to the gaining of acceptance of planning objectives.) For the system to change, driving forces must be either increased or decreased.

Forces Contributing to Acceptance of Plan

In making the diagnostic assessment, the planner first lists those forces that contribute to achieving acceptance of the plan. Such forces would include:

1. *Organizational capacity of the planning organization.* Does it have positional legitimacy? What influence does the organizational constituency have?
2. *Composition and influence of the planning constituency.* Is the cooperative system related to all elements of the action system? Does the cooperative system have the motivation to complete its task? Does the cooperative system have the energy and commitment to campaign for acceptance of the plan? What influence does the cooperative system have over decision centers related to the plan?
3. *Intensity and breadth of need that initiated planning activity.* Is the need well established? Is there sufficient understanding of the need? Is the need recognized beyond the decision centers? Can the broad base of the need act as a contributory force for acceptance on decision centers? Can the solution satisfy needs of other organizations and interests? Can a solution enhance the aims of other organizations and interests? Can the solution generate a broad base of support?
4. *Feasibility of solution.* Can the plan be implemented?
5. *Conventional wisdom of action and community systems.* Does the solution fall within the general belief systems of the community? If not, can the belief systems be altered? Are there forces operating to alter the belief system?

OBSTACLES TO ACCEPTANCE OF PLAN

A second list includes obstacles to acceptance of the plan. These are called restraining forces, and the objective is to reduce them to permit acceptance of change.

Restraining forces, of course, are the obverse of driving forces. The fact that the plan is unrelated to a recognized need would suggest that an obstacle is the absence of need. Further, if the cooperative system has no influence over decision centers, then the decision centers must be viewed, at least, as potential obstacles. Nonetheless, there are obstacles not related to driving forces. These include:

1. *Habit.* Are there ingrained procedures militating against change? Is the present method of operation providing satisfactions unlikely to be given up?
2. *Creation of potential community conflict.* Will the plan solution generate conflict among community groups? Will the plan solution create more problems than it solves?

Forces Interfering with Acceptance of Plan

There is one further list the planner should catalogue as part of his or her diagnostic assessment; it is made up of what are called *interference forces*. Identified by Lippitt and his colleagues,[3] interference forces are not specific obstacles to a plan, but in effect can act as obstacles. They interfere with the possibility of the plan being accepted. In addition, they are the most difficult to deal with, because they may be either real or imagined. Interference forces could include:

1. *Lack of resources.* Is there a loss of funds once the planning has been initiated? Are there insufficient resources (funds, equipment, personnel) to implement the plan?
2. *Lack of commitment.* Once the planning process has commenced, has the cooperative system begun to lose its commitment to the plan? Has the planning process drained the energies of the planning staff and the cooperative system?
3. *Interpersonal conflicts.* Is there likely to be any emotional negative responses coming from any individual or group proposing the plan?

4. *Fear.* Is the plan likely to create fear or mistrust because of the nature of the plan's proponents? Does the plan solution create distrust or fear?

DECISION-MAKING STRATEGIES

Clearly there are but two ways in which decisions become accepted.[4] One is simple *agreement.* Agreement occurs wherever the decision center accepts the recommendations or conclusions of the proposal makers, that is, those proposing the plan.

The second is *compromise.* Compromise is a decision-making method that arises whenever the decision center withholds judgement on the basis that the recommendation or conclusions are either at the moment unacceptable, or can be modified. In this event, two possibilities are likely. The proposal makers and the decision center can enter into a bargaining phase until agreement is reached, or those proposing the plan can devise techniques that will force the decision center to enter into bargaining.

Roland Warren makes a distinction between *issue consensus and issue dissensus* situations which is helpful here.[5] In an issue consensus situation, there is either basic agreement on the way an issue should be resolved, or there is likelihood that basic agreement can be reached once the issue is fully considered.

In an issue dissensus situation, important parties either refuse to recognize the issue or oppose the solution of the proposal maker.[6]

There are three strategies related to issue consensus, or the agreement form of decision-making, and there are two related to issue dissensus, or the compromise form of decision-making.[7] Figure 10–2 depicts the strategies and relationship of each to the basic form of decision-making.

Decision-making strategies are the means for implement-

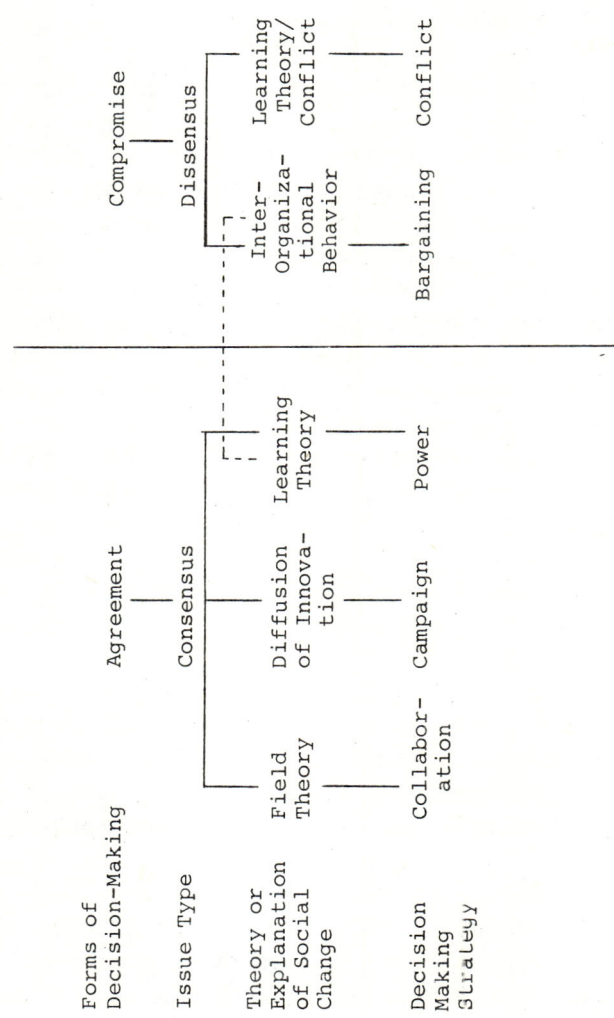

Figure 10-2 Diagram of decision-making strategies and their relationship to basic forms of decision-making and theories or explanations of social change.

ing social change objectives. Each decision-making strategy, therefore, presupposes assumptions related to particular theories or explanations of social change. Outlined, also, in Figure 10-2 are the relationships of decision-making strategies to theories or explanation of social change as explained in Chapter 5.

A decision-making strategy, however, may be based on the assumptions of more than one theory or explanation of social change. Only the most dominant relationships are depicted.

It should be pointed out, as well, that the distinction between agreement and compromise is not discrete but represents points on a continuum. Moreover, the decision-making strategies as described here are described as ideal types. In practice, decision-making strategies are not pure types and are not discrete. More than one strategy may be used in achieving the acceptance of a decision. Elements of one strategy, furthermore, may be used in another. For clarity and exposition, however, the strategies of decision-making are described as discrete and ideal types.

STRATEGY OF COLLABORATION

Collaboration is frequently viewed as synonymous with consensus and agreement. As a strategy of decision-making, however, it serves to reach unanimity and consensus through the active involvement of specifically identified individuals in the planning process.

Collaboration is a highly popular method of reaching decisions. It is nonthreatening and comfortable. It subscribes to the folk belief that men and women of goodwill can work out differences and agree on common goals for the good of the group, or the organization, or the community. Of course, this is not always so; yet it is a frequently used strategy for arriving at decisions.

Technology

The strategy of collaboration relies for its effectiveness on the methods and techniques of group dynamics, specifically the techniques related to the assumptions of *field theory*. The interaction of those involved and their subjection to group norms is designed to create an atmosphere in which problem solving and decision-making can take place.

The participants are both the *target* of the decision, and the *medium* or *technology* in which individual attitudes and behavior can be altered in terms of group objectives.

Conditions for Effectiveness

A primary condition of the strategy is the selection of the "right" people. The collaboration strategy assumes—and there is sufficient empirical evidence to support the assumption—that individuals engaged in a group problem-solving activity are more likely to support decisions arising out of a group effort than they are to support a decision individually. (See Chapter 5).

But the assumption holds only for the members of the group. The collaboration strategy is appropriate in planning, therefore, when those who have control and authority over the requisite actions to be taken are involved.

The cooperative system, in other words, is made up of those decision centers that will be required to make a decision regarding the plan.

For fulfilling this condition, recruitment and selection techniques must be carefully prepared at the outset. The decision centers are first identified and then a plan is devised for recruitment. In any such recruitment plan the recruiter has to have sufficient influence or status to persuade the individual to participate in the planning enterprise. Failure to recruit a decision center vitiates the use of the strategy.

A second condition for the effectiveness of the collaborative strategy is motivation to plan and implement the decisions of the plan. Certainly, motivation to plan is a critical condition in all strategies of decision-making. But the collaborative strategy presupposes that the decision centers are involved in the planning effort. Therefore, the emphasis in relation to motivation is the willingness of the participants to engage initially in a joint planning effort that in all likelihood will affect their activities. Equally important is the necessity to maintain the motivation as the participants move toward an awareness of the decisions that will be made and their willingness to accept the decisions.

Initially there must be some form of stimulus to begin the change or planning effort; a stimulus, in other words, to engage in planning. Such stimuli could include:

1. A recognized dissatisfaction with current conditions. One example is a threat in the loss of position or status of one or more decision centers. Another example is the recognition that current procedures are failing to achieve intended objectives. And a still further example is external pressure such as edicts or threats.
2. The possibility of a reward is another stimulus for planning. Rewards can include the enhancement of the position of one or more of the decision centers. Tax incentives or grants-in-aid are further concrete examples that act as stimuli to initiate planning.

During the planning phases (latter part of problem identification phase, goal phase, and planning element phase) the emphasis is on maintaining the motivation to plan and accept the decisions that are made.

A third condition for effectiveness is open and undistorted communication. There are two aspects to the condition of communication. One is functional. The more the participants are involved in working through the problem-solving activity, the more the motivation is maintained and the more likelihood that the participants will become committed to the solution or decision. Obviously, therefore, the participants will have to communicate with each other freely in working through the problem-solving and planning activity.

The second aspect is the dynamics of the communication patterns among the participants. For communication to be functional, the planner has to devise techniques for opening up communication. At the outset of any group activity, communication tends to be minimal and guarded. This is best illustrated by referring to an analytical device developed by Luft and Ingham called the Johari Window.[8] (See Figure 10–3.)

The Johari Window is an illustration of relationships in terms of awareness. Cell 1 is the area in which behavior and motivation are known to the individual and others. Cell 2 is a blind area in which others can see things in an individual of which the individual is unaware. When criticized or threatened, for example, an individual may become defensive but be unaware that he or she is acting in that manner.

Cell 3 represents things an individual knows but does not reveal to others. Hidden agendas are examples. Matters about which an individual has sensitive feelings are other examples. The fourth cell is an area of unknown activity both to the individual and to others. An example is deep-seated fears.

During the initial stages of a group activity, as we have said, individuals are not open and free to communicate ideas or

	Known to Self	Not Known to Self
Known to Others	1 Open	2 Blind
Not Known to Others	3 Hidden	4 Unknown

Figure 10–3.

impressions. A period of testing is required to see if an individual and his ideas are comfortably accepted. The individuals, using the Johari Window example, tend to be represented as in Figure 10–4.

There is a great deal that is unknown. Individuals tend to keep from revealing their impressions and as a result, Cell 3 is dominant.

As the group members interact and become comfortable with one another, Cell 1 dominates (Figure 10–5). One of the tasks of the planner is to facilitate communication and thereby create an openness for discussion. The intention is to reduce hidden agenda and create a climate in which people can work together.

Holding regular meetings is one technique for achieving those intentions. Another is the actual participation by individual participants in specific planning tasks. The more complex the planning problem, the more difficult it is to do this. One device, however, is to partialize the problem and involve participants in various partialized tasks.

It is the planner, however, who can best provide the means for opening communication channels. He or she can raise questions at meetings, direct questions to certain individuals, and clarify observations and comments. In fact, it is the planner's performance and skill that is the best means for creating a climate in which communication becomes free and undistorted.

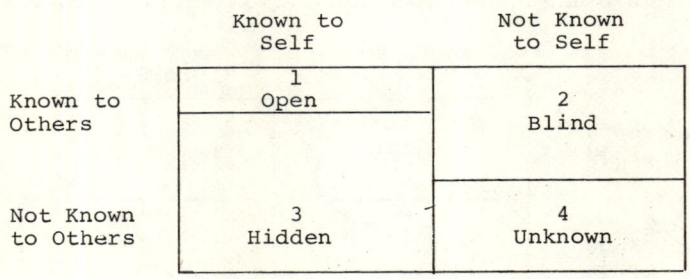

Figure 10–4.

	Known to Self	Not Known to Self
Known to Others	1 Open	2 Blind
Not Known to Others	3 Hidden	4 Unknown

Figure 10–5.

A fourth condition is the need to develop a group identity. As indicated earlier, it is usually easier for individuals to change their attitudes when they are part of a group than when they are not. (See Chapter 5.) The change that takes place in the group context stems from the individual's desire to live up to group norms. The more, therefore, the participants identify with the group as a whole, the more likely they individually will accept group-made decisions. Moreover, when members identify with each other as a group, they become more motivated to complete the tasks they have initiated as a group.[9]

A number of techniques are used to create group identity. One is to publicize the activities of the group both within the planning organization constituency and to the community at large. Within the organization, the importance of the group's efforts needs to be continually underscored. Regular reports to the organization's board of directors or authority board is one means to fulfill this objective.

A second technique is the use of news releases and other public relations activities to provide recognition of the group to the community. It is common and effective to issue news releases whenever a new planning group is formed. Not only does this provide group identity, but further, it offers status incentives to the group members.

Operationally, it is important that a new group begin to learn to work with each other before hard decisions have to be made. In the early planning phases, consequently, tasks should be selected that are easily accomplishable and accomplishable over a short period of time. This gives group members an understanding of each other, helps to create openness, and develops confidence in problem solving.

Phase in Planning Diagram at Which Strategy Is Initiated

The collaborative strategy is initiated at the very outset of the planning process. Once the requisite actors—that is, the decision centers—are recruited, the primary emphasis is to create conditions and an environment within which the participants:

- Identify the problem.
- Work through the solution.
- Select goals.
- Select objectives or plan elements for achieving the goal.

Acceptance and agreement is implicit. This is a basic assumption of the strategy, viz., individuals are more likely to support a decision and equally important, more likely to carry it out if they have had a part in discovering the need for change and if they share in the solution to that need. Participation, in other words, creates commitment to objectives.

We have spent considerable time in describing the conditions necessary for the effectiveness of the collaborative strategy. One reason, of course, is that it is a popular form for decision-making. But more important, as indicated in Chapters 7 and 8, consensus is the basic strategy for decision-making *within the cooperative system.* For the cooperative system to be an effective agent of change, it must be unified. To achieve unity, it must be in agreement on the decision it wants to be accepted. To achieve that agreement, collaboration is the necessary strategy for the internal decision-making activities of the cooperative system.

Strategy of Campaign

Frequently the problem confronting any individual or group attempting to get a plan approved is first trying to get some attention to the plan itself, before even trying to get the plan adopted. The issue the plan purports to resolve first does not appear to command attention. The initial task, consequently, is to generate enthusiasm for the plan; to persuade decision centers that the plan is important, necessary, and therefore needs to be accepted and implemented. In this context, the entire act of decision-making can be compared to a contest in which the objective is to "win over" decision centers to a proposal's cause. The appropriate strategy is the *campaign strategy*.[10] One or all three factors dictate the use of the campaign strategy:

1. Decision centers are indifferent to the proposal the plan purports to resolve.
2. There are conflicting or other issues that place the plan proposal low on the decision center's or community's priority.
3. Decision centers are unaware of the importance of the issue the plan intends to resolve.

The ultimate target of change, as a general rule, is external. It is a legislative group, an administrator or an organization that needs to be persuaded to accept the plan. Nonetheless, individuals or representatives of the change target may be involved in the planning process. They can serve a linkage function to other decision centers. Therefore, the target of change is more correctly depicted as a combination that is partly external and partly internal.

The campaign strategy implies, also, a broader concept of the change-target principle. It assumes that decision centers need to be supported in making decisions. An intent, therefore, is to influence a number of organizations and groups to support the plan proposal. In this respect, such groups are considered initially as change targets until they agree to support the plan proposal. They then become neighboring systems of support.

Technology

The primary technology of the campaign strategy is *diffusion of innovation*. Field theory is also used to guide the work with the primary planning group or the cooperative system. The cooperative system is the change agent in the campaign strategy.

There are two basic techniques in diffusion of innovation used in this strategy. One is the *campaigning* technique, which is similar in many respects to the technique used by fund raisers and political organizers.

There are two prongs to the campaigning technique. One is publicity. The success of the technique requires a carefully orchestrated publicity campaign involving news media, testimonials, and community meetings.

The publicity drive is designed to present the "case" for the plan. The objective is to heighten awareness and to create an immediacy for resolving the plan proposal. The plan proposal should be seen by the community at large as resolving an urgent and critical need.

The second prong of the technique is *organizing;* that is, recruiting individuals, groups, and organizations to support the plan proposal. The objective is to spread the base of support for the plan. The more widely the base of support for the plan, the more likely it is that decision centers will accept the plan.

Conditions for Effectiveness

There are three conditions necessary for the effectiveness of the campaign strategy.

The first is that the plan proposal cannot be conflictual in nature or likely to generate conflict. This does not mean that there cannot be opposition. On the contrary. The strategy is frequently employed given the likelihood that there will be opposition. In the event of opposition, the intention is to win it over, neutralize it, or make it insignificant through organizing a broad base of support.

If there is, however, the likelihood of significant conflict, the conflictual issues must be resolved before any planning can begin—assuming, of course, that the campaign strategy is to be used as opposed to other strategies, such as bargaining or conflict.

A second condition is the capacity and ability to recruit a broad-based support effort for the plan. Two techniques are required to master this condition.

One is the initial recruitment of the cooperative system. Recruitment of cooperative system members begins with the design of the action system chart as described in Chapter 8. Cooperative system members maintain a communication and influence link to action system members and act as the agent of change for acceptance of the plan.

At each stage in the planning process, cooperative system members report to their action system reference group. The objectives are threefold. One is to maintain support for the planning activity. The second is to create a positive environment for acceptance. And the third is to receive feedback on the feasibility of the plan's acceptance. The feedback activity, incidentally, may lead to modification of the plan.

The relationship of the cooperative system to action system reference groups may be sufficient to develop a broad support for the plan. On the other hand, it may be necessary to organize a campaign *effort* if the following conditions exist:

1. There are insufficient members in the cooperative system to link up with a range of organizations and interests.
2. There is an inability to generate broad interest among the action system for the plan.

3. There is a need to reduce the proportionate amount of opposition.

A campaign effort is a broad-based organization of individuals and groups recruited for the purpose of creating support for a plan proposal. Except for the top leadership in the campaign effort, rarely are the participants who are involved in the campaign itself involved in the development of the plan. Their function is to sell the plan as an issue, much as a fund-raising solicitor seeks pledges or a political volunteer solicits votes for a candidate. The campaigners, therefore, must themselves be sold on the plan proposal before they begin.

A successful campaign effort follows four principles. The first is that the top leadership in the campaign must be able to recruit other community and group leaders. Secondly, the campaign organization is established on a "straight-line" basis. A chairperson is selected, who in turn recruits division chairpeople, who in turn, recruit other persons to solicit organizational support for the plan. How many individuals are needed or whether further sectioning of the campaign organization is necessary depends on how large an effort is needed. One rule of thumb is that an individual should not be responsible for more than seven to nine other individuals.

Thirdly, the organizational framework should cut across functional rather than geographical lines. Unlike fund raising or political organizing, soliciting of individual support is not necessarily desired. The aim is to seek support from organizations and groups. Figure 10–6 is a sample organization chart for a campaign effort in planning.

The aim of the individual recruiters is to seek direct organizational support. They solicit testimonials, letters of support, and make speeches at organizational meetings. Incidentally, and equally important, publicity—news releases, for example—is used to back up the work of the recruiters.

The fourth principle is to establish and follow a time schedule for the campaign effort. The time schedule provides an

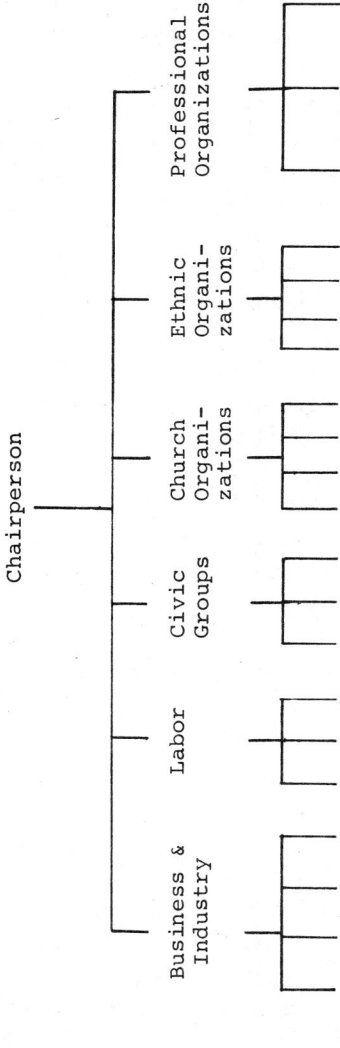

Figure 10–6 Sample campaign organization chart.

orderly direction for the campaign effort. Further, it points out each step necessary until the completion of the campaign. Consequently, the time schedule is helpful in evolving the campaign plan.

The time schedule is drawn up in reverse, from the last date of an activity to the first. *Example:* The deadline date for recruiting civic organization support is September 30. Training of recruiters for civic organizations should be held by September 20. Before such recruiters can be trained, they need to be recruited; the deadline date, consequently, for recruiting civic organization recruiters is September 12, and so forth.

Another condition for the effectiveness of the campaign strategy is the need to generate publicity. Publicity is a means for setting the agenda for planning. It does not necessarily influence people to act, but it does create an awareness of a plan or issue. It puts, in other words, the plan in front of the community.

Moreover, publicity acts as a support for planning participants. It maintains momentum and acts as an inducement for their efforts. It creates a feeling that they are engaged in an important activity.

Phase in Planning Diagram in Which Strategy Is Initiated

The campaign strategy, as a general rule, is used at the outset of the planning process. The intention of the strategy is to generate momentum and enthusiasm for the acceptance of the plan, and win adherence to the cause. Widespread communication is needed at each phase of the planning process. At the goal-setting phase, for example, it is desirable to publicize the planning goals through meetings with organizations and groups. Members of the cooperative system meet with organizations to secure their acceptance of the goals. This is done at successive phases. Publicity is also used to explain the objectives and progress of the plan.

When it is necessary to organize a campaign effort, however, the phasing is different. A campaign effort is initiated only at the plan acceptance phase, because of the difficulty in maintaining a campaign organization over a long period of time. The plan as developed is viewed as an issue. The campaign effort is designed to seek acceptance of the plan as developed.

The explanation of further strategies of decision-making will be contained in the next chapter. A summary of the strategies is in Chapter 11.

NOTES

1. At this point, a distinction should be made between a plan and an issue or issue proposal. We have implicitly defined a plan as a product of study and identifying solutions to a problem. In that respect, it is a rational process of problem solving.

    An issue or issue proposal is a statement of what an individual or group desires. It may or may not be preceded by any planning whatsoever. Fluoridization of water, an increased budget appropriation, or a policy modification are examples of issues. This is not to say that any of these issues could not be preceded by study or analysis. The point is that they need not be.

    We will use the term "plan" throughout the explanation of decision-making strategies. The reader should keep in mind that there is a distinction between plan and issue. Moreover, the reader should also recognize that certain strategies are more appropriate for issue resolution than plan resolution. This will be explained later.

2. Kurt Lewin, *Field Theory in Social Sciences.* (New York: Harper & Brothers, 1951), pp. 202–212.

3. Ronald Lippitt, et al., *The Dynamics of Planned Change,* (New York: Harcourt, Brace, 1958), pp. 86–88.

4. Rejection has been ruled out as a decision-making mode. Rejection is the absence of acceptance, and our interest is in describing ways in which decisions become accepted, not rejected.

5. Roland L. Warren, *Social Change and Human Purpose,* (Chicago: Rand McNally, 1977), pp. 126–129.

6. Ibid., p. 127. Warren also includes an intermediate term, *issue difference,* but inclusion of the issue difference situation is not necessary for the purposes here.

7. A third issue dissensus related strategy is sometimes proposed. That is the strategy of *rebellion.* Certainly rebellion is an organized means for bringing about acceptance of a decision. It is, however, not a strategy that fits the conception of planning outlined in this book.

   The strategy of rebellion is designed to bring about the radical restructuring of institutions. The case itself is always a moral one in the minds of the proponents. None of the issues is negotiable, because that would compromise the moral integrity of the case and the proponents. Any compromise is on technicalities, not the issues themselves. Those using a strategy of rebellion would, therefore, reject participation of any individuals or groups who did not subscribe wholeheartedly to the case and the aims of the proponents.

   The effectiveness of the strategy, moreover, depends on an articulate and charismatic leader who can demand allegiance and obedience to the cause of the group. Whether planners can assume such a role stance may be questionable. Whether they should assume such a role is another question. A role stance that eschews participation and requires obedience contradicts the theme of this book.

8. Joseph Luft, *Group Processes,* (Palo Alto, Calif.: National Press Books, 2nd Ed. 1970), pp. 11–20.

9. Michael S. Olmstead, *The Small Group,* (New York: Random House, 1959), pp. 69–70.

10. The reader should be familiar with Roland Warren's explanation of the campaign strategy of social change which serves as a basis for our campaign strategy of decision-making. Warren, op. cit., pp. 133–137.

Chapter 11

THE DECISION PHASE OF PLANNING: PART II

STRATEGY OF POWER

Power, as we defined it earlier, is the ability to control an actor who has authority over assenting to or withholding action requisite to the adoption of a proposal.[1] Individuals are capable of attaining power through the control of wealth or control of institutions; access to information or legitimated authority; or control over roles, past actions, or friendship patterns. Whether it is possible or desirable to exercise power to influence decisions in all instances is questionable. Nonetheless, it is a means for achieving acceptance of a decision, or if used in conjunction with other strategies, a means to influence decisions.

Quite simply, the power strategy is defined as achieving acceptance of a decision by virtue of controlling or applying a sanction (positive or negative) to someone (change target) who has control or authority over an action necessary for the adoption of a proposal. The power strategy presumes that the change target is an external decision center. Rarely is the change target involved in the process of arriving at the decision. If so, it is primarily for symbolic reasons—to give the outward appearance that the planning entity is "representative"; or to give a sense of participation to the change target.

Technology

The technology of the power strategy depends on the ability and willingness to use sanctions. The technology is related in many ways to learning theory. The exercise of power involves a complex system of rewards and punishments. A decision is influenced either in response to a favor or the anticipation of a favor; or it is influenced in order to avoid painful consequences—the exercise of a coercive technique.[2]

The techniques of the strategy are pressure or salesmanship. The latter is preferred. The power or influence figures attempt to "sell" or use their own status to pursuade to agree to a decision.

The use of pressure, on the other hand, is too expensive. Power, as Banfield has noted is like capital. If it is to be used, it should be used for investment purposes, to increase the stock of capital. In community planning activities, actors with power tend to be reluctant to use pressure. Convincing a decision center to agree to a decision for the good of the community, or for the good of the organization, or for his or her own good is preferred. Nonetheless, pressure, indeed even bribes, are not excluded as techniques of the strategy. They are employed, however, when the stakes are high or there is likely to be self-interest gain.

Conditions for Effectiveness

There are three conditions that govern the effectiveness of the strategy. One is the willingness of the power holder to exert the required influence. If there is little to be gained, or no return from exercising the influence, it is unlikely to be used.

Planning activities, nonetheless, are highly potential sources of accruing status and thereby influence. The potential success of a planning project itself can be used as a technique for inducing a community or organizational leader to exercise influence. Yet the influence used cannot be at the expense of other influence or statuses. Business executives, for example, cannot afford to engage in activities, however successful, that may alienate customers or clients.

The nature of the planning proposal and the nature of the decision, therefore, influence an individual's willingness or nonwillingness to use his or her stock of power.

The second condition of the strategy is the willingness of the change target to respond to the powerholder's pressure. On the one hand, the willingness may be related to the change target's hierarchical position in relation to the powerholder and further may be required to obey the demand of the powerholder.

Within an organizational system this may apply. In community planning activities, the example is less applicable. Individuals may be scaled hierarchically according to status or position but rarely are ordered to agree to a decision.

What is a more likely example is that the change target responds to a "favor." A favor may be owed and the powerholder may be calling in the debt. In this instance, however, the powerholder recognizes that influence capital is being used up.

On the other hand, the change target may be willing to respond to the powerholder even though he or she may be able to resist the pressure. This willingness is in response to any one of three factors. One is to increase the stock of the change target's own capital or power. Another is a quid pro quo, one favor in exchange for another. And a third (unfortunately) may be in response to a bribe.

In some instances, the strategy of power may result in trade-offs and compromise. Despite the pressure that may be exerted, the change target may insist on negotiating features of the plan. The strategy, consequently, is not limited to situations of consensus and agreement. It can be employed, and frequently is, when there is little likelihood of agreement. The intention is to "force" agreement. The strategy, therefore, is related to either consensus *or* dissensus conditions.

Phase in Planning Diagram at Which Strategy Is Initiated

The power strategy is executed almost entirely at the acceptance phase in the planning process. The powerholders (community elites, legislative elites, organizational elites) agree on a decision and at the acceptance phase pressure specific change targets to accept the decision. During early planning phases, the powerholder may engage in informal contracts to determine a sense of how likely it will be for the potential decision to be accepted. This is a sensing technique, and formal attempts to secure acceptance are delayed until the decision is finally arrived at.

DECISION-MAKING STRATEGIES RELATED TO COMPROMISE

Compromise arises when there is a lack of consensus on how to reach a decision. The proposed decision may be unacceptable in whole or in part. An agreement may be made to seek a mutually acceptable decision through modifications of the proposed decision. This agreement to compromise may be made willingly or by force and threat.

Compromise exists, too, when the decision center modifies its position rather than modify the proposed decision. This occurs more commonly when force is used. The decision center is forced to accept the decision of plan.

In planning there are two strategies related to the compromise form of decision-making: bargaining and conflict.

Strategy of Bargaining

Bargaining is the process used in negotiating an agreement between two or more parties. As defined here, it is a deliberate rather than an accidental strategy in which two or more parties agree to negotiate differences and thereby arrive at a mutually satisfactory agreement.

In the bargaining strategy, the change target is generally external to the proposers of the plan. The proposers of the plan are the change agents. In some instances, representatives of some of the change target may be involved in the plan development. The target relationship to the change agent is mixed, therefore, but primarily the target is external.

Technology

There are three conditions for the effectiveness of the strategy. The first is a group of individuals must be firmly committed to the objectives of the plan. This is a critical condition because division among individuals supporting the plan weakens the ability to negotiate.

Similar to the collaborative strategy, field theory techniques are used to assess and develop consensus and unanimity. In addition, however, it is also necessary to use more direct techniques to secure commitment. Actual declarations of support, including votes, need to be taken periodically. The plan supporters, in other words, make contractual agreements with one another.

A second condition is the negotiating skill itself. Frequently, in community planning activities, bargaining is a result rather than a strategy for securing acceptance of a decision. The process tends to be haphazard and a conclusion emerges after a series of random trade-offs.

A more deliberate method of negotiation used in the context of bargaining is suggested here. The bargain, that which is agreed upon, arises out of purposeful negotiation. For negotiation to be successful, the following factors are necessary:

Prior to the Negotiation Process

1. A single person must be selected to be the negotiator for the negotiating team. He or she must be both a respected leader for the constituency of the plan proposers and be able to articulate the issues.
2. The negotiating team, that group selected by the constituency, should have a clear understanding of the issues that are negotiable. Certainly the total plan is not negotiable. But elements of it are. Before the negotiation begins, therefore, the negotiable elements need to be identified. It is not an uncommon practice, incidentally, to add to a plan or proposal issues that can be used as negotiable trade-offs. There is, however, a "bottom line" beyond which the plan or issue would be compromised by further negotiations.
3. Careful preparation is critical to the success of negotiations. The negotiating team should work together, including rehearsals, in order to be fully prepared for the negotiation. Under no circumstances should the team overestimate itself or the jurisdiction of its case.

During Negotiation

1. Discussions should begin around areas of common agreement. By avoiding controversy at the outset, it is easier to reach favorable decisions on the different issues.
2. All-or-nothing decisions should be avoided if possible. An attempt should be made to reach decisions through the selection of alternatives.
3. Allow the other party to save face. Humiliating an antagonist may be personally satisfying, but it can create an insurmountable obstacle to reaching decisions.
4. Keep the negotiations focused on the plan. In this respect, support points by facts. The plan itself should be the major premise for bargaining.

A third factor necessary for the effectiveness of the strategy is to create conditions that can lead to negotiation. Negotiation presupposes that an organization has the capacity or "issue threat" to bring another organization or decision center to the bargaining table. In the union-management field, the trade union uses the threat of strike to initiate bargaining. In the community planning field, of course, this is not possible. Yet there are issue threats in community planning that can lead to bargaining.

One is a legislative mandate. An organization with positional legitimacy in a specific field can enjoin others who are bound within that field to bargain. Area-wide health planning agencies, for example, can enforce health decision centers to bargain on health issues. The agency uses its mandate as the threat.

A second kind of issue threat is the influence a planning group or organization may have over resources. Community elites can use their influence to insist on negotiation. An organization with a large constituency can use the membership base as a threat to initiate bargaining. The membership base is seen as a political lobbying or voting force.

A third issue threat is the threatened use of turmoil. To avoid "problems," decision centers can be brought to bargaining. The threat, however, has to be real and the organization employing it must be viewed as one capable of carrying out the threat.

Phase in Planning Diagram at which Strategy Is Initiated

Strategy of bargaining is initiated at the plan acceptance phase. The plan proposers often use many of the publicity techniques of the campaign strategy to announce planning goals and objectives. This is used to prepare the conditions for bargaining. Decision centers should be fully aware that a plan is in process. In this way, the negotiation process becomes a technique in and of itself.

Strategy of Conflict

Conflict is a strategy of decision-making best described by its techniques than by anything else. To be fully correct, it is not a decision-making strategy, but a tactic to achieve bargaining. Yet conflict has also been recognized as a strategy of social protest. Gamson, for example, finds that it has been a highly successful strategy for achieving acceptance of a plan or issue.[3]

The conflict strategy accepts the premise of the traditional community power theorists; that power in a community is hierarchical and that decisions reflect the interests of dominant groups. The strategy suggests, however, that another source of power or influence is an organized and committed constituency. By confronting decision centers with a large committed constituency, it is assumed that a plan can be accepted or brought to negotiation by force.

Even though the assumptions about community power may be incorrect or oversimplified (see Chapter 1), a strategy using conflict as a means of achieving plan acceptance should not be dismissed. The strategy has the ability to obtain accommodations from decision centers both from its inherent strength of members and its choice of tactics: demonstrating, distributing leaflets, boycotting, and picketing, among other common weapons.

When describing the collaborative strategy, it was explained that the strategy assumes that the change target is always involved in the planning process, and that the involvement itself is the medium through which the plan becomes accepted; the exact opposite holds for the conflict strategy. The target is external to the planning group and is *never* involved in the planning process. Indeed the more the change target is perceived as an external antagonist to the group proposing the plan, the more a beneficial effect this may have in creating group cohesion and commitment.

It should be pointed out that the agitation and disruption techniques used in the conflict strategy are not designed to engender violence. Violence may result, but it is not an intention of the group employing the strategy.

Technology

The basic technology of the conflict strategy is related to learning theory. The objective is to weaken the behavior of specific identifiable decison centers. Rather than use established or positive reinforcement techniques, negative reinforcers are primarily used. Picketing and disruption are negative reinforcement techniques.[4] The pickets and disrupters act as mediators in applying the negative reinforcement. If the decision center agrees to consider negotiation, then the negative reinforcement is no longer needed, or in B. F. Skinner's words, "the aversive stimuli is removed."[5]

Once the agreement to bargain is established, a second technology negotiation, as described above, becomes necessary.

Conditions for Effectiveness

In some respects, the conflict strategy is similar to the campaign strategy. The difference often is in character rather than in substance. Like the campaign strategy, a primary condition for the effectiveness of the conflict strategy is the need for a strongly committed planning group or cooperative system. The commitment has to be more intense than the campaign strategy because, as it shall be seen, the consequences are more significant.

The success of the conflict strategy also requires a broad base constituency of support. Where the campaign strategy, however, focuses on recruiting a variety of organizational and group support, the conflict strategy recruits individual support. The constituency of the conflict strategy is made up of a group who share a common interest, who believe they are—or actually are—the victims of some inequity and are unable to remedy the inequity through customary institutional channels. Examples may be low income housing tenants, welfare recipients, students, and ethnic groups.

The recruitment techniques are person-to-person. The intention is to develop a broad membership base from among the defined constituency. In some instances, dues may be charged to support the organizing effort and to develop membership identification with the organization.

Where it may be necessary (for financial reasons or even to create a much broader base of membership) to recruit members from outside the defined constituency, a separate classification is necessary. Such membership classifications are termed "friends" or "associates." Because of the anomalous relationship, it is difficult to retain associate member classifications for more than a year or two, unless considerable effort is devoted to organizing associate memberships. One consequence, however, is that the more effort put into the organizing of associate members, the more the associate members may become defining agents of the organization using the conflict strategy.

A second condition of the strategy is the necessity for people to engage in disruptive activities. Few individuals are willing to participate in picketing or demonstrations. They are traumatic activities often subjecting the participant to ridicule, and, conceivably, physical harm. There is, therefore, a fear and reluctance to participate in protest activities.

To overcome the fear and reluctance, rehearsal and role playing exercises are useful and necessary techniques. The intention is to develop confidence in carrying out the techniques of conflict. Practice can develop confidence. It is necessary, then, to simulate conflict by using role playing conflict techniques before they are carried out in practice.

A third condition is publicity. Much like the campaign strategy, the conflict strategy is used to raise the plan proposal to a high priority in the community or organization's decision level. Without publicity, the techniques of conflict go unnoticed, and the change target toward which the conflict is directed can ignore the tactics and the plan proposal.

A final condition is the necessity to follow through on negotiations once the change target agrees to bargaining. The skills and techniques previously outlined under the bargaining strategy apply here.

The importance of skillful use of negotiating techniques, however, cannot be overemphasized. The conflict strategy is a means for initiating and bringing about change, but *not* a means for sustaining change once it occurs. For the change to be sustained it needs to be institutionalized. Negotiation is the means for institutionalizing the change.

Phase in Planning Diagram at Which Strategy Is Initiated

Conflict strategy is executed during the acceptance phase of the planning process. In fact, it is only executed in the acceptance phase. The plan is developed, converted to an issue, and the strategy invoked with surprise and drama. The last serves as a technique for publicizing the issue.

STRATEGY CONSEQUENCES

The effectiveness of a particular strategy of decision-making depends on specific conditions and assumptions peculiar to the strategy itself. Moreover, each strategy has its own advantages and disadvantages. The selection of a particular strategy, therefore, will depend on two conditions. One is its organizational fit; that is, it needs to be consistent with the organization's mandate, as well as the organization's capacity to use the strategy. The second is the consequences of the strategy; whether the consequences are to be desired or avoided.

The organizational requirements of the *collaborative strategy* are minimal. It lends itself to use by most planning organizations. It does, however, achieve limited objectives and is inconsistent in organizations seeking broad institutional changes. It would, for example, be inappropriately used by conflict oriented organizations.

The overriding demand is the ability of the organization to recruit the required decision centers as participants in the planning process. One further organizational requirement is the need for staff who have skills in planning and human change dynamics.

A primary consequence of the collaborative strategy is the way in which the decisions are made. Basically it is antithetical to the rational calculus approach of traditional planning. It shifts the focus from a search for rational means for achieving predetermined goals to an actual search for common goals themselves. The emphasis is upon means, therefore, rather than ends; towards developing conditions that enable the participants to arrive at a commonly agreed on decision rather than a commitment to planning as a method of problem solving.

There is, consequently, a likelihood that the least satisfactory of decisions will be made. Within the group system trade-offs can be frequent. The group sacrifices one decision in the hope that certain members will agree to another decision, which can contribute to a condition where no one is satisfied.

The campaign strategy has the fewest organizational limitations. It can be used by any organization. It does require, however, considerable organizational skill and time. For organizations with limited staff, this may be an obstacle.

There are, likewise, few if any consequences contrary to planning organization objectives. There is the likelihood that an organization that skillfully uses the campaign strategy may impose its values on the community. But all organizations endeavor to achieve this aim. And that is the essence of the interest group theory of decision-making.

The ability to offer status incentives is the primary organizational requirement of the *power strategy* of decision-making. Community elites are in and of themselves status producing individuals. Their membership enhances the status of an organization. At the same time, their own prestige is enhanced by associating with the high status organizational members. It becomes necessary, therefore, to restrict membership to elites in decision-making. Other individuals may be recruited and may be necessary for the carrying out of activities of the organization. In this case, it is necessary to create two levels of membership; not publicly stated, of course.

The consequence of the power strategy is that decisions reflect the interests and views of the elites. Their views become the definer of organization policy and plans.

The organization requirements of the *bargaining strategy* are primarily administrative. Once the decision is made to use bargaining as a strategy, management techniques become the dominant operational procedure. The planning team takes on the responsibility of negotiation. Planning activities cease until the negotiation is worked out.

The consequence of using the bargaining strategy is that a second party or other parties become defining agents of the planning decision. Bargaining obviously implies compromise. And the compromise is a resultant, not a decision, dictated by all parties involved in the bargaining process. The strategy, therefore, limits the decision-making influence of the planning organization.

The organizational consequences of the *conflict strategy* are related to recruitment of participants. The techniques used in the strategy limit recruitment. Business executives and professional people, for example, will refuse to participate in an activity that appears likely to have harmful effects on their business or ability to serve clients.

The conflict strategy works best for organizations committed to a cause rather than to specific issues or services. (See Chapter 4.)

PLANNING DIAGRAM ACTIVITIES RELATED TO CHAPTER

As explained in the previous chapter, it is difficult—if possible at all—to pinpoint the time at which a planning outcome becomes accepted. Acceptance can be a process that starts at the beginning of a planning activity and occurs simultaneously with the conclusion of a plan. Or it can occur at any time after the development of a plan as a consequence of a campaign for acceptance of the plan. The planning diagram, therefore, suggests events and activities that can occur at any point in the process of planning, up until implementation.

The singularly critical event in the decision-making phase is conducting a diganostic assessment (Event 41). This assessment may be an extension of the preplanning diagnostic assessment (Event 2). It is, nonetheless, an important step in planning. It suggests the appropriate decision-making strategies (Event 42), and, as well, what roles the cooperative and action systems (Events 43 and 44) will have in the decision-making phase.

Summary

In the past two chapters, the basic strategies of achieving acceptance of planning decisions have been described. The selection of any decision-making strategy depends first on a diagnostic assessment of acceptance, and secondly, the organizational capacity to utilize a particular strategy.

Figure 11–1 is a composite of the decision-making strategies explained in these chapters.

STRATEGY	DESCRIPTION	RELATIONSHIP OF CHANGE TARGET TO PLANNING GROUP	TECHNOLOGY OF CHANGE	CONDITIONS FOR EFFECTIVENESS	TECHNIQUES	PLANNING PHASE AT WHICH STRATEGY IS INITIATED
Collaborative	Agreement reached through discussion and joint problem solving	Internal	Small group theory (Lewin)	• Decision centers represented • Willingness to change is present • Communications • Group identity	• Recruitment and selection • Diagnostic assessments • Meetings, reports, self study • Status, publicity	At outset only
Campaign	Agreement reached through organization, publicity, involvement, and persuasion	Some internal Some external	Group theory Publicity Organizing	• Planning group committed to objectives • Capacity to develop broadbased organization • Need to generate publicity issue can be acceptable to community	• Group method • Formal cooptation • Organization and coalition • Public relations	At various stages
Power and/or Influence	Agreement reached through persuasion and/or pressure	External, but some can be coopted as internal	Group cohesion Pressure Salesmanship	• Ideological acceptance of strategy by community • Willingness to exert influence • Inability or willingness of targets to accept	• Inducements • Trade-offs	At final acceptance phase... informal communication can begin at earlier stages

Figure 11-1 Summary of decision-making strategies.

Bargaining	Compromise reached through negotiation and bargaining	Primarily external—may be some decision targets involved	Bargaining and negotiation	• Committed group • Skill at negotiation • Ability to bring decision center to bargaining table	• Organizing • Bargaining technology • Formal legitimacy or threat	At final acceptance stage
Conflict	Compromise reached through disruption to bargaining	External only	Disruption Bargaining	• Committed group • Large constituency • Ability and willingness to disrupt • Follow through on negotiation	• External enemy • Organizing • Creating felt need • Role playing	At final acceptance stage only

Figure 11-1 (continued).

NOTES

1. See Chapter 1 for definitions of requisite actors and how they should be identified.
2. An explanation of power-coercive strategies for creating change can be found in Robert Chin and Kenneth D. Benne, "General Strategies for Effecting Changes in Human Systems," Warren G. Bennis, et al., *The Planning of Change* (New York: Holt, Rinehart, and Winston, 3rd ed., 1976), pp. 22–45.
3. William Gamson, *The Strategy of Social Protest,* (Homewood, Illinois: Dorsey Press, 1975).
4. Morton L. Arkava, *Behavior Modification: A Procedural Guide for Social Workers,* (Missoula: Department of Social Work, University of Montana, 1974), pp. 14–15 and 54–59.
5. B. F. Skinner, *Beyond Freedom and Dignity,* (New York: Knopf, 1971), pp. 28–32.

Chapter 12

INTRODUCING AND CARRYING OUT THE PLAN: FINAL DESIGN AND PLAN CUT-OVER PHASES

We have identified six phases in the planning process. For purposes of emphasis it is possible to reduce these phases to three discrete stages; namely: *developing* the plan, achieving *acceptance* of the plan, and *implementing* the plan. It is to this final stage, implementing, or carrying out, the plan, that we now turn.

There are two phases in the implementation stage of planning. One, the "final design phase," is the point at which the plan as accepted is introduced. Responsibilities are assigned, resource allocations are made, and the plan is put into practice.

A second phase, "plan cut-over phase," is composed of monitoring activities. It is during this phase, too, after any minor adjustments are made, that steps are taken to see that the plan becomes institutionalized.

FACTORS INFLUENCING IMPLEMENTING THE PLAN

The effectiveness, and thereby, the success of a plan is not achieved merely because it has been accepted and sanctioned by a decision center. A plan is only successful if it is carried out as designed. This is not to suggest that there needs to be rigid adherence to all program elements of a plan. Indeed plan formulation and implementation are interdependent processes. How a plan is to be implemented will influence its design, and equally important the design will influence the way a plan can be implemented.[1] What is meant, however, is that once a plan has been accepted, "reasonable" efforts are carried out to implement all the plan's program elements. If any modifications are made, they are made to accommodate the objectives of the plan to changing or unforeseen conditions.

If there are substantial changes to be made, particularly if they can compromise the objectives of the plan, they should not be made without approval of the decision center that accepted the plan *and* the cooperative system.

It should be pointed out here that the cooperative system is not discharged once a plan is accepted. It remains in existence until the completion of the cut-over phase. The cooperative system provides an important change function during the implementation of the plan. It is a watchdog over the implementation activities. If necessary, it can serve also as an advocacy group for implementing the plan.

The implementation of a plan is an integral part of the *social change* process of planning. Social change, as was noted in Chapter 5, involves three stages, beginning with an awareness of the need and desire for change; through the actual change itself, which may involve trial and evaluation; to the final adoption of stabilization of the change effort. During the adoption stage, the objective is to devise means for making the change permanent. If techniques for making the change permanent are not provided, individuals will revert to preexisting levels of attitude and behavior.

Resistance to Implementation

Resistance to change during the implementation phase tends to be different in character than resistance during the acceptance phase of planning. The resistance is subtle and takes the form of *passive aggression*. The resisters will manifestly agree with the plan, primarily because they or a decision center with authority over their actions has accepted the decision. Quietly, however, they will refuse to carry out the program elements. The excuse may be that the plan does not work. Indeed, in some instances the plan may actually be sabotaged, making the resisters' behavior a self-fulfilling prophecy.

It also must be recognized that resistance to implementing a plan may occur simply because of ignorance. The plan has been accepted but not correctly communicated to those responsible for carrying it out. An ambiguous or incorrectly communicated plan is a form of resistance to a plan's implementation, but the source of the resistance is the plan, not those charged with the responsibility of carrying it out.

Facilitating Implementation

Many of the factors that contribute to a plan's being accepted by a decision center are also factors that facilitate its being implemented by those responsible for carrying it out. These factors include the following:

1. The plan is recognized by those who are to carry it out as a response to a *real need*. No attempt should be made to introduce the plan unless an assessment is made of this awareness. (See below.) If there is a lack of awareness of the need, then a program for spreading an awareness of the need is a necessary first step.
2. The planning group is recognized as having *legitimacy*. Resistance is often encountered in carrying out a plan if those responsible for carrying it out do not trust or believe the planning proposal group. Within organizations the planning group (planner and cooperative system) must seek to legitimate itself with those responsible for carrying out the plan.

3. The plan is *specific* to the problem it is proposed to solve. Not only must a plan be recognized as responding to a need, but also the program elements that are devised are understood as specific solutions. The greater the specificity of the plan elements, the easier they are to implement.
4. The plan has a *widespread base of support.* Those responsible for carrying out the plan should see that the plan itself has support from a number of constituencies. This is a primary function of the cooperative system and the accepting decision center.
5. The plan is capable of being *understood.* A plan not understood is difficult at best to implement. The plan should be presented in a way that it is understandable.
6. The plan is *technically* accurate. The accuracy of a plan, of course, is an essential component for its successful implementation. Often, however, the accuracy of the plan may have to be demonstrated to those responsible for carrying out the plan. This can take the form of pretesting certain program elements before the plan is formally introduced. During the pretesting, representatives of the implementing group can be involved. This incidentally assists in making the plan persuasive in nature and eases its implementation.

OBSTACLES TO IMPLEMENTATION

Although the above factors are those that improve the capability of implementing a plan, there are some common obstacles that frustrate the implementation of a plan. The planner should be familiar with these obstacles.

Insufficient Resources

Most plans require resources, personnel or material, to carry them out. If the resources are not available for carrying out a plan, it can be for one or two reasons. There never were enough resources to carry out the plan, or once the plan was accepted resources suddenly became unavailable. If the reason is that there never were enough resources, then the plan (can also read planner) was at fault. Resource determination for carrying out a plan should be made in the plan element phases. (See Chapter 9.)

If, however, the necessary resources become suddenly unavailable it is difficult to hold anyone at fault. Unexpected and unforeseen events can occur in any situation. A crisis, for example, can occur in one sector of a community, organization, or economy, that can drain resources that otherwise could have been used for the carrying out of the plan. The only solution is to hold the plan in abeyance until resources become available.

Lack of Effective Demand

Some plans depend on consumers for their implementation. Urban renewal planning is one example. Social service delivery planning is another.

In the case of urban renewal, the evidence regarding the importance of effective demand is startling. In the mid-1950s, the urban renewal objective was redevelopment of slums, primarily in the central business districts. The federal government underwrote a portion of the costs, which made the resale of the land and rebuilding of the slums highly successful.

The Golden Triangle in Pittsburgh, the Archway in St. Louis, and Government Center in Boston are visual symbols that slum clearance and rebuilding worked. Flushed with such success, renewal agencies expected the process to repeat itself elsewhere. Once the concept of redevelopment was extended outside the central business districts of large cities, however, redevelopment planning became more difficult. One reason was that the land was not as attractive and thus demand—effective demand—was not forthcoming.

Similar problems, although not so dramatic, occur in social service delivery planning. Social service programs are designed and consumer demand is found either wanting or critical.

One criticism has been that social service consumers are not represented in the planning process. This is a fair criticism but not an entirely warranted one. A half dozen or so consumers represented on a planning project do not represent the views of all consumers. Statistically, in fact, they represent only their own views. Thus they are not a reliable source of effective demand.

The issue with both redevelopment planning and social service delivery planning is insufficient analysis of consumer demand. Plans that depend on effective demand should be market tested. Such testing is usually done during the plan element phases. The function of testing is to determine the feasibility of the program. At that point changes in program elements can be made to fit the effective demand principle.

Certainly it is true that the best tested product may fail. Despite the overwhelmingly favorable market analysis of the Edsel, for example, it did not sell. Nonetheless, this has not deterred manufacturers from test-marketing products.

Changed Decision Center

The acceptance of a plan depends on specific decision centers. If they change, this may place the implementation of the plan in jeopardy. This occurs, frequently, where there is little support for the plan beyond the original decision center. If such is the case, the only recourse is to begin anew the campaign to gain acceptance of the plan with the new decision center.

False Assumption of the Decision Environment

This is an interesting reason why a plan does not get implemented. It happens frequently, and often people are unaware that the plan's objectives are not being realized. A myth is created and the myth becomes reality.

What occurs is that a plan is constructed with reasonable objectives, reasonable expectation, and with considerable open and acknowledged support, yet it fails to be implemented. Ironically, and unknowingly, those who support the plan may act to frustrate its implementation. The proposed plan operates on one set of assumptions of how decisions are made while in reality the decision-making process operates on another, usually latent, set of assumptions. An example may help to explain this conundrum.

One observation made about the delivery of social services in this country is that there is a disparity between services funded and service needs. In relation to the total social welfare needs some services are overfunded, while others are scarcely funded. Often, the solution to the problem is to conduct a needs assessment planning study with the objective of establishing a priority ranking of needs. The priority ranking of services according to needs is to be used as a basis for the allocation of funds.

It is a logical basis for the allocation of scarce funds. Frequently, however, the priority plan fails—for two reasons:

First, services funded in one year tend to get funded in the next year. There is, in other words, rarely a drop-off of services once started. This is true both in the public and the voluntary social services field. Nixon's unsuccessful attempt to dismantle the poverty program is one example. The other example is the refusal of the March of Dimes organization to disband once a cure for polio was discovered.

Any program once initiated develops a constituency of its own. The constituent members, paid and volunteer, receive satisfactions from the participation in the organization. To maintain the satisfactions, they will both resist the dissolution of the organization and protect its status and influence.[2]

Secondly, the overall appropriations for social services remain relatively unchanged from year to year. Increases in allocations barely, if at all, keep up with inflationary costs. Whatever increases that might become available are eaten up in salary raises. From a practical standpoint, therefore, there are no additional funds available to implement a priority allocation plan.[3]

Priority plans, however rational they appear to be, often run into difficulty. They tend to be incompatible with the way in which allocation decisions are made.

The implementation capability of a plan, consequently, depends on the relationship between the decision-making method proposed in a plan and the way in which decisions are actually made. If the plan operates on one set of assumptions about how decisions are made and the decision-making processes are operating on another set of assumptions, the plan cannot be implemented. The only recourse is to change one or the other set of assumptions.

Plan Depends on "Wished-for" Behavior

Probably the most common reason for the failure to implement a plan is the belief that it will be carried out. This is termed "wished-for" behavior, and a plan that depends on such behavior rarely if ever succeeds.[4] This obstacle to implementation was alluded to at the outset of the chapter and refers to the caveat that a plan will not necessarily be implemented merely because it has been accepted.

Incidentally, there is a distinction between this and the previous obstacle to implementation. The assumption behind the previous obstacle is that the plan is at fault and thus is incapable of being implemented. A plan, however, that depends on wished-for behavior is capable of being implemented. The fact that the plan is not implemented is not a fault of the plan, but a fault of the procedures or lack of procedures used for changing wished-for behaviors into coordinated behaviors for carrying out the plan.

The primary objective of the final design phase of planning is to explain how wished-for behaviors, as described in the plan, can or will be carried out. It is the translation of a planning decision—agreed upon and accepted—into an administrative decision. The achievement of an administrative decision requires a set of procedures that in effect is a plan for implementing the administrative decision. The activities listed in the planning diagram in the final design and plan cut-over phases are designed to achieve that objective. *It is a plan for implementation.*

PROCEDURES IN THE FINAL DESIGN PHASE

Certainly, the most efficacious method for implementing a plan is through the involvement of those responsible for carrying out the plan. If the group developing the plan is also responsible for implementing, it is reasonably safe to assume that the plan will be carried out. Nonetheless, substantive procedures[5] will be needed to specify how the plan should be implemented, including such items as the specification of policy changes, the development of instructional manuals, or guides, and the allocation of functional responsibilities.

When, however, those responsible for carrying out the plan were not involved in developing or achieving acceptance of the plan, which is frequently the case, more detailed implementing procedures are necessary. Implementation is viewed as the initiation of a change process. Those responsible for carrying out the plan are defined as the target group of the change. The decision center that accepted the plan becomes the sanction for implementation, and, therefore, legitimate the change activity-implementation of the plan.

With the above conditions in mind, the first step in the final design phase is a diagnostic assessment of the target group. Similar to the preplanning and the decision-making diagnostic assessments, the objective is to gauge the willingness of the target group to accept the change, in this instance to carry out the plan. The assessment includes:

1. The target group's awareness of the need for the plan.
2. The target group's level of understanding of the plan.
3. The target group's attitude toward the proposers of the plan.
4. The target group's customary procedures that would have to be altered or changed as a result of the plan.

Once the assessment is completed, the next step is to organize for implementation. Operating under the assumption that those involved in a decision-making activity will tend to be committed to the decisions that they have devised, the preferred technique is to organize an implementation committee composed in whole or in part of the target group. The implementation committee uses collaborative and campaign strategies to win acceptance of the plan. (See Chapter 10 for descriptions of these strategies.)

The primary objective of the implementation committee is to devise procedures required for carrying out the plan. The plan is accepted as given. It is presumed to be a solution to a problem that has been endorsed and accepted. Any modification of the plan or its program elements, consequently, should receive prior approval from the accepting decision center and the planning cooperative system. It is implicitly assumed that approval has also been sought from the planning agency's formal policy constituency. This approval is obtained by the cooperative system, which periodically reports on the implementation progress to the formal policy constituency.

In securing implementation of the plan, the implementation committee is responsible for a number of activities. It must first overcome any resistance to the plan. In addition, it is responsible for the setting up of an implementation time schedule, the selection of training of personnel to carry out the plan, the devising of policy changes in relation to the plan's objectives, the establishment of guidelines and instructional manuals, and the overall supervision for the carrying out of the plan.

Once these activities are completed, the administrative sanctions are obtained and approval is given to carry out the plan. The next phase is a review process; that is, the monitoring of the plan as it moves into operation or practice.

Plan Cut-Over Phase

It is only after a plan is in operation for a period of time that the unworkable elements become identified. The objective, therefore, during the cut-over phase is to test the plan after it has been in use a reasonable period of time—six months to a year. If there are elements of the plan that are not working or have not been implemented, a determination has to be made to see whether this is the fault of the plan element itself. Modifications to the plan or a restudy of the implementation of the plan are appropriately made at this point.

Once the plan cut-over phase is completed, any necessary organization and institutional changes are made final at this point.

The plan is determined completed, and a report is submitted to the planning agency's formal policy constituency. If a cooperative system was involved in the planning, it is discharged at this point.

Planning Diagram Activities Related to Chapter

As explained in Chapter 9 consideration to implementation factors is given as early as the plan element phases (Events 38 and 39; identification of administrative and operational decision centers). These are preliminary events, the purpose of which is to gauge the readiness of specific individuals to implement the plan.

Except in a general way it is difficult to list all the events and activities for the implementation phase of planning. How extensive the implementation activity needs to be will depend on the diagnostic assessment conducted at the outset of the final design phase. This event (49) defines the scope of the implementation activities.

SUMMARY

The implementation of a plan requires two operations. One is introducing and carrying out the plan. To do so, however, requires a *plan* for implementation that is designed to ensure that the plan can and will be carried out.

The second operation is a review process that monitors the carrying out of the plan. The aim is to see that the program elements of a plan are being put into practice as designed.

NOTES

1. John Friedmann, "A Conceptual Model for the Analysis of Planning Behavior," *Administrative Science Quarterly,* Vol. 13, No. 2 (September 1967), pp. 240–243.
2. See David L. Sills, *The Volunteer,* (New York: Free Press, 1957), pp. 253–270.
3. There is also an explanation of this phenomenon on the national level. See Aaron Wildersky, *The Politics of the Budgetary Process,* (Boston: Little, Brown, 1964).
4. This is a term used by Herbert Simon. See Herbert A. Simon, *Administrative Behavior,* (New York: Macmillan, 1968), pp. 105–106.
5. Herbert Simon describes the problems of securing the acceptance of a plan from an administrative perspective. He views it as an element of coordination and makes a useful distinction between procedural and substantive coordination. Procedural coordination establishes the lines of authority and outlines the sphere of activity for organizational members. Substantive coordination specifies the content of work activities. Simon, op. cit., pp. 10, 110–153.

Chapter 13

THE ROLE OF THE PLANNER

The role of the planner is not a single or uniform one. It is varied, it is complex, and it is constantly changing. It is, moreover, defined and shaped in the process of interacting with others in designing and achieving common objectives. At one time skills in data collection, analysis, and design were the principal, if not exclusive, requirements of the planner's role. Now skills related to the social process component of planning are also required. Primarily these are the organizing and the political skills or what Bolan has termed the "social relations" role of the planner.[1]

Some reference was made to this facet of the planner's role in Chapter 2. The role was defined as including procedural and interactional skills. The procedural skill is related to function; that is, knowing how *to do* or *to carry out* the total range of functions required of planning. The interactional skill refers to the planner's ability *to engage* with others in carrying out a *collaborative* process of planning. In Chapter 8, qualities of the interactional skill were identified. These were diagnosis, working with groups, and empathetic analysis.

In this chapter the intention is to be more specific about the role of the planner. We are interested in two factors about the planner's role—what are the roles, and what are the influences that define planning roles? The former is sometimes referred to as the functional roles of the planner.[2] The latter is an interpretative characteristic of role. It is not enough to know what roles planners can be expected to perform, but it is also important to know what specific role is called for in a specific instance. This is the analytic factor of role.

Functional Roles

There are seven major functional roles of planning.

Planner As Analyst

This is the commonly recognized and basic role of the planner. It refers to the planner's function as an expert in the analysis and synthesis of data and phenomena.[3]

The analytical skills include the planner's ability to examine and look at a problem; to design data collection methods and strategies; and to identify consequences of various courses of action.

It includes, also, the program development requirements of planning—how to take data, for example, and use it operationally to define elements of a plan.

And equally important, the planner as analyst includes the creative skills of planning. Solutions are consequences of analysis. But they are also the consequence of imagination. To take the analysis and creatively apply it to solutions is an important function of planning, equally as important as data analysis.

An ancillary aspect of this role is the planner's analytical function in relation to a substantive field of practice. Planning is not carried on in a single community agency, but in a variety of specialized organizations. The organizations are related to a specific field of practice, such as health, poverty, transportation, social services, and housing among others. Planners working in such organizations tend to have specific knowledge about the substantive field of practice in addition to planning knowledge. Frequently this is referred to as a "state of the art" knowledge. A simple example is knowledge of grant and funding procedures in a particular field.

The analytic role in the substantive field of practice includes knowledge of the field itself along with skills in analyzing trends and issues in the field. It also includes an understanding of the common practices of the field. These are the folkways of the field, the customary way things are done.

Planner As Organizer

The function of organizing is twofold; one, to bring citizens and groups into the planning process; and, two, to develop a constituency of support for a plan. All planning requires political and organizing skills to some degree. The extent of organizing necessary will depend on the nature of the plan, the power of the client system, and the nature of the decision system.[4]

What is meant by organizing skills is a variety of activities designed to involve individuals in planning. It refers to the identification of various types of citizen leadership, the ability to develop recruitment programs for citizens, the development of citizen leadership, the creation of commitment to the planning activity, and to motivating individuals and groups to seek acceptance of planning objectives.

Another set of organizing skills includes committee management; that is, planning and executing different kinds of committee activities, from small group meetings to large community meetings. Included also is the role of diagnosing the dynamics of group meetings to facilitate the work of the group.

There is, too, a political aspect to the organizing role. This includes the ability to assess and utilize the decision-making process of organizations and communities. It includes skills in identifying centers of influence and control, the capacity to determine their effectiveness in influencing decisions, and the skill in concerting influence to achieve action.

Planner As Broker[5]

Frequently, planning involves interactions between and among organizations. Coalitions may be formed, or there may be competition between organizations for the right to plan and organize a program. The planner, therefore, may be required to act as an intermediary between organizations and groups, or indeed, even between groups within the same organization. The role is one of coordinating and integrating the varying desires of groups who have a stake in the outcomes of a plan.

The broker role requires an ability to mediate issues; to understand and use negotiating skills; to use techniques of persuasion and to bargain elements of a decision.

Planner As Advocate

Advocacy has been identified as both a traditional and an emerging role of the planner. In the former instance the planner acts as a reformer for planning and welfare issues.

Frederic Law Olmstead, Daniel Burnham, Jacob Riis, Jane Addams, and Robert deForest are examples of early reformers and activists.

In the latter instance, about which much was written in the 1960s, the planner acts as an advocate for a specific client group.[6] The client may be organized around its own needs—aged, poor, women; or, it may be organized around a specific issue—fair housing, environment, health. Organizing is a principle element of advocacy, because successful advocacy requires an organizational constituency. But the advocacy role implies that the planner, too, become involved directly in advocacy activities. In some instances and for certain types of "grass roots" organizations, the planner is the spokesman for the client.

As an advocate, the planner has to employ a wide variety of political skills—bargaining, persuading, convincing and influencing. It includes publicity skills as well as speaking, conducting meetings, and staging media events.

Planner As Enabler

A contrasting role to that of the advocate is the role of the enabler. Where the advocacy role calls for direct and active leadership, the enabler role calls for an indirect leadership. The intention is to act as a facilitator in guiding others to achieve their own objectives.[7]

It is important not to confuse this role with the early city planning conception of the technician role of the planner. In that role the emphasis is on the planner offering advice and guidance but leaving the ultimate decision-making to the client group or policymakers.[8] This is an element of the enabler role. But the enabler role has a further premise and that is that the planner focuses also on enabling the client system to develop its own leadership skills. In that light the planner may not at times even provide *suggested* answers or alternative answers. He or she may have questions that stimulate insight into answers. The emphasis, in other words, is on encouragement and support.

As an enabler the planner has to be skillful in diagnosis, able to work comfortably with a wide variety of different individuals and groups, and to be knowledgeable and skillful in the dynamics of committee work.

Planner As Educator

The planner has two roles in his or her capacity as an educator.

One is the role of educating society about the purpose and function of planning. This involves public speaking and the writing of articles and books about planning. It includes, too, the role of the planner as an educator for aspiring planners. This can include lecturing in high schools and universities. It can also include providing internship opportunities in planning organizations.

The second aspect of this role is the educational relationship between the planner and the client system. Both the planner and the client are involved in knowledge transactions. The planner shares analytic information, or what John Friedmann suggests is "processed knowledge" in the development of a plan. The client shares personal knowledge; that is, knowledge of his or her own and the community's practical experience.[9]

With the cooperative system, the sharing of the planner's analytical information is done at various events in the planning process. At the outset, it is frequently formalized and referred to as an orientation to the planning problem. (Note suggested Events 9 and 10 in the planning diagram.)

Planner As Publicist

Publicity plays an important part in planning. Prior to a planning activity, publicity creates an awareness of the planning problem in the community. Norton Long has suggested that because of the role of newspapers, publicity aids in placing an issue on the community or public agenda. As a chronicler of events in news columns and special features, the newspaper provides an organizing medium for community elites and provides them with information about things in general. In a sense, comments Long, the newspaper is a prime mover in setting the community agenda.[10]

Publicity is also an aid to the planning constituency. It maintains public interest in an issue as the planning process proceeds. It also serves to enhance the status and image of the planning constituency. In turn, this acts as a motivating and energizing force for the constituency.

Publicity skills include public speaking, preparing reports and brochures, and writing news releases and articles. In small agencies with limited staff, the planner may have to handle all publicity activities. In large agencies, specialized public relations or public information staff may be employed. All planners, however, should know the value and use of publicity techniques. Indeed, it is even worthwhile for planners to have some experience in writing news releases.

The foregoing are the most common roles planners can be expected to perform. There are others—administrator, researcher, grantsman, financial analyst, consultant, for example; but these tend to be specialized roles for particular activities.

It is important to state again that there is no single exclusive role of planning. There is a variety of roles that planners are expected to perform. Over the course of a planning episode a planner may exercise a half dozen different roles. Indeed, a planner may exercise more than one role simultaneously. The enabler, publicist, and educator roles, for example, may all be utilized at the same time.

What determines the use of a particular role, and how that determination affects the planner is related to the second aspect or analytical facet of the planner's role.

The Term Role

Role, as we intend now to use it, is a behavioral concept. It signifies what a person occupying a specific *position* actually does. The position, in other words, is a definer of the role. A role, however, is not acted out in isolation from others or without a context in relation to others. A role is performed in relation to how others expect the role should be performed. A further definer of the role is the individual himself or herself. Thus the individual expectations also influence how the role should be performed. What defines a role, therefore, is:

1. The expectations of the person occupying a position.
2. The expectations of others interacting with the position.
3. The position itself.[11]

Planning Expectation of Role

When an individual assumes a position in an organization, there is agreement about the generally accepted behavioral requirements for the position. There is a position or job description written or implied. A secretary, for example, is aware that the position requires typing, filing, taking dictation, and the like. There is, in other words, a normative expectation for the position.

Any position description, however, must allow for latitude. No description can adequately cover all conceivable expectations. Changing circumstances and time will cause different interpretations of the description.

The degree of latitude that can be allowed for interpreting a position description depends primarily on the nature and requirements of the organization. In a military organization, for example, the degree is quite limited and prescribed.

In professional organizations, on the other hand, the latitude or zone of accepted behavior for the role is generally extensive or wide.[12]

Planning organizations fall into the latter category. Position descriptions are rare, or if defined, defined in general terms because of necessity. Planning is a professional practice requiring individual judgment. It is also a practice involving art as well as science. As a consequence, the individual planner is a significant determinant of the planning role.

The planner's expectations of how the role should be performed is influenced primarily by two factors: one, previous experience and training, and two, the individual's personality.

Previous Experience and Training

One source of expectations for role performance is past experience. Individuals tend to rely on experiential behavior to guide them in understanding how they should be expected to perform. Where there is little nominal guidance for performance, such as in much of human services planning, experiential behavior tends to be a major guide.

Training, professional training in particular, has a marked influence. One function of professional training is to socialize the individual into the professional role.

In a changing practice environment, this may and often does produce strain. This was evident in city planning and social work in the 1960s. In response to changing conceptions about their respective professions, for example, schools of social work and city planning began to shift the emphasis of professional education. One emphasis was to stress the role of the practitioner in involving agencies in the process of bringing about societal changes. The practice organizations reacted critically. In social work, practitioners are now included on teams of evaluators for accrediting social work schools. In city planning, the accusation was made that planning schools were not training students to be planners, as evidenced by an article in *Planning* entitled, "Why Can't Johnny Plan."[13]

Whether the accusations were factual or not is irrelevant here. The point is that professional training does significantly influence the planner's own expectations of how the role shall be enacted.

Personality

A number of studies have suggested that an individual's personality attributes influence role performance.[14] For example, reticent people tend to reject roles that require a great deal of interaction with other people. Activist-oriented individuals, on the other hand, prefer such roles. Activists, however, tend also to enact leadership roles, and as a consequence, find it difficult working in collaborative relationships with such groups as citizen organizations. The tendency is to provide direct leadership rather than to assist the group in providing its own leadership.

Values

Values are another definer of a person's own expectations for role performance. Unlike personality, which suggests that the individual has limited choice in influencing a role, values represent a conscious and deliberate choice. That choice may be influenced certainly by other factors, some of which may be controllable, such as educational preparation; and some of which may not be controllable, such as the availability of a job. Nonetheless, values imply choice.

Individuals may elect to work only for planning organizations that are mandated to serve a select client group: low income populations, women, or public housing residents. For others the choice may be to work in a substantive planning area such as alcoholism, health, or social services. And for still others there may be no preference whatsoever. In all events, however, the value preference will influence the way the person expects the role to be enacted.

EXPECTATIONS OF OTHERS

A significant determinant of role is the expectation of others—supervisors, colleagues, clients, citizen or interest groups, professional organizations. Any position involves a system of social relationships—an individual interacting with others, in which both share functions in defining results or outcomes. In the process of planning, as we noted, planners are inevitably involved in social relations with other individuals, groups, and organizations. It is these interactions that help to shape how the planner is expected to perform.

Certainly it is not possible in one chapter to explain adequately all the external determinants of the planning role. We will focus, therefore, on the most critical: the organization, client system, and cooperative system.

Type of Planning Organization

The organization in which one works is obviously a crucial determinant of how a role gets enacted. Indeed, there is much in organizational theory devoted to explaining the function of sanctions used by organization to influence role performance.[15] We are, however, less interested with this aspect of defining role expectations than in explaining how the function of an organization influences role expectations.

One category of role determination is the scope and type of the planning organization. For example, studies suggest that neighborhood organizations require an activist-leader role of planner.[16] The planner is expected to be an advocate for the neighborhood group. The same role expectation is held out for planners working with issue-oriented organizations. The objective is to serve as an advocate for the citizen group. In regional or metropolitan planning agencies, on the other hand, the traditional role of planner-analyst predominates.[17] Performance is structured and organized.

Differences in role expectations can be found also along other organizational dimensions. Planners working for voluntary agencies practice an enabler role.[18] The planner's leadership function is indirect. In city public planning organizations, the role is more directive. Partly, this is a historical expectation and partly a reflection of organizational influence.

Voluntary organizations depend on citizen leadership for influence. Thus, the planner acts to stimulate and develop this voluntary leadership. It would be counterproductive, therefore, for the planner to compete with the volunteer for leadership.

In public planning organizations, the planner has customarily exerted a leadership role. It has not been inconsistent, for example, for a city planner to be a dominant figure both in planning and in the society as witnessed by the performance of Robert Moses in New York.

Client System

It is difficult to separate the client system from the planning organization. Some writers view both as one and the same. In some instances this is true. But as conceptualized in this text, the client system is the formal policy constituency, that entity (an individual or group or a formal organization) that employs the planner. Thus a distinction between the client system and organization is necessary.

The planner and client system are engaged in a collaborative relationship. It is fundamentally an interactional and reciprocal relationship in which each influences the other's performance, scope, and function.

The planner, however, is not a passive agent of the client system. The planner's function is to broaden the client system's understanding of planning issues and technical problems. Basically the relationship is a partnership. Each must assume responsibility for sharing in the task of the planning.

The role of the planner will depend, too, on the background and experience of the citizen group. Low income citizens with little experience in community activities rely on the planner for leadership and direction. One study of antipoverty planning in low income neighborhoods suggests, however, that the expectations of the citizens is not to be dominated by the planner. Neighborhood groups expected the planner to work through and with them in advocate and activist roles.[19]

If on the other hand, the citizen group is sophisticated in planning or community activities, the opposite is the case. The citizen group exerts considerable demands and expectations on the planner. The planner will be expected to provide technical assistance on aspects of a planning proposal. The citizens, however, will expect to have a significant voice in making the decision, as well as negotiating through the politics of decision-making. The role of the planner in this instance will be as enabler. The function will be to facilitate the planning activities.

Cooperative System

The cooperative system or planning constituency is engaged in a direct and immediate relationship with the planner. This type of working relationship is explained in Chapter 8. In this chapter our interest is in helping the planner understand the scope of the role relationship.

The cooperative system defines its relationship with the planner in terms of its own background and experience in planning. Cooperative systems made up of individuals with little previous experience in planning or community endeavors will tend to rely on the planner for leadership in direction. This can be dysfunctional if the objective is for the planning constituency to act as an agent for change.

If, on the other hand, the cooperative system is sophisticated in planning and community activity, the exact opposite is the case. The planner tends to be put into a subservient role. This is more true if the cooperative system is recognized for its sophistication. The danger in this case is that the cooperative system will not recognize the planner's function and contributions to the planning process. The outcome *may* reflect the politics and values of the cooperative system rather than other interests or data.

Both of these are extreme characterizations of cooperative systems. Planners may not be able to exert—at least for too long—an authoritarian role, and planners would reject a totally submissive role.[20] The relationship, similar to that of the planner's relationship with the client system, is a cooperative and reciprocal one. The planner may help to identify principal problem areas and thus play a leadership role. He or she may play a supportive or enabler role; that is, the planner may assist the cooperative system in achieving its aims. The choice of these roles is one that is worked out in cooperation with the cooperative system. It is also worked out in relation to the particular requirements of the planning activity itself—which is the position description.

EXPECTATIONS OF THE POSITION

A role has a situational context. It exists within a social system or organization and thus is defined in part by that context. We may talk about the role of the planner in general, that is the functional expectations. But the functional expectations may and usually do differ from one position to another and from one organization to another—and they can differ along a variety of dimensions. We, however, are interested in three dimensions.

A planner working exclusively for such a planning agency as a city planning commission or a regional planning organization will have a set of position expectations different from that of a planner working within a department that exists in a direct service agency, such as a public social services organization. In the latter instance the planner is confronted with all the difficulties of a specialist in a nonhost setting. The planner's position is an ancillary one, albeit important, but still ancillary to the main functions of the organization. The emphasis and attention is given to the direct service functions. The planner consequently finds that there is a continuing need to legitimate the planning function. Considerable time needs to be spent "touching bases" with important operational personnel. The purpose is to overcome resistance and to avoid resentment.

The second dimension is the hierarchical rank in the organization. Staff planners will have one set of norms for expectations in relation to planners in administrative positions. Staff planners tend to be involved in specialized activities. Their role will be limited and prescribed. The larger the planning organization, the more prescribed the role will be.

There is a tendency in large organizations for the position to become bureaucratized. The freedom to innovate becomes curtailed and the emphasis is on fulfilling regulatory functions rather than planning functions.

A third dimension is the task environment. Emerging studies of organizations suggest that one determinant of organizational structure is the certainty and uncertainty of task performance.[21] Organizations with an uncertain and volatile task environment (mental care giving organizations, for example) are characterized by a need to engage in coordination-integrative roles. Organizations with predictable and certain task environment (container manufacturing companies) roles are structured and the staff operates under standardized procedures.

On the whole, planning operates in an uncertain task environment. Within the domain of planning organizations, however, relative variations can be found. The task environment in physical planning agencies, for example, is more certain than that in human service planning organizations.

As a consequence, the planning position in human service organizations tends to call for roles that place emphasis on coordination and legitimation. Planning procedures vary and the planner often relies on adaptive strategies. In physical planning organizations, in contrast, planning procedures are somewhat more structured. There is a common set of procedures from one organization to the next, thereby permitting standardized position description. These organizations are labelled "professionally mature organizations" by one researcher.[22]

SUMMARY

Planning roles are varied and complex. There is no single role expectation. Planners are called on to execute a variety of roles.

What influences a role are a number of factors—the individual's own background, personality, and values; the organization and client system; and the position itself. It is important for a planner to understand who is defining the role. This requires an analytical perspective.

NOTES

1. Richard S. Bolan, "The Social Relations of the Planner," *Journal of the American Institute of Planners,* Vol. 37, No. 6 (November 1971), pp. 386–396.

2. Henry Fagin, "Advancing the 'State of the Art,'" Ernest Erber (Ed.), *Urban Planning in Transition,* (New York: Grossman, 1970), pp. 128–129.

3. Ibid., p. 129.

4. Bolan, op. cit., p. 395.

5. Some would suggest that the broker role is part of the planner's political role. See Francine F. Rabinovitz, *City Politics and Planning,* (New York: Atherton Press, 1969), pp. 90–98.

6. See Paul Davidoff, "Advocacy and Pluralism in Planning," *Journal of the American Institute of Planners,* Vol. 3, No. 4 (November 1965), pp. 331–337.

7. This is a traditional though not an exclusive role of community organization. See Murray G. Ross, *Community Organization,* (New York: Harper and Row, 1955), pp. 211–218.

8. Rabinovitz, op. cit., pp. 11–17.

9. John Friedmann, *Retracking America: A Theory of Transactional Planning,* (Garden City, N.Y.: Anchor Doubleday, 1973), pp. 171–185.

10. Norton Long, "The Local Community as an Ecology of Games," *American Journal of Sociology,* Vol. 64, No. 3 (November 1958), pp. 259–260.

11. Concepts about role have been taken from Neal Gross, Ward S. Mason, and Alexander W. McEachern, *Explorations in Role Analysis* (New York: Wiley, 1958), pp. 48–69.

12. This is a variation of Barnard's concept of the zone of indifference; that is, that zone within which an individual will unquestionably accept the orders of a superior. See Chester I. Barnard, *The Functions of the Executive* (Cambridge: Harvard University Press, 1968), pp. 167–169.

13. Melvin R. Levin, "Why Can't Johnny Plan," *Planning,* Vol. 42, No. 8 (September 1976), pp. 21–23.

14. Jack Rothman, *Planning and Organizing for Social Change* (New York: Columbia University Press, 1974), pp. 53–58. See also Bolan, op. cit., p. 389.

15. See, for example, Herbert A. Simon, *Administrative Behavior* (New York: Macmillan, 1961).

16. Rothman, op. cit., pp. 46–71, 61–66.

17. Donald A. Kreuckeberg, "A Multivariate Analysis of Metropolitan Planning," *Journal of the American Institute of Planners,* Vol. 35, No. 5 (September 1969), pp. 319–325.

18. Rothman, op. cit., pp. 61–106.

19. Neil Gilbert, "Neighborhood Coordinator: Advocate or Middleman," *Social Service Review,* Vol. 43, no. 2 (June 1969), pp. 136–144.

20. See Richard Bolan's discussion of this. Bolan, op. cit., p. 90.

21. Charles Perrow, "A Framework for the Comparative Analysis of Complex Organizations," *American Sociological Review,* Vol. 32, No. 2 (April 1967), pp. 194–208; Paul R. Lawrence and Jay W. Lorsch, *Organization and Environment* (Cambridge, Mass.: Graduate School of Business Administration, Harvard University, 1967); Jay W. Lorsch and John J. Morse, *Organizations and Their Members: A Contingency Approach* (New York: Harper and Row, 1974).

22. Donald A. Kreuckeberg, "Variations in Behavior of Planning Agencies," Administrative Science Quarterly, Vol. 16, No. 1 (June 1972), pp. 192–202.

Chapter 14

TYPOLOGIES OF PLANNING

All planning, as we have insisted, is a product of social and cognitive processes. The aim of this book has been to stress the social or political processes of planning.

This is not to suggest, however, that there is a single framework, type, or style of planning. That may have been the view in the 1950s. What was characteristic of planning research in the 1970s, however, was the growing evidence that there is no "best" type of planning. Today, planning types and styles are seen as a consequence of the planning organization's purpose, the organizational structure of the planning agency, the character of the decision environment, planning knowledge and skills, and the scale or type of outcome desired.[1] The type or model of planning, therefore, is *contingent* on organization, task, and decision environment.[2]

A task preliminary to that assertion is the identification of the various kinds of planning. What are the types of planning and how can they be classified? That is the purpose of this chapter: namely, to outline some of the major types of planning.

Ways of Classifying Planning

There are any number of ways of classifying planning. One way is by field of practice—e.g., health planning, social services planning, transportation planning, and the like. This type of classification is not only for nominal reasons. By classifying planning according to fields of practice, it is possible to compare ways in which planning is approached in each of these fields. Are there differences in methods? What influence does structure have on planning? What, if anything, is the degree of certainty or uncertainty in the task environment of different fields of practice?

Another way of classifying planning is by scale of outcome—innovative planning,[3] adaptive planning,[4] responsive planning,[5] incremental planning.[6] A series of questions can be asked about this classification beginning with the simple question about the need for such an array of scale. What, for example, is the distinction between adaptive planning and incremental planning? What is the measure of innovative or incremental? Would it be more helpful, as the economist Schumpeter has done, to merely distinguish between a planning outcome that produces a "creative response" (an outcome that is outside the existing range of existing practice) and an "adaptive response" (an expansion of an existing practice)?[7]

Planning can also be classified by the type of outcome (policy plan, operational plan, single use plan) or the scale of the planning task (societal, community, neighborhood, organization). These types of classification are useful for comparing methods with outcome or task. What, for example, is the appropriate method type of planning at the neighborhood level?

Still further ways to classify planning are by method and by value orientation. The former is a methodological classification; that is, it specifies ways of accomplishing a planning task. The latter is a prescriptive classification—how planning *should* be conducted.

It is these latter two classifications of planning that will be the emphasis of this chapter.

INSTRUMENTAL CLASSIFICATION

Planning, as was pointed out earlier, is a means or premise for decision-making. Planning, therefore, has an instrumental or method characteristic. It is a method, in other words, for arriving at decisions. There are five methods of planning which are classified here.

Rational/Comprehensive

The traditional or classical conception of community planning is the rational/comprehensive model. The essential feature of the classical model is that a planning commission as the guardian of the public interest assumes that no aspect of community development is beyond its responsibility. From this perspective, the commission establishes long-term goals expressed by a master plan. Short-term, small-scale development decisions are measured against the yardstick of the master plan.[8]

Rational/comprehensive planning has a scientific bias. It proceeds from the enunciation of a goal, and analytical techniques are used to achieve the goal. Of course, the effectiveness of the model depends on the capability of assembling and analyzing data.

The effectiveness depends also on a consensus environment. Unless there is agreement on the goals and aims, as well as a willingness to grant autonomy to the planning unit, the rational/comprehensive model cannot work.

Remedial Planning

Where the rational/comprehensive model proceeds from a goal premise, remedial planning proceeds from a quite different perspective. The salient characteristic of remedial planning is that it is initiated in response to a dissatisfaction or a painful situation. The aim is to move away from the dissatisfaction or pain rather than toward some goal or end state.

Remedial planning resembles a search process. The intention is to identify objectives that on the one hand solve the problem and on the other hand are acceptable to a number of related interests. One feature of remedial planning is that part of the process includes identifying resistance points and developing strategies for overcoming the resistance. In the interaction between attempting to overcome resistance and developing solutions, an agreed upon plan emerges. The plan tends to be only marginally different than the status quo. A major consequence of remedial planning is that it produces incremental changes.[9]

Strategic Planning

Strategic planning is a form of planning that rejects the principle of comprehensiveness but accepts the premise of planning as a rational process. While recognizing that the environment influences the planning process and that the planner's knowledge is bounded or limited, the object of strategic planning is to select particular issues or problems and resolve each independently. The assumption is that energies directed towards overextended total plans are wasteful.[10] However, by concentrating on key issues, planning best serves its primary function: the application of conscious and deliberate methods to control the futures.

A principal characteristic of strategic planning is that it emphasizes seizing the initiative and taking advantage of opportunities. It begins with a procedure of identifying issues for planning. Following that step, strategies are designed to solve a problem or take advantage of and promote opportunities.[11]

Strategic planning is common in most large industrial firms. It is seen as an annual and ongoing process of identifying objectives and defining overall corporate strategy.

Allocative Planning

To use the terms "allocative" and "planning" together may seem to be a redundancy. Economists, for example, define planning as an allocative function. It is the Friedmann conception of allocative planning, however, that is referred to here. He defines it as the "distribution of limited resources among a number of competing users."[12]

Allocative planning, it has been found, is the major type of planning practiced by state social services agencies.[13] It is partly a consequence of the annual requirement for social services planning.

Under Title XX of the Social Security Act, each state must prepare a comprehensive social services plan. The ostensible purpose of the plan is to develop a program and network of social services that meets the needs of the individual state's citizens. (The plan also serves as an eligibility requirement for federal funds.)

Title XX planning takes place within a highly political and competitive environment. There is a wide variety of public and private agencies dependent on Title XX funds. There are others seeking to be included as recipients of Title XX funds. Tactics of negotiation, bargaining, and even conflict are used to influence the allocative decisions.

As a result, the existing network of social services is assumed; and the Title XX planning endeavor becomes a means of designing an allocative process that responds to the demands of the environment and in some ways reflects the objectives of the planning task.

The consequence of this interaction—that is, the environmental demands and the task of planning—produces four different kinds of allocative planning.

1. *Linear programming.* Linear programming is extrapolated allocations. Allocations of resources are based on a prior year's allocation, which serves as a base point. Increases or decreases in the overall pool for allocation are shared by all users. If, for example, there is a 10 per cent decrease in the funds available for allocation, each user will get 10 per cent less than the previous year's allocation.

2. *Performance budget planning.* Performance budgeting is a term that originated with the Hoover Commission Report in 1949. It is basically a formalized cost accounting scheme. The intention of performance budgeting is to estimate costs of performing agency or organizational functions.[14]

Performance budget *planning* is characterized by the establishment of accounting methods, budget procedures, and system reports. Potential recipients of allocations are required to submit budget reports. Allocative decisions are then based on maximizing the efficiency and productivity of outputs as reflected in the budget report submissions. Considerable attention is given to devising evaluating and monitoring techniques for budget reports and expenditures.

There is, moreover, a line item review of budget requests. Line items not related to productivity or to improving the efficiency of outputs are disallowed.

3. *Process budget planning.*[15] In process budget planning, allocative decisions are seen as part of a negotiating process. The allocative decisions are based on not just a review of budget request, but also on a collaboration between the unit requesting the allocation and the allocating unit. The process may be formalized and indeed include elaborate budget panels involving consumers and users of service.

The process, however, may not be structured. It may exist as an informal process in which influential users bargain over budget decisions with the budgeting unit or its superiors, including legislative superiors. An agency, for example, may appeal its budget decision to the state legislature.

The salient feature of the budget process planning method is that it is an activity in which bargains are struck and allocations are negotiated. The assumption, as with the decision-making strategy of collaboration

outlined in Chapter 10, is that if the process is working effectively, the outcomes will be favorable to all.
4. *System budget planning.* System budget planning is a method combining analysis with budgeting. It is a means for systematizing decisions and analyzing program objectives. What it purports to state is that the heart of the allocation decision is the validity and effectiveness of specific programs. The allocation of resources is seen as a *means* not an end in the process of improving and developing programs. The basis of the system budget planning is that built into the budget process is a systematic comparison of alternative courses of action.

Characteristic of the system budget planning approach is the attempt to be comprehensive in making decisions. Emphasis, too, is on developing methods for improving data collection and quantitative analysis. Examples of techniques used in system budget planning are cost-benefit analysis, PPBS, and zero based budgeting.

Organizations may use more than one type of allocative planning. In some instances, for example, an organization may use a performance budget planning approach with one segment of recipient agencies and a system budget planning approach with another. It may, too, use more than one type with all agencies. Both system budget planning and process budget planning can be used simultaneously.

Issue Focused Planning

Issue focused planning is a type of planning that is used primarily to achieve acceptance and implementation of goals and objectives. The emphasis is on designing strategies that will overcome resistance to a plan or issue.

Some may argue, and rightly so, that issue focused planning is not planning at all. It is merely a phase or stage in the planning process. Nevertheless, planning models have been proposed that emphasize implementation almost to the exclusion of planning.

Community organization oriented planning is one example. John Friedmann's conception of "action planning" is another.[16] Practice examples would include much of the poverty program planning done in the 1960s.[17] A current example would be planning practices by consumer oriented organizations such as described in Chapter 3.

PRESCRIPTIVE CLASSIFICATION

Another typology of planning is based on a prescription of how planning *ought* to be conducted. All planning models, whether they are a product of analysis or not, are to some degree prescriptive. They purport to describe how to go about achieving planning results.

Some, however, are principally the consequence of research. Braybrooke and Lindblom's strategy of disjointed incrementalism is a good example. Braybrooke and Lindblom explain that the disjointed incrementalism strategy is merely a formalizing of a procedure that policymakers do in fact use. The strategy itself grows out of Braybrooke and Lindblom's observation of practice.[18]

Prescriptive models, on the other hand, are derived wholly from value premises. They are based on an assertion that this is the way planning should be practiced, irrespective of any study or analysis of practice. Six models are described here.

Community Integration

The achieving of planning results or goals is incidental to those who advocate an integrationist perspective for planning. The function of planning is to bring a community together, to enhance cooperative attitudes and practices, and to provide a framework for learning how individuals in a community can learn how to work together.

The community integrators insist, further, that the integration goal of planning should always be paramount. Short run material gains are misleading and deter society from achieving the purposeful "good life." The objective of planning is not to achieve a new nursery, water system, or housing project, but an increased capacity for citizens to undertake other cooperative projects.[19] In fact, according to proponents of community integration, by focusing only on planning goals, planners are treating only half of the community system, "and perhaps not the most important half at that."[20]

Advocacy Planning

In the late 1950s and early 1960s, a spate of articles and research reports questioned the public interest assumptions of city planning. Planning, it was revealed, did not serve the public or community-wide interest, primarily because all interests did not have an opportunity to be involved in community planning decisions. The planning commission, therefore, represented one interest and more often than not the powerful and influential interests of a community.

Arguing that it was possible to redress the balance, Paul Davidoff proposed the concept of advocacy planning.[21] Democratic urban government, he argued, must operate to include not exclude citizens in the planning and decision-making processes. Inclusion, moreover, meant that the citizen would be well informed about the underlying reasons for planning proposals and be able to respond to them in the technical language of professional planners.[22] Advocacy planning is the means for carrying out the process of including an informed citizenry in planning. Working on behalf of community groups, particularly low income groups, advocate planners would act as *proponents* of specific substantive planning solutions.[23]

Radical Planning

One of the more recent and significantly different prescriptive orientations to planning is radical planning. Radical planning begins with the assertion that modern planning, the rational/comprehensive model and modified variations of that model, are elitist, centralizing, and change resistant. The planner and planning systems tend to perpetuate and preserve a societal system that is technocratic and removed from the citizenry. Such actions foster a mass alienated society.

Radical planning would transform society. It is a concept of planning based on system change and a decentralized means for making decisions. Decentralization is a critical feature of radical planning. The vision is of a communal society focusing on human development and an ecological ethic. The consequence would be a form of planning that fosters spontaniety and produces innovative results. The planner, moreover, would be an active agent of change.[24]

Normative/Functional

These two prescriptive forms of planning are included in combination because they represent two divergent ideologies and also two contentious views of planning.

Functional planning concentrates on means. Goals or ends are assumed as given. The planning function is to devise methods and procedures for achieving goals, irrespective of how the goals are defined.[25]

There is an implicit belief under the view of functional planning that better information leads to better policy decisions. There is a view, too, that the goals need not be questioned because they are "correct." The goals are considered to be the product of political decisions and thus outside the realm of the planner.

Normative planning, on the other hand, extends the function of the planner to an analysis of goals. Moreover, the planner, it is argued, has a responsibility to scrutinize goals, to determine the purpose of the planning activity. He or she cannot assume a neutral, value-free stance in regard to goals. Not only is value-free planning impossible, according to those who argue for a normative view of planning, but also the planner has an ethical responsibility to be concerned about the goals of planning.[26]

Participatory Planning

We have noted in this book that there are two bases for advocating citizen participation in planning. One is the practical argument that planning results will tend to reflect more accurately the needs of a community or constituency than if a planner tried to determine the needs. There is some evidence to support this assertion.

A second and prescriptive orientation takes the position that citizens *should* participate in planning activities regardless of any practical results. The cultural history of America is a constant effort to strengthen the active role of citizens in community and governmental affairs. Citizen participation, therefore, is part of the philosophic traditions of America.[27] Citizens should participate in planning activities, not for any pragmatic reason, but simply because it is a good, in and of itself.

An underlying theme of this book, we should hasten to add, is the prescriptive basis for citizen participation. We have also pointed out the practical reasons.

Educative Model

An emerging orientation of planning is to view the planner as both an educator and student in the planning process. Planning, consequently, is defined as part of a learning process for the planner and the client. John Friedmann's concept of "transactive planning" is a representative example.[28]

Transactive planning, explains Friedmann, is a response to

a communication gap between technical planners and clients. To close the gap, a continuing series of personal, and primarily verbal, transactions between planners and clients is necessary. The transactions are through a medium of dialogue in which two kinds of knowledge are shared. One is the processed and analytical knowledge of the planner and the other is the experiential knowledge of the client. By sharing this knowledge, a process of mutual learning takes place.[29]

Friedmann points out that the growing technocracy of our society demands a decision-making method based on mutual learning. It is necessary, he explains, to join scientific and technical intelligence with personal knowledge at the critical points of social intervention in order to avoid decision-making at the exclusive hands of the technocrat. Transactive planning, he maintains, is the most appropriate method for achieving this linkage.[30]

Significantly, a growing concern with the rise of technocracy and a consequent fear that decision-making would fall to a meritocracy gave rise to the social work method of community organization in the 1920s. Community decisions, it was observed by one analyst, Eduard Lindeman, were becoming more and more the province of specialists. To counter this drift, he proposed a working relationship between the "democratic process and specialism." The working relationship was defined as *community organization.*[31]

Summary

In the 1950s and 1960s, two vying conceptions of planning were prevalent. One was a rational/comprehensive model and the other was an incrementalist model.

There is a growing realization, beginning in the 1970s, that such an "either/or" conception of planning is questionable. Two principles have been advanced:

1. There is no "best" type or style of planning;
2. The type or style of planning is contingent on the planning organization, the nature of the planning task, and the decision environment.

Planning can be classified along a number of typologies: by field of practice, by scale of outcome, by type of outcome, by method, by prescription, and by scale of planning activity.

In this chapter two typologies of planning were outlined: methodological and prescriptive.

NOTES

1. See for example, Donald A. Krueckeberg, "A Multivariate Analysis of Metropolitan Planning," *Journal of the American Institute of Planners,* Vol. 35, No. 5 (September 1969), pp. 319–325; Donald A. Krueckeberg, "Variations in Behavior of Planning Agencies," *Administrative Science Quarterly,* Vol. 16, No. 2 (1971), pp. 192–202; Thomas D. Galloway and Riad G. Mahayni, "Planning Theory in Retrospect: The Process of Paradigm Change," *Journal of the American Institute of Planners,* Vol. 43, No. 1 (January 1977), pp. 62–71.

2. Studies of organizations reveal a similar development. There is no preferred structure for organizations. An organization's structure depends on the environment within which the organization operates. See Charles Perrow, "A Framework for the Comparative Analysis of Organizations," *American Sociological Review,* Vol. 32, No. 2 (1967), pp. 194–208; John J. Morse and Jay W. Lorsch, "Beyond Theory Y," *Harvard Business Review,* Vol. 48 (May–June 1970), pp. 61–68.

3. John Friedmann, *Retracking America: A Theory of Transactive Planning,* (Garden City, N.Y.: Anchor Doubleday 1973), pp. 59–61.

4. John Friedmann, "A Conceptual Model for the Analysis of Planning Behavior," *Administrative Science Quarterly,* Vol. 12; No. 2 (September 1967), pp. 230–232.

5. H. Glennerster, *Social Service Budgets and Social Policy* (London: George Allen and Unwin, 1975), p. 26.

6. Amatai Etzioni, *The Active Society* (New York, Free Press, 1968), pp. 270–273.

7. Joseph A. Schumpeter, "The Creative Response in Economic History," *The Journal of Economic History,* Vol. VII, No. 2, (November 1947), pp. 149–159.

8. Richard S. Bolan, "Emerging Views of Planning," *Journal of the American Institute of Planners,* Vol. 33, No. 4, (July 1967), p. 234.

9. Disjointed incrementalism, mixed scanning, and feasible planning are variations of remedial planning. See David Braybrooke and Charles E. Lindblom, *A Strategy of Decision* (New York: Free Press, 1963), pp. 102–104; Amatai Etzioni, op. cit., pp. 282–309; Robert Morris and Robert H. Binstock, *Feasible Planning for Social Change* (New York: Columbia University Press, 1966).

10. Andreas Faludi, *Planning Theory,* (New York: Pergammon Press, 1973), pp. 210–211.

11. Glennerster, op. cit., p. 27.

12. Friedmann, *Retracking America: A Theory of Transactive Planning,* op. cit., p. 52.

13. Edmund M. Burke and Victor A. Capoccia, "Social Service Planning Under Title XX: A Report to HEW" (Mimeographed, 1978).

14. Bertram M. Gross, "The New Systems Budgeting," *Public Administration Review,* Vol. 29, No. 2, (March/April 1969), pp. 119–120.

15. This and the following term, "system budget planning," have been adapted from two sources. Allen Schick, "Systems Politics and Systems Budgeting," *Public Administration Review,* Vol. 29, No. 2, (March/April 1969), pp. 137–151; Glennerster, op. cit., pp. 88–116.

16. John Friedmann, "Notes on Societal Action," *Journal of the American Institute of Planners,* Vol. 35, No. 5, (September 1969), p. 312.

17. See, for example, Peter Marris and Martin Rein, *Dilemmas of Social Reform,* (New York: Atherton Press, 1967), particularly p. 111.

18. Braybrooke and Lindblom, op. cit., p. 81.

19. Murray Ross, *Community Organization* (New York: Harper & Row, 1955), p. 48.

20. David Popenoe, "Community Development and Community Planning," *Journal of the American Institute of Planners,* Vol. 33, No. 4, (July 1967), p. 264.
21. Paul Davidoff, "Advocacy and Pluralism in Planning," *Journal of the American Institute of Planners,* Vol. 31, No. 4, (November 1965), pp. 331–338.
22. Ibid., p. 332.
23. Ibid., p. 333.
24. Steven Grabow and Allan Heskin, "Foundations for a Radical Concept of Planning," *Journal of the American Institute of Planners,* Vol. 39, No. 2, (March 1973), pp. 106–114.
25. Faludi, op. cit., pp. 171–172.
26. Richard S. Klosterman, "Foundations for Normative Planning," *Journal of the American Institute of Planners,* Vol. 44, No. 1, (January 1978), pp. 37–46.
27. Fagence provides an excellent summary of these views. Michael Fagence, *Citizen Participation in Planning,* (New York: Pergammon Press, 1977), pp. 17–49.
28. Friedmann, *Retracking America: A Theory of Transactive Planning,* op. cit, pp. 171–193. See also Grabow and Heskin, op. cit., p. 112.
29. Friedmann, *Retracking America: A Theory of Transactive Planning,* op. cit., pp. 171–193.
30. Ibid., pp. 190–193.
31. Eduard Lindeman, *The Community* (New York: Association Press, 1921).

INDEX

Acceptance phase of planning, 100, 132, 177, 211, 215–229, 252, 253, 255
Action planning, 213, 292
Action system, 148–150, 173, 178, 192, 193, 206, 208–209, 213, 231, 251
  composition of, 165–168
  consensus type, 168–169, 185
  defined, 164–165
  dissensus type, 169, 185
Addams, Jane, 271
Advocacy
  as organizational role, 73, 171
  as planning role, 271–272, 278
  as strategy of citizen participation, 90, 102–104
  as strategy of planning, 15, 82–84, 107, 293
Alinsky, Saul, 102, 135–138
Allocative planning, 288–291
Altshuler, Alan A., 42, 82, 172
American Institute of Architects, 51
Arnstein, Sherry R., 74
Arrow diagram, 152–155
Atlanta, Ga., 29
Authority, 33, 48–50, 52, 80, 165

Baltimore, 67
Banfield, Edward C., 33–36, 40, 54–56, 124, 135, 165–166, 239
Bargaining
  as strategy of decision making, 231, 242–244, 246, 248, 250, 253
  as used by organizations, 126
Barnard, Chester, 47, 48, 122–124, 187–191
Bartholemew, Harland, 51, 52
Behavioral change strategy of citizen participation, 92–95
Behavior modification, 120, 121
Bolan, Richard S., 26, 57–59, 162, 196–197, 202
Boston, 49, 57, 213, 259
Braybrooke, David, 117, 292

Brzezinski, Zbigniew, 72
Burnham, Daniel, 51, 271
Campaign strategy of decision making, 127, 229–235, 246, 249, 264
Chapin, Stuart F., Jr., 213
Change
  forces toward, 111–115, 124–126, 128, 130, 132–138, 153–154, 216–218
  interference forces, 219–220
  restraints on or obstacles to, 112–115, 153–154, 216, 218–219, 256–263
Change agent, 111, 115–117, 120, 130, 132–134, 137–139
  organization as, 126–127, 171, 230, 242
  planner as, 128, 133, 270–272, 295–296
Change target, 111, 116, 121, 124–128, 132, 137–139, 233, 238, 242, 245, 263–265
  classified, 131–133, 252–253
Change technology, 111, 117–118, 120–121, 125–128, 132, 138, 230, 239, 242–244, 246, 252–253
Chicago, 51, 54, 56, 67, 124
Chicago City Council, 55
Chicago Housing Authority, 54, 55
Citizen participation, 12–14, 27, 212
  characteristics of in planning, 65–68
  and civil rights, 72–73
  and decision making, 76–79
  in issue politics, 72–74
  in poverty program, 69–72
  strategies of, 89–107
  in urban renewal, 66–69
Citizen role in planning, 74–76, 84–85, 160, 198–199, 212
City planning, 12, 276, 278, 281
Civil rights movement, 72
Clark, Terry, 32
Cleveland, 82

Client system in relation to role of planner, 270, 273, 279
Cognitive processes of planning, 16–17, 173, 196–200, 207–208
Collaborative strategy of decision making, 222–228, 242, 248–249, 252, 264
Community action program, 70–71
Community Chest, 9
Community integration type of planning, 292–293
Community leader, 38–40, 56, 124, 232, 244, 249–250
Community organization method, 81, 91, 93, 213, 292–293, 296
Community organizations, 39–40, 46–48, 101, 182–183
Community power
 and action system, 165–166
 characteristics of, 29–36
 and influence, 37–39
 as strategy of change, 107, 128, 140
 as strategy of citizen participation, 101–102
 as strategy of decision making, 238–241
 theories of, 28–36, 245
Conflict
 as explanation of social change, 110, 134–140, 231
 as strategy of citizen participation, 102–104
 as strategy of decision making, 245–248, 250
 as technique, 79, 102–104, 126, 134
Consensus environment for change or decision making, 18–19, 78, 168–169, 171, 185, 241, 287
 and cooperative system, 228
 and issue, 220–222
Cooperative system
 and action system, 170–171
 as advocacy group, 171, 208–209
 composition of, 223
 defined, 169–170
 in implementation process, 256, 258, 269
 and organizational theory, 123
 as planning entity, 178, 186–191, 193
 and planning process, 204–206
 and role of planner, 273, 280–282
Cooptation
 defined, 97–99
 as strategy of citizen participation, 90, 99–101
 as technique, 126
Cuba, 92

Cut-over phase of planning, 151, 157, 203, 255, 265–266

Dahl, Robert, 30–31, 57
Davidoff, Paul, 82
Decision center, 217, 223, 228, 229, 239, 246, 256, 258, 260, 263, 270
 administrative, 150, 210
 operational, 150, 210
Decision making
 and citizen participation, 76–83
 community, 25–46, 55–56
 decentralized character of, 26–28
 and facts, 167
 interest group process style, 79–83
 legislative process style, 76–79
 and planning, 147–152, 195, 213, 216
 and pluralism, 83–84
 strategies of, 160, 211, 220–254
 studies of, 29–39
 town meeting style of, 77
Decision phase of planning, see Acceptance phase of planning
deForest, Robert, 271
Diagnostic assessment, 129, 154–155
 acceptance phase of decision making, 150, 154, 216–220, 251
 implementation, 151, 155, 263–264, 266
 preplanning, 148, 154, 180–184, 191
Diffusion of innovation, 110, 128–134, 140, 153, 230
Disjointed incrementalism, 15, 292, 299
Dissensus environment for change or decision making, 168–169, 185, 241
 and issue, 220–222
Durden, Dennis, 96

Economic Opportunity Act, 71
Educative model of planning, 295–296
Education-therapy strategy of citizen participation, 90–92
Etzioni, Amitai, 62
Exchange theory, 106

Fagence, Michael, 83
Field theory, 110, 112–119, 122, 126, 130, 140, 154, 223, 230, 242
Final design phase of planning, 151, 156–157, 203, 255, 263–266
Formal policy constituency, 161–163, 173, 178, 180–182, 191, 193, 264, 279
Friedmann, John, 96, 169, 213, 273, 289, 292, 295–296
Functional community, 81
Functional planning, 294

INDEX 303

Gamson, William, 39, 245
Goal setting phase of planning, 149, 155–156, 192, 195–196, 202–207, 209–210
Gordon, Chad, 37

Hartford, Conn., 52
Headstart program, 70
Health planning, 49
Health Systems Agency, 49
Hirten, John E., 213
Hiedt, Sarajane, 20
Hoover Commission Report, 290
Human services planning, 12–13, 259, 286, 289–291

Implementation phase of planning, 156, 157, 209, 210, 215, 255–267
Incentives or inducements, 47–48, 63, 123–124, 182–183, 189–191, 249–250
Initiating set, 178–180, 183, 191
Interorganizational behavior as explanation of change, 110–111, 121–128, 135, 140
Interest group decision making, 79–83
Issue focused planning, 291–292
Issue oriented organizations, 191, 192
Issue politics, 72–74, 84

Johari Window, 225–227

Kennedy, John F., 78, 97
Kropotkin, 134

Leahy Clinic, 49
Learning theory, 110, 118–121, 126, 130, 140, 239, 246
Legislative type of decision making, 76–79
Legitimacy, 79, 99, 104, 127, 147, 158–159, 177, 179–180, 201, 257, 263
 as compared with authority, 48–51
 defined, 48–49
 types of, 51–61
Lewin, Kurt, 112-113, 115, 217
Lewis, Oscar, 92
Lindblom, Charles, 117, 292
Linear programming, 289
Lippitt, Ronald, 113–116, 129–130, 219
Long, Norton, 273
Luft, Joseph, 225

Machiavelli, Nicolò, 29, 50
Maine, Sir Thomas, 110
March, James G., 120

March of Dimes, 261
Martino, R. L., 148
Mazziotti, Donald F., 83–84
Minneapolis, 82
Motivation for planning, 177–193, 224
Mumford, Lewis, 110
Myerson, Martin, 54, 56

Nash, Peter, 96
Needs assessment, 261–262
Negotiation techniques of bargaining strategy, 242–244, 246, 248, 251, 271
Neighborhood Legal Services, 70
Newark, N.J., 70, 213
New England, 77
New Haven, Conn., 30, 31
New York City, 57, 213
Nixon, Richard, 70, 71, 261
Normative planning, 294–295
Nuttall, Ronald, 37, 57–59, 213

Oakland, Calif., 70
Olmstead, Frederick Law, 51, 271
Organizational behavior, 39–40, 46–48, 122–128, 182, 186–191, 278
Organizational constituency, 161–162, 174, 218
Organizational enhancement, 124–126, 128, 182–183
Organizational legitimacy, 51, 54–57, 158, 160–174
Operant conditioning, 120, 121

Parsons, Talcott, 134
Participatory planning, 295
Pavlov, Ivan, 118
Performance budget planning, 290
Pittsburgh, 57, 70, 213, 259
Plan element phase of planning, 150, 156, 195, 201, 206–211, 259, 260
Planner's role, 57–61, 268–274
 advocate, 271–272
 analyst, 269–270
 broker, 271
 with cooperative system, 186–189
 designer of the future, 197–198
 educator, 272–273
 enabler, 272
 interactional, 59–60, 268
 organizer, 270–271
 procedural, 59–60, 268
 publicist, 273–274
 social and cognitive processes of, 196–202
Planning, types of
 action, 213, 292
 advocacy, 15, 82–84, 107, 293
 allocative, 288–291

community integration, 292–293
disjointed incrementalism, 15, 299
educative, 295–296
functional, 294
health, 49
human services, 12, 286, 289–291
issue focused, 291–292
linear programming, 289
normative, 294–295
participatory, 295
performance budget, 290
poverty, 292
priority, 261–262
process budget, 290
radical, 294
rational/comprehensive, 11, 287
redevelopment, 259–260
remedial, 287–288
strategic, 288
systems budget, 291
transactive, 15, 295–296
voluntary, 80–82, 96, 278
Planning diagram, 147–157, 163, 171–173, 185, 191–193, 202, 207, 209–210, 228, 234–235, 241, 244, 248, 250–251, 265–266, 273
Planning constituency, 161, 163–164, 174, 218, 273
Positional legitimacy, 51–54, 80, 158–160, 174, 244
Poverty program, 69–72, 91
planning, 292
Power strategy of decision making, 238–241, 249–250
Priority planning, 261–262
Problem definition phase of planning, 148, 154–155, 157, 192
Process budget planning, 290
Program planning budgeting systems (PPBS), 291
Public interest, 78–80, 82–84, 293
Public relations and publicity, 173, 185, 190–191, 206, 230, 232–234, 247, 272–274

Radical planning, 294
Rational/comprehensive planning, 11, 287
Rebellion strategy of decision making, 237
Remedial planning, 287–288
Representativeness, 79, 87, 95, 99, 170
Requisite actions, 33–36, 165–166, 238
Riis, Jacob, 271
Rogers, Everett, 129–131
Role legitimacy, 51, 57–61, 159, 268, 281–282
Ross, Murray G., 91, 213
Rostow, Walt, 110

St. Louis, Mo., 51, 259
San Francisco, 51, 204, 205
San Francisco Bay Area Conservation Commission, 204, 205
Scheuch, Irwin K., 37
Schoderbeck, Peter B., 148
Schoop, E. Jack, 213
Schumpeter, Joseph, 286
Selznick, Philip, 99
Sentiment groups, 166–167
Shriver, R. Sargent, 69
Shurtleff, Flavel, 51
Skinner, B. F., 118–120, 246
Social change, 108–141, 147, 153–154, 256
Social Darwinism, 134
Social process concept of planning, 16–19, 147, 173, 196–202, 204–206, 208–209, 268, 285
Social work, 276
Sower, Christopher, 179
Staff supplement strategy of citizen participation, 96–97
Strategic planning, 288
Syracuse, N.Y., 29, 70
Systems budget planning, 291

Tennessee Valley Authority, 99
Title XX (of the Social Security Act), 18, 46, 181, 289
Toffler, Alvin, and anticipatory democracy, 77
Transactive planning, 15, 295–296
Truman, President Harry S., 127

U.S. Bureau of the Budget, 70
U.S. Department of Health, Education, and Welfare, 95
U.S. Department of Housing and Urban Development, 91, 95, 159
U.S. Office of Economic Opportunity, 70, 91
U.S. Urban Renewal Administration, 67, 69
United Way of America, 13, 40, 101
Urban renewal, 66–69, 91, 159, 182, 259–260

Voluntarism, 96–97
Voluntary community planning, 80–82, 96, 278

Walker, Robert, 57
Warren, Roland, 91, 121, 175, 176, 220
Willie, Charles V., 166
Women's rights movement, 72
Work plans, 207–208, 210

Zero based budgeting, 291